WITHDRAWN

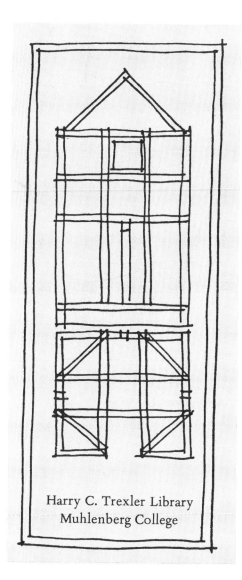

Harry C. Trexler Library
Muhlenberg College

WITHDRAWN

AFRICAN SOCIETY TODAY

Inequality in Africa

This study of inequality in Africa not only rejects the orthodox approach of the World Bank and the International Monetary Fund, which neglects income distribution and advocates greater external economic reliance, but also the statist Lagos Plan of Action, which supports comprehensive planning, large capital-intensive state firms, and increased government intervention in peasant prices. Wayne Nafziger's political economy analysis shows how the colonial legacy, the contemporary global economic system, and the ruling elites' policies of co-opting labour, favouring urban areas, distributing benefits communally, and spending on education to maintain inter-generational class exacerbate discrepancies between regions, urban and rural areas, and bourgeoisie and workers, even under 'African socialism'. The author's policy discussion eschews technoeconomic solutions, arguing that reducing inequality requires democratising political participation as well as economic control.

AFRICAN SOCIETY TODAY

General editor: ROBIN COHEN

Advisory editors: O. Aribiah, Jean Copans,
Paul Lubeck, Philip M. Mbithi, M. S. Muntemba,
O. Nnoli, Richard Sandbrook

The series has been designed to provide scholarly, but lively and up-to-date, books, likely to appeal to a wide readership. The authors will be drawn from the field of development studies and all the social sciences, and will also have had experience of teaching and research in a number of African countries.

The books will deal with the various social groups and classes that comprise contemporary African society and successive volumes will link with previous volumes to create an integrated and comprehensive picture of the African social structure.

Also in the series

Farm labour. KEN SWINDELL
Migrant laborers. SHARON STICHTER
The politics of Africa's economic stagnation. RICHARD SANDBROOK
The African worker. BILL FREUND
African capitalism: the struggle for ascendancy. PAUL KENNEDY

INEQUALITY IN AFRICA

Political elites, proletariat, peasants and the poor

E. WAYNE NAFZIGER

*Department of Economics,
Kansas State University*

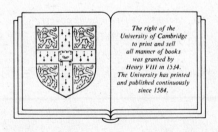

The right of the
University of Cambridge
to print and sell
all manner of books
was granted by
Henry VIII in 1534.
The University has printed
and published continuously
since 1584.

CAMBRIDGE UNIVERSITY PRESS

Cambridge

New York   New Rochelle   Melbourne   Sydney

Published by the Press Syndicate of the University of Cambridge
The Pitt Building, Trumpington Street, Cambridge CB2 1RP
32 East 57th Street, New York, NY 10022, USA
10 Stamford Road, Oakleigh, Melbourne 3166, Australia

© Cambridge University Press 1988

First published 1988

Printed in Great Britain at the University Press, Cambridge

British Library cataloguing in publication data

Nafziger, E. Wayne
Inequality in Africa: political elites,
proletariat, peasants and the poor. –
(African society today).
1. Social classes – Africa   2. Social
classes – Economic aspects – Africa
I. Title   II. Series
305.5'096   HN780.Z956

Library of Congress cataloguing in publication data

Nafziger, E. Wayne.
Inequality in Africa.
(African society today)
Bibliography.
Includes index.
1. Income distribution – Africa.   2. Poor – Africa.
3. Peasantry – Africa.   4. Elite (Social sciences) –
Africa.   5. Africa – Economic conditions.   I. Title.
II. Series.
HC800.Z9I5I36 1988   339.2'096   87–24263

ISBN 0 521 26881 8 hard covers
ISBN 0 521 31703 7 paperback

TM

To John F. Due

CONTENTS

FIGURES AND TABLES

ACKNOWLEDGEMENTS

I did the research for this book during five trips to Africa, beginning in 1964–5, with funds from the American Philosophical Society, Kansas State University (KSU), the University of Denver Graduate School of International Studies, the Social Science Foundation, and the Midwest Universities Consortium for International Activities. Richard Sklar, John F. Due, Carl Eicher, Kusum Nair, Irving Leonard Markovitz, Robin Cohen, David Hirschmann, Bola Okuneye, John Exdell, Jarvin Emerson, and many other scholars helped my research. I received generous help from librarians at KSU, the Institute of Development Studies (Sussex University, Brighton), the Oxford University Institute for Economics and Statistics, the Institute of Development Studies (Nairobi), Boston University's African library, and Northwestern University's Africana library (especially curator Hans Panofsky). Colleagues responding to my talks to the Institute of Development Studies and the Department of Economics, University of Dar es Salaam, Tanzania (19 November 1982), and the African Studies Association (US), New Orleans (23 November 1985), contributed to the study. I thank Margaret Grosh for permission to use material in chapter 3 from our joint research, Richard Sandbrook and Cambridge University Press for permission to use the map of Africa, and the US Department of Agriculture's Economic Research Service for data used in fig. 3. Elfrieda, Brian, and Kevin Nafziger tolerated incoveniences, leaving me more time for research. I am grateful to all these, but I am solely responsible for weaknesses.

GLOSSARY

Balance on current account – An international balance comprising exports minus imports of goods and services, plus net grants, remittances, and unilateral transfers received (see table 4).

Commodity terms of trade (net barter terms of trade) – The price index of exports divided by the price index of imports. For example, if export prices increase 10% and import prices 22%, the commodity terms of trade drop 10%, that is, 1.10/1.22 = 0.90.

Economic growth – The rate of growth of GNP per capita.

External economies – See spillovers.

Formal sector – Government sector and firms with 10 or more employees in the private sector.

Gini index of inequality – A measure of concentration that indicates how far a distribution is from perfect equality. It ranges from a value of 0 representing perfect equality to 1 representing maximum inequality (e.g., where the richest individual has all the income).

GDP (gross domestic product) – A measure of the total output of goods and services, which encompasses income earned within a country's boundaries. This includes income earned by foreign residents and companies, even if it is transferred abroad, and excludes income earned by a country's residents and companies abroad.

GNP (gross national product) – A measure of the total output of goods and services, which encompasses income earned by a country's residents. This includes income by the country's residents abroad, and excludes income earned domestically by foreign residents.

GNP per capita – GNP divided by the population.

IDA-eligible countries – Poor countries eligible for International

Development Association concessional loans.

Immiserisation – Falling average economic welfare.

Import substitution – Domestic production replacing imports.

International balance of (merchandise) trade – Exports minus imports of goods.

International balance on goods and services – Exports minus imports of goods and services (see table 4).

Investment in human capital – Expenditures on education, training, research and health, enhancing a person's future productivity.

Monopsony – A single buyer of a product.

Oligopoly – An industry with few sellers, with interdependent pricing decisions among the firms in the industry.

Parastatal enterprises – Public corporations and statutory boards owned by the state, but responsible for day-to-day management to boards of directors, at least partially appointed by the state.

(Price) elasticity of demand – The absolute value of the percentage change in quantity demanded divided by the percentage change in price. Values more than one are elastic, and less than one, inelastic.

Primary products – Food, raw materials, and organic oils and fats.

Progressive taxes – Tax structure where people with high incomes pay a higher percentage of income in taxes.

Quintile – Fifth (e.g., first quintile is the bottom 20%).

Real economic growth – Inflation-adjusted growth in GNP per capita (usually expressed per annum).

Regressive taxes – Tax structure where people with low incomes pay a higher percentage of income in taxes.

Relative economic gap – GNP per capita of the developed countries as a multiple of the developing countries.

Spillovers – Cost advantages rendered free by one producer to another, so that the social profitability of production exceeds its commercial profitability.

Surplus – Output minus wages, depreciation, and purchases from other firms.

Terms of trade – Same as commodity terms of trade.

Total economic growth – The rate of GNP growth.

ABBREVIATIONS

DCs	Developed countries
ECA	UN Economic Commission for Africa
EEC	European Economic Community
EIU	Economist Intelligence Unit
FAO	Food and Agriculture Organisation of the UN
IFPRI	International Food Policy Research Institute
ILO	International Labour Office
IMF	International Monetary Fund
LDCs	Less developed countries
MNCs	Multinational corporations
OECD	Organisation for Economic Cooperation and Development, which includes the US, Canada, Western Europe, Japan, Australia, and New Zealand
V	Weighted coefficient of variation – a measure of relative dispersion (standard deviation relative to the mean)

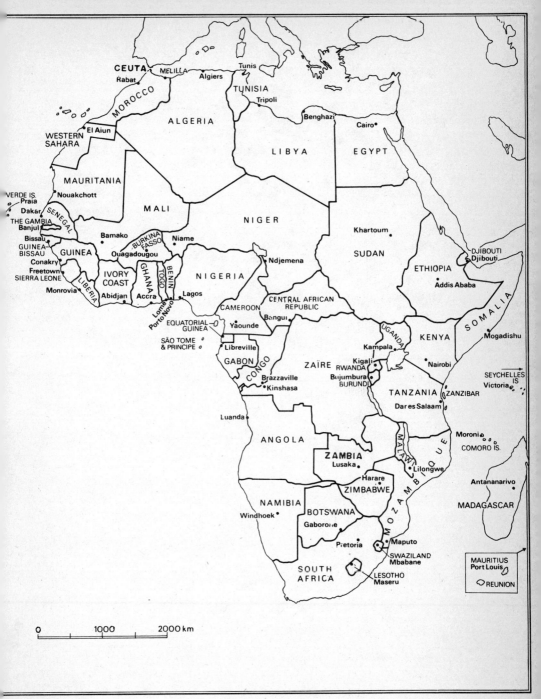

African states and principal cities

§ 1 §

EQUALITY AND GROWTH
TRADEOFF OR INTERLINK?

Economic growth probably cannot solve the problem of widespread poverty unless attention is given to how income and property are distributed. For LDC poverty increased in the 1960s and 1970s even though overall growth surpassed UN targets. Growth can be a misleading indicator of economic development, as poverty, unemployment, and income inequality can increase with growth.

But though LDC poverty generally grew more slowly than population so that poverty *rates* fell, in subsaharan (black-ruled tropical, excluding South and Arab North) Africa both poverty numbers and rates rose. The ILO (1981) estimates poverty rates in Nigeria increased, 1960–80, while it was the fastest growing African economy. Subsaharan Africa (without Nigeria) achieved virtually no growth in the two decades after 1965. The few data available indicate growing inequality from the 1960s to the 1970s, which together with stagnation, means increased poverty rates.

ECA's twenty-fifth anniversary projection (1983b) of past trends forward to 2008 envisions a nightmare of explosive population growth pressing on physical resources and social services. Maintaining past trends means degrading human dignity for the majority, with a rural population surviving on intolerable toil, disastrous land scarcity, and a worsening urban crisis, with more shanty towns, congested roads, unemployed, beggars, crime, and misery alongside the few unashamedly demonstrating greater conspicuous consumption, shopping at national department stores filled with luxury imports. The consequences of extreme wealth and poverty would be social tensions and continued financial crises threatening national sovereignty.

IS AN INVERTED U INEVITABLE?

Sandbrook (1985) argues that 'Income inequality [in Africa] is not, strictly speaking, an aspect of economic crisis. Unequal distribution is common in the early and middle stages of capitalist development, and therefore is often linked with growth rather than stagnation.'

Indeed the economists' prevailing view, first advocated by Nobel laureate Kuznets (1955), is that LDC inequality follows an inverted U-shaped curve, first increasing and then decreasing with economic growth. Initially, growth results in lower income shares for the poor and higher income shares for the rich.

Why is a dualistic subsistence-modern economy supposed to produce an upside-down U? Inequality increases as growth begins in a subsistence agrarian economy (output for the cultivator's family use) through the expansion of a narrow modern sector (primarily manufacturing, mining, and processing), especially worsening where foreign natural-resource exploitation triggers growth. The income shares of the poorest 60% and middle 20% (fourth-highest quintile) decline significantly, while the share of the top 5% increases strikingly – particularly where traditional or foreign elites dominate.

Once countries move beyond this early stage, further development generates no change in shares for the top 5%. At an LDC's highest income level, broad-based economic advances benefit middle-income groups to the rich's relative disadvantage, at least if government enlarges its economic role. However, the top 5%'s share rises if natural-resource exploitation increases.

The relative position of the poorest 60% typically worsens as the modern sector competes with the traditional sector for markets and resources. The poor's declining share occurred when peasants became landless workers during the European land consolidation of the sixteenth through nineteenth centuries, when high-yielding varieties of grains were first used on commercial farms in India and Pakistan, and when the colonial government established plantations in Africa. Even when growth becomes more broadly based, the poor increase their shares only when government widens their opportunities for education and training (Adelman and Morris, 1973).

While the evidence for the inverted U is strong when you classify countries *in a given time period* by per capita income levels, the necessary *individual country data over time* are lacking (Nugent, 1983). And the inverted U-shaped pattern, even if assumed historically accurate, is not inevitable, but a consequence of economic policies. Greater third-world inequality during the 1950s and 1960s is a result of policies placing the highest priority on growth, while incorrectly assuming benefits 'trickle down' to the poor. Moreover, many African countries, like other LDCs, emphasised the growth of the urban-oriented, highly technological, highly mechanised production of

Western-style consumer goods. They neglected production patterns based on indigenous tastes, processes, and resource endowments.

THE LEGITIMACY OF INEQUALITY

In defending inequality, Bauer (1981) contends that wealth and income concentrations cannot be attributed to differential political and economic power. Indeed 'the accumulation of wealth, especially great wealth, normally results from activities which extend the choices of others'. Most income inequality is due to people differing in 'their ability to perceive and utilize economic opportunities... Economic differences are largely the result of people's capacities and motivation'. Equality of opportunity, not equality of results, is important.

Bauer rightly points out variations in people's endowment and motivation, but fails to see how these are highly correlated with the advantages that are a legacy of the superior environment, education, and influence those with wealth (especially inherited) have.

I show (1977, 1978) that in both the West and LDCs, children from upper classes and established business families use the advantages of their parents – property, influence, status, and so forth – to obtain the education, training, experience, concessions, and capital to become disproportionately successful in economic activities, especially business enterprise. Wealth and position facilitate the possession of greater opportunities like greater information, superior access to training and education, a lower discount of future earnings, larger firm size, and lucrative agreement (Dobb, 1926). Below I demonstrate that contemporary African political and economic elites use power and wealth to acquire education and investment opportunities to maintain their families' positions at the top of the class system.

THE EFFICIENCY OF INEQUALITY

Economists widely maintain that inequality, by spurring high capital formation rates, benefits the poor, since accumulation raises productivity and average material wellbeing. Papanek (1967) asserts a conflict 'between the aims of growth and equality' such that 'great inequality of incomes is conducive to increased savings'. Ul Haq (1966), an eloquent spokesman for meeting LDC basic needs while World Bank economist in the 1970s, contended while Pakistani planner in the 1960s: 'The underdeveloped countries must consciously accept a philosophy of growth and shelve for the distant future all ideas of equitable distribution and welfare state. It should be recognised that these are luxuries which only developed countries can afford.' His policy conclusion was that 'additional output should be distributed in favour of the saving sectors'. His was 'basically a philosophy of growth as opposed to a philosophy of distribution [and] is indispensable in a period of "take-off"'. As Pakistani planner in the 1980s, he stated views similar to those he had held in the 1960s.

Stolper (1970), head of the Economic Planning Unit preparing Nigeria's First National Development Plan, 1962–8, argued that 'a very good case can be made that premature preoccupation with equity problems will backfire and prevent any development from taking place'. Indeed, Nigeria's first plan stressed production and profitability, not distribution.

MY PREMISES

Unlike Bauer, most Western development scholars do not make their value presuppositions explicit (see Nafziger, 1976). Social scientists frequently work as consultants for Western or LDC political, bureaucratic or business elites, and accept their goals. Higgins (1968) explicitly states 'there are enough countries where the political power elite does want economic development to keep economists busy for some time to come'. Let me state my value premises concerning inequality.

Many economists support political elites' maximising economic modernisation, while waiting for a later stage of development to emphasise income distribution (*ibid.*). Yet the initial distribution of income and physical and human capital is a crucial factor determining the trend in inequality. People who already own property, hold an influential position, and have a good education are in the best position to profit once growth begins. Thus, a society with initial income inequality that begins growth is likely to remain unequal or become more so, whereas one with small disparities may be able to avoid large increases in inequality. It may not be possible to 'grow first and redistribute later', because early socio-economic position may largely fix the pattern of distribution, at least until much higher income-levels are approached. Reducing poverty and inequality requires immediate priority through land reform, mass education, and other means, rather than leaving redistribution until after growth has taken place.

Even if you assume that inequality spurs capital accumulation and growth, it may not be prudent for the LDC poor to favour inequality, thus risking their children's health and nutrition to bequeath a fortune to their grandchildren. Promoting saving through inequality is more costly than other alternatives like using the state to promote both equality and capital accumulation (Robinson, 1949).

If society tolerates inequality to promote saving, a large part of higher incomes is wasted in providing the rich with luxuries. Kaldor (1975) argues that progressive taxation may stimulate capital accumulation by curbing luxury spending that distorts investment. Before progressivity, too much is invested in industries catering to the rich. Afterwards, some investment shifts from luxury production to necessities. Thus, there are fewer conflicts between African income redistribution and capital accumulation than is commonly believed.

How do we evaluate whether inequality is justified? Assume a society adheres to Rawls's (1971) first principle of equality of basic rights and duties. Should we not reward an innovator or risk-taker whose new techniques improve the country's productivity, income, health, and welfare? For example, the Nigerian government has to pay incomes far above average to spur researchers, innovators, administrators, financiers, and marketing experts to use time and money to develop a safe, effective spray to kill the tsetse fly, thus eliminating trypanosomiasis, a disease attacking people, cattle, goats, and transport animals in southern Nigeria. Suppose poor Nigerians agree that the extra remuneration for tsetse-fly project personnel is preferable to using these funds for alternative wants. This fulfils Rawls's second principle: inequalities of wealth and authority are just if they result in compensating benefits for everyone, particularly the least advantaged.

I accept Rawls's second principle in evaluating income distribution. Yet African political elites, like those everywhere, often justify policies furthering their economic interests in terms of compensating benefits for the population at large. We must look at whether government's 'modernising' policies, ostensibly in the general interest, may not benefit merely the tiny elite that controls the state's levers.

One rule of thumb is that a development project should pay for itself in the long run, unless the programme creates positive spillover effects or redistributes income in a clearly desirable way. A programme that does not pay for itself, where the recipient of the service is not charged an economic price, involves a subsidy to him. Since the alternative to a subsidy is resource allocation to another project, the burden of proof should fall on the subsidy's advocate.[1] The rule would be consistent with, for instance, subsidies to distribute milk or maize to low-income families, but not to provide automobile allowances for senior civil servants in higher-income brackets.

CAN AFRICAN GOVERNING ELITES IMPROVE INCOME DISTRIBUTION?

Kenya's 1979–83 and 1984–8 Development Plans indicate reduced income inequality and poverty as major objectives. In the 1967 Arusha Declaration, TANU (Tanganyika African National Union), led by President Julius K. Nyerere, made a commitment to a socialist transformation and a 'war against poverty' and inequality. Political leaders in Nigeria recognised, beginning in the late 1970s, how little its oil-fuelled economic boom reduced poverty and income concentration.

These and other African states expressed their economic goals in summit declarations and resolutions by heads of governments at Organisation of African Unity meetings and ECA documents in the late 1960s and 1970s, which culminated in the Lagos Plan of Action (29 April 1980) (OAU, 1980). The Plan's major pillars were improving income distribution, eradicating poverty and unemployment, democratising development, promoting increasing national self-reliance, accelerating self-sustained development, and speeding up regional economic integration (Adedeji and Shaw, 1985).

Why should a governing elite be interested in distribution? Would not its major concern be to consolidate its position by using its control of state machinery? Ng'ethe (1980) assumes no ruling group has an economic interest in relinquishing control or redistributing to other classes, and thus none will want to improve income distribution. So governing elites will only engage in public-relations exercises to blur class contradictions.

Radical economists think a socialist revolution is the only way to reduce capitalist inequalities. Indeed inequality in socialist countries declined after their revolutions, and their income concentrations are generally lower than mixed and capitalist countries. The greatest income inequalities are between property-owners and wage-earners. Under socialism, where the state or community owns most capital and land, profits, rents, and interest are distributed to society as a whole.

Thus, Cuba's income distribution improved substantially after its 1959 revolution through expropriating property, giving tenants ownership of houses and small farm holdings, guaranteeing employment for able-bodied workers, slashing wage differences between managers and workers, subsidising food and bus prices, and emphasising spending on health, education, and other public services (Seers, 1974). And China's land reform, agricultural collectivisation, and other redistributive policies increased income equality sharply between liberation in 1949 and 1957 (although not after 1957) (Nafziger, 1984).

The 1970s' ratio of incomes of the richest fifth to the poorest fifth in China, about 9:1, was less than India's 11:1, the Philippines' 14:1, Mexico's 15:1, and Brazil's and South Africa's 25:1, but about the same as Sri Lanka's 9:1, and more than Taiwan's or South Korea's 5:1. Non-socialist Taiwan, South Korea, and Sri Lanka pursued less radical strategies than China to reduce income concentration in the 1960s and early 1970s. Taiwan and South Korea redistributed land in the early 1950s, provided credit and extension services for small farmers, emphasised education, and expanded labour-intensive manufacturing. Sri Lanka not only expanded education, but spent 10% of GNP on food subsidies, including a free weekly rice ration of 0.5–1 kilograms for each person (*ibid.*; Jain, 1975; Eberstadt, 1979).

In the mid 1970s, the share of the bottom 60% in these three non-socialist countries was high, so that Ahluwalia *et al.* (1979) list them as LDCs performing well in income distribution. For Taiwan, the income shares of the poorest 60% was 38%, for Korea 32%, and for Sri Lanka 35%, which even compared favourably to the 36% of Yugoslavia, the only socialist LDC with data.[2] Thus, some non-socialist LDCs have income inequalities as low as socialist LDCs. This suggests that African countries can reduce income concentration without a socialist revolution and in some instances even without radical political change.

Moreover, China, Taiwan, and South Korea were all among the nine fastest-growing LDCs, while having low and declining inequality 1950–75 (Morawetz, 1977), suggesting that Africa, too, can pursue strategies of both rapid growth and income redistribution.

To maintain control or avoid political discontent, political elites may invest in mass educational and health programmes, and even undertake asset redistribution. Alternatively, ruling elites may be divided, so that factions back income redistribution policies to obtain support from disadvantaged classes as they become politically mobilised. Moreover, economic interests can cut across class lines. Workers and industrialists paying wages dependent on food prices want cheap food, while landlords join with peasants to press for high food prices.

Elites and masses may be united by similar communal and regional economic interests. Sometimes these common interests are more apparent than real. Political elites can build patron–client relationships to accentuate the precolonial and colonial identification with ethnic, regional, and linguistic communities, and use these sentiments to transfer potential hostility from class discrepancies within their communities to the rulers and subjects of others.

In Africa, both new and higher levels of political mobilisation add pressures to the governing elites. With negative economic growth in much of Africa, increasing inequality means higher poverty rates. Accelerating economic growth may be the most satisfactory *political* approach to meeting these rising demands. Thus, Mexico, with an annual growth of more than 3% from the early 1960s to the mid 1970s, experienced a decline in the relative income share of the poorest 60%, but their absolute incomes grew by about 2.5% yearly. On the other hand, Niger's annual 2% decline during the same period resulted in a fall in the absolute incomes of the bottom 60% of the population, even though their relative income share increased (Nafziger, 1984; World Bank, 1976). When the income pie is not enlarged, as in many parts of Africa, inequality is an especially severe problem. Any gains the underprivileged classes make are at the expense of the more privileged classes. Such a redistribution from higher-income to lower-income classes is difficult to achieve politically. However, when the GNP pie grows, the slices can be bigger for both privileged and underprivileged groups. Thus increasing the economic pie slices for Africa's poor requires attention to both growth and income distribution.

Most scholars believe there will be poverty in Africa, regardless of how income is distributed. They see a growth–equity tradeoff, where improved income equality cuts into growth. But Ahluwalia's empirical study (1974) finds no correlation between economic growth and income inequality in LDCs.

Indeed African ruling elites are often not only anti-egalitarian but also anti-growth, hurting small farmers' incentives, appropriating peasant surplus for parastatal industry, building parastatal-enterprise size beyond management capacity, and using these inefficient firms to dispense benefits to clients. Regime survival in a politically fragile system requires marshalling elite support at the expense of economic growth. Spurring peasant production through market prices and exchange rates interferes with state leaders' ability to build political support, especially in urban areas.

We need to view the growth–equity relationship dynamically. Statically, the US Department of Agriculture (1980), which assumes a given level of output, is correct in contending that even if food consumption in Africa were evenly distributed, its average nutritional standards would still be below the minimum requirements. But over time, reducing the arbitrary, wasteful, and capricious policies by ruling elites in large parts of Africa (like Ghana, Zaïre and Uganda) would not only reduce inequality but also increase future average incomes and food consumption, through making more funds available for productive projects. Redistributing output and wealth and providing incentives for small producers would reduce poverty, affecting not only current incomes but also future investment, educational, and occupational decisions.

Economists' assumption of widespread equality–growth tradeoff results from a neglect of political considerations and their legitimations. Political leaders stress the tradeoff as a way of rationalising policies that reduce equality, as well as growth, at the expense of their and their clients' interests. Few voices question the tradeoff, especially when mass political participation is lacking.

§ 2 §

RESEARCH WITHOUT STATISTICS
WHAT ARE THE QUESTIONS?

NATIONAL INCOME DATA

African GNP per capita data are only roughly indicative of differences in average economic welfare. The ECA (1985) laments that

> A variation of the order of 20 per cent is a fair indication of the range of precision of most data. Such differences are especially serious in agriculture, where most current data concerning food crops and livestock are based on so-called 'eye estimates', i.e., the educated guesses of agricultural officials, since most countries do not undertake objective surveys.

For Stolper, heading Nigeria's Economic Planning Unit in the early 1960s involved *Planning without Facts* (1966). Analogously, writing on African economies today, if not completely without facts, is still based on limited and poor quality data.

INCOME DISTRIBUTION DATA

Income distribution data are usually less accurate than GNP statistics. The ILO's 1984 survey of 100 African income-distribution studies found grave weaknesses in individual-country data frequently used for crossnational comparisons (Lecaillon *et al.*, 1984). The survey found only nine African countries with reliable and comparable measures of household income concentration. Few African countries offer enough data for a rigorous, quantitative analysis of the dimensions and trends in poverty and income inequality.

Moreover, as Rimmer (1984) points out, scholars often do not indicate how income and the units sharing in it are defined. Also, the factual basis of the estimates is sometimes unclear. Some figures appear to have been produced on a very slender basis, but are frequently cited, gaining credence with each subsequent citation. A case in point is Ahluwalia (1974), whose source for Sierra Leone cites the *Freetown Daily Mail*, which drew its information from the advance report of a 1966–8 household survey of the urban Western province, not representative of a primarily rural country. Additionally, the report measures only money income. Futhermore, it is not possible to compute Ahluwalia's figures from the original data.

The problem is not only having the data but interpreting them. Because of the lack of comprehensive rural income distribution data, Lee (1983) looks at 'partial indicators' like land distribution. He calculates a Gini coefficient of 0.45 for Côte d'Ivoire's (southern) forest zone. While Lee considers this high, it is low compared to 0.53, the average Gini for land distribution in 15 other Afro-Asian countries, and 0.84, the average for 14 Latin American countries (Squire, 1981). Moreover, although Lee indicates that larger farms have a larger number of residents per farm, he does not include this when calculating the Gini. When Gbetibouo and Delgado (1984) use Lee's data, but include average number of residents per farm as well as imputed subsistence income, they calculate a Gini for *income* distribution for the same region of 0.20, a low degree of inequality. One reason why income distribution is so much more equal than landholdings is that small farms are worked much more intensively.

Because of these problems, I have checked the sources, comparability, and meaning of inequality figures carefully. Despite the weaknesses indicated, the available evidence – macro and micro, quantitative and qualitative – can help us build a general picture of African poverty and income inequality at a given date, and enable us to compare these data to other LDCs (Ghai and Radwan, 1983).

BASIC-NEEDS MEASURES

Measures of African inequality have some limited value, but we must go beyond these data to look at class, regional, and ethnic disparities, to identify deprived groups, and to analyse the degree of equality of opportunity and upward mobility. Streeten *et al.* (1981) prefer measures of basic needs like nutrition, education, health, sanitation, water supply, and housing to measures of poverty and inequality, even though they admit that basic-need satisfaction is highly correlated with income distribution. Yet these measures usually lack information about the distribution by income classes. Thus, overall infant mortality and life expectancy rates in the United States fail to disclose the differentials between the majority white population and minority black and native American populations. Likewise aggregate indicators for Ghana hide differences between the more affluent south and poorer north, and for Liberia differences between Americo-Liberians (descendants of freed slaves from the US in the early nineteenth century) and the 'tribal' population.

Basic-need indicators like caloric consumption (as a percentage of requirement), life expectancy, infant survival, primary enrolment rates, literacy rates, piped water access, and housing availability are highly correlated with GNP per capita when all countries are included. But correlation coefficients drop substantially when you analyse only LDCs (*ibid.*), a partial reflection of GNP's limitations in measuring welfare, especially for the bottom 40% of the population.

DATA AND POLICIES

How much does the lack of data hamper African income-distribution policies? Stolper's reason (1970) for giving up equity concerns to concentrate on growth is the fact that 'in no African country do we have really good information on existing distribution of income or wealth'.

In a similar vein, Okigbo (1975) asks:

> How poor are [Nigeria's] poor and what economic distance separates our poor, so defined, from our rich? It would soon be found that this question cannot be answered until we have cleared away a number of conceptual cobwebs and resolved some statistical difficulties of measurement. It is tempting to rush to promulgate social policies without first establishing the reference points for assessing their subsequent efficiency.

In Nigeria, there is much ignorance about income, employment, physical health, food and nutrition, literacy, water supply, and sanitation. Data are so lacking that the ILO (1981) indicates that making policy is like trying to run through the forest in the dark without a torchlight.

Yet Nigeria, like the rest of Africa, cannot wait for highly reliable time-series data on income distribution to promulgate policies to reduce poverty and inequality. Weak though the data may be, they clearly indicate the necessity to take action. And waiting for good data might mean fossilising income and power discrepancies long before anything is done.

THE QUESTIONS AND APPROACHES OF THIS STUDY

Neo-classical economists (dominant today in the US, Britain, and elsewhere) still use the natural-law paradigms of late-eighteenth-century French physiocracy and Adam Smith's classicism to analyse capitalism and socialism. Neo-classicists usually write in the passive voice so that we can rarely identify the major economic actors. The state does not give subsidies; subsidies are given. Interests in government do not set a price of foreign currency above market rates; the foreign-exchange rate is set or exchange controls are promulgated. (See Nafziger, 1976, for a detailed critique of neo-classicism.)

World Bank economists (e.g., 1981a, 1984a, 1986a) mirror the best and worst of neo-classicism. They criticise African states for keeping farm prices far below market rates, dampening farm producer incentives, transferring peasant savings to large industry, expanding the loss-ridden parastatal sector, protecting and subsidising highly inefficient capital-intensive enterprises, setting exchange rates that discourage exports and encourage imports, and neglecting the maintenance and recurrent costs of new activities. My subsequent chapters not only show the validity of the Bank's criticisms but indicate how these state policies increase inequality.

But the World Bank, particularly during A. W. Clausen's presidency, 1981–6, neglects adverse international economic factors, advocates greater reliance on external technical advice, calls for fewer restrictions on foreign capital, extols Malawi's low price distortions and small-farmer emphasis, and no longer emphasises reducing poverty and income inequality. Indeed its adjustment loans consolidate IMF insistence, when lending to avert African balance-of-payments crises, that the country reduce social (often anti-poverty) programmes. Later I indicate how external economic linkages contribute to income concentration (chapter 6), and that Malawi's policies are not very market-oriented and are biased toward large-scale estate agriculture (chapter 7).

But this study rejects not only the neo-classical approach but also the alternative 'socialist' (actually statist) approach African elites advocate in the Lagos Plan of Action. Most of the Plan's goals mentioned earlier are incontrovertible. But later I criticise the detailed comprehensive planning, large parastatal firm expansion, capital-goods and heavy-industry development, increased state intervention in peasant price-setting, and the introverted development strategy that the Plan emphasises. Indeed a major theme of this book is how elites use the state to pursue economic policies that support their interests at the expense of Africa's poor and working classes.

My 'political economy' approach, like the neo-classicists', not only analyses state policies toward markets, but also examines interests controlling or contending to dominate these policies. Unlike Anglo-

American orthodox economists, I view parastatal losses from expansion beyond market size and management capacity as not merely a techno-economic problem, but also as one of political elites expanding the state sector to disperse benefits to themselves and their clients. Moreover, I recognise the African ruling elites' insight into the contribution of external economic ties to stagnation and income concentration. However, I also discuss how policies of these elites exacerbate inequalities between them and the working classes.

Chapters 3 and 4 set the stage for subsequent political–economic analysis by looking at Africa's position in the global income distribution, and poverty, inequality, and immiserisation in Africa since 1965. Chapter 5 shows how colonialism affected the rules and institutions for trade and investment, foreign economic ties, class relationships, and the level of economic development among various regions and communities after independence. I explore how the contemporary global economic system influences income discrepancies in chapter 6.

Africa's dependence on capitalist DCs, like the US, Canada, Western Europe, and Japan, hampers Africa's economic development. DCs use military and political strength, superior resources, and transnational economic ties with Africa to keep it dependent. African countries become highly dependent on DCs (and international agencies like the IMF and World Bank) for trade, aid, investment, technology, political support, and military assistance, training, and equipment. Economic, political, and military power enables DCs to transform conflicts of economic interests between them and Africa into harmonies of interest between the countries' elites. Large portions of the African political elite and bourgeoisie rely on, and profit from, aid and support from Western countries for position, success, and even survival.

Economic and political interests of African elites depending on activities of foreigners are constraints on internal economic policies. Domestic elites, because of their dependence, protect foreign interests, often at the expense of local economic interests. African elites often act in harmony with outside economic interests, even when military force and aggressive diplomacy are absent (Galtung, 1971).

The common interest between Western and African elites corresponds to disharmony of interests in African countries. As chapter 7 points out, transnational ties, as well as domestic political factors, result in substantial inequalities in both capitalist and socialist countries.

The following types of interest conflicts and income discrepancies exist in Africa: those between the political elite and the working class; the urban and rural classes; the upper and lower elites; the 'comprador' and national elites; and the different regional or ethnic elites. Chapter 8 examines the conflicts and discrepancies between Africa's state bourgeoisie and working class. Chapter 9 looks at the labour aristocracy, income differences among workers, the unemployed, rural discrepancies, and male–female inequalities. Chapter 10 analyses how education maintains class from one generation to another. Chapter 11 shows how policies of urban bias increase urban–rural inequalities and rural poverty. The effect of an export boom (like Nigeria's oil boom in the 1970s) on income distribution is the subject of chapter 12. Chapter 13 indicates the importance of regional and ethnic discrepancies in explaining inequality in Africa. The final chapter discusses approaches to reducing inequality.

§ 3 §

AFRICAN INCOMES IN GLOBAL PERSPECTIVE

The international economy is an interdependent system, where the welfare of peasants, workers, business people, civil servants, and political elites in Africa are linked to decisions made by DC economic policymakers. Many Africans, especially elites, compare their material levels of living with those of rich countries. This chapter examines the position of Africa's rich, poor, and middle class in the global income distribution.

METHOD

Grosh and Nafziger (1986) calculate 1970 global household income distribution by using an aggregation technique that requires data on GNP and populations, on national, household income-distribution (by deciles from the lowest tenth, 1, to the highest tenth, 10), and on Kravis purchasing-power coefficients, which seek to convert from GNP in local currency to US dollars by using an index that measures the relative purchasing power of the two currencies at home, rather than by using the exchange rate. This coefficient multiplied by an African country's nominal GNP gives a higher GNP that more accurately reflects real income differences.

Grosh and I multiply the GNP per capita for each decile for each country by its Kravis coefficient to obtain the decile's GNP per capita in international adjusted dollars (I$). Once we rank the more than 1,000 deciles (all deciles for all 124 countries, each with more than 1 million people) from the lowest (the 1.33 million people in Tanzania's bottom decile, who average I$46) to the highest (the 0.04 million in Kuwait's top decile, who average I$118,000), we divide the roughly 3,600 million people into ten deciles, each with 360 million people.

Table 1. *Global income distribution*

(1) Population deciles	(2) Fraction of total income earned	(3) I$ GNP per capita of decile upper limits
1	.006	202
2	.010	293
3	.015	422
4	.019	588
5	.029	882
6	.042	1,322
7	.069	2,236
8	.122	3,847
9	.201	6,878
10	.487	—
Gini coeff.	.636	
Mean per capita GNP		2,499

GLOBAL INCOME DISTRIBUTION

Table 1 indicates global income distribution. The Gini index of inequality for the world distribution, 0.64, is more than that for the nation with the greatest household income inequality. Global income distribution is more unequal than that within any single country because it adds the effect of crossnational disparities in GNP per capita to that of internal inequalities.

REGIONAL INCOME DISTRIBUTION

North America (Canada and the US – Gini = 0.39) and Europe (0.47) have both narrow crossnational disparities in real GNP per capita and low internal inequalities. Asia (0.64), which combines East Asia, Southeast Asia, South Asia, and Japan, but excludes China and the Middle East, accounts for 43% of the world's population. The high income concentration in Asia, whose incomes range from Japan to Bangladesh, is representative of the world's wide, crossnational income disparities. Although its internal income distributions are high, Africa has intermediate inequality (Gini = 0.56) between Latin America (0.54) and the Middle East (0.61). The reason for Africa's moderate regional inequality is that it includes only low- and lower-middle-income countries (except for South Africa), and thus narrower crossnational disparities than Asia. Yet subsaharan Africa's inequality is higher than any of Asia's three, more homogeneous, regions (table 2).

SOUTH AFRICA AND BLACK-RULED AFRICA

Inequality is of serious concern even when poverty rates, by third-world standards, are not low. In 1976, the GNP per capita of black South Africans was $420, roughly the same as that for Africa as a whole. Yet this low income for 19 million blacks (as well as $1,120 for almost 2 million Asians and $900 for almost 1 million coloureds) appals the world community when compared to the $5,240 income per capita for the 4.5 million white South Africans, higher than Britain's $4,180. In the early 1970s, life expectancy, an indicator of health, was 52 years for black South Africans compared to 46 for Africa generally, but 65 for white South Africans and 72 for DCs. During the same period, income concentration in South Africa was the world's highest, with the income share of its top 10% households (virtually all white) 57% compared to 48% for Brazil (the LDCs' highest), and 37%, the DCs' highest. Moreover, South Africa's top 10% held at least 75% of the wealth, a share in excess of any Western country (World Bank, 1978b; Nattrass, 1979; McLaughlin, 1979; McGrath, 1977, 1984; Jain, 1975). South Africa's inequalities are a microcosm of global inequalities, with whites highly over-represented among the affluent and non-whites disproportionately poor.

WORLD INCOME DECILES

How much of a given decile consists of members of particular world regions? The first (lowest) decile of the global income distribution consists of 360 million individuals (213 million (59%) from South Asia, 46 million (12%) from subsaharan Africa, 57 million (16%) from China, 30 million (8%) from Southeast and East Asia, 7 million (2%) from the Middle East, 3 million (1%) from Latin America, and 4 million (1%) from Eastern Europe and the USSR) who received between 42 and 202 adjusted US dollars. The results of these calculations for all ten deciles are plotted in fig. 1. Each bar represents one decile of the global distribution. The divisions within each decile show the proportion of it constituted by different world regions. This figure indicates that there are subsaharan Africans (as well as East and Southeast Asians, Middle Easterners, Latin Americans, and Eastern

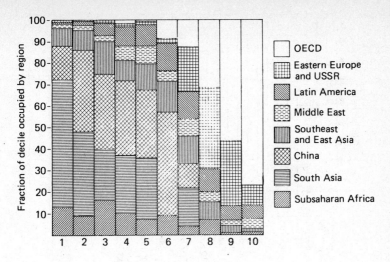

Fig. 1   Global income deciles

Europeans) in every decile of the world population. Even when South Africa is not included, subsaharan Africa is represented in the first nine deciles.

What decile corresponds to the median income (i.e., with half the households having incomes above and half below) for each world region? For South Asia it is the second decile (10th – 20th percentile), for subsaharan Africa and China the fourth, for Southeast and East Asia the fifth, for the Middle East and Latin America the sixth, for Eastern Europe the eighth, and for the OECD the ninth.

Let us compare the deciles of African countries with those of other countries. In fig. 2, the scale on the left goes from world decile one to ten. The country lines extend through all of the world deciles in which that country has citizens. Thus, Kenyans are in the first through eighth deciles, while Britons are in the seventh through tenth.

Fig. 2 and table 1, column 2 show that a poor Frenchman (global decile 4, I$422–588) is poorer than a Zambian with median income (43rd percentile in decile 5, I$588–882) and that a poor Briton (decile 7, I$1,322–2,236) is richer than a rich Ethiopian (decile 6, I$882–1,322). (Today Zambians and Ethiopians are probably worse off relative to Western Europeans than in 1970, the reference year.) Although any number of such comparisons can be made, a word of caution is necessary. The extremes of the distributions are cut off because the data are presented in deciles. Thus, the highest incomes

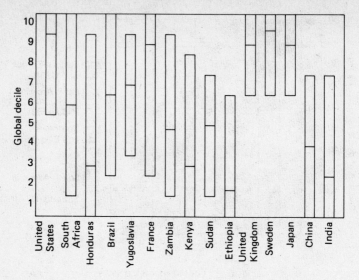

Fig. 2   Crossnational comparisons (with line for median percentile)

portrayed here are averages of the top 10% of the population. This hides the differences between the well-to-do and the extraordinarily rich. Thus, the common perception that the top 1–2% income earners (the most affluent politicians, civil servants, military officers, and business people) in Kenya, Zambia, and other African countries have greater access to material goods than the median-income American (at the 90th global income percentile) or median Briton (at the 85th percentile) is still consistent with the global income distribution data.

The extremes of poverty are also somewhat under-represented in these figures. However, this distortion is less severe because a person's income cannot permanently fall below a subsistence income.

CONCLUSION

Subsaharan Africa's 1970 median income is at the world's 31st percentile. About 70% of Africans (including South Africans) are in the bottom half of the global income distribution. Chapters 5 and 6 indicate how global economic relationships helped contribute to Africa's stagnation and inequality.

§ 4 §

THE GREAT DESCENT
INEQUALITY AND
IMMISERISATION

Africans entered the 1960s' UN First Decade of Development (DDI) with high expectations. A majority of African states (24) received political independence in that decade. National leaders planned economic strategies to overcome the barriers to economic growth during the colonial period.

Kwame Nkrumah, Ghana's president, 1957–66, prophesied in 1949 that 'If we get self-government, we'll transform the Gold Coast into a paradise in ten years' (Killick, 1978). Even Indian economist Patel (1964) saw enormous potential for Africa. According to him, Africa's arable land was more than twice that of Latin America or China, and nearly one and a half times that of India, but with only half India's population, and a climate ideally suited for many crops. Moreover, the agricultural distance between the industrialised countries and Africa 'is much narrower than is commonly imagined'. Indeed the distance separating farm scarcity from surplus was not difficult to cover. Patel explained that an annual industrial growth of 7–9% could bring Africa to DC levels in 40–50 years. Hance (1967) found 'no justification for pessimism regarding the future of many [African] countries; there is need for greater realism, and it is realistic to aim towards far higher standards than prevail today'.

The UN General Assembly (1962), in proclaiming DDI, indicated the objective to 'accelerate progress towards self-sustaining growth of the economy of the individual nations and their social advancement so as to attain in each under-developed country a substantial increase in the rate of growth, with each country setting its own target, taking as the objective a minimum rate of growth of aggregate national income of 5 per cent at the end of the decade'.

Although in 1969 the Pearson commission decried 'the widening gap between the developed and developing countries', LDC growth has been at least as fast as that of DCs. Morawetz (1977) indicates that

21

Table 2. Poverty and income inequality (by income groups and LDC regions)

	Population (ms) 1984	1984 GNP per capita (US$)	Annual growth rate, GNP pc (%) 1965–84	% of pop. in poverty 1975 p.p. adj. (a)	Life expectancy at birth (years) 1984	Poorest 20% share/ richest 5% share 1970
LDC regions						
Subsaharan Africa	406.1	382	0.8	51	49	0.155
South Asia	972.9	258	1.6	47	55	0.288[b]
Southeast Asia	377.3	640	4.1	59	59	0.215
East Asia	69.8	2,853	6.6	7	69	0.384
China	1,029.2	310	4.5	27	69	0.227
Middle East	181.9	1,266	4.0	18	57	0.116
Latin America	386.2	1,741	2.8	14	65	
Country income groups						
LDCs	3,577.1	589	2.9	37	60	0.198
Hi-in. oil ex.	18.8	11,250	3.2		62	
DCs	733.4	11,430	2.4		76	0.443
Socialist	389.3				68	

Note: Subsaharan Africa does not include South Africa. Southeast Asia contains the Philippines. LDCs comprise the low- and middle-income countries in World Bank, 1986b. DCs are non-socialist only. Socialist includes only Soviet and Eastern European. High-income oil exporters consist of the United Arab Emirates, Kuwait, Saudi Arabia, Libya, and Oman.

Sources: Ahluwalia et al., 1979; Eberstadt, 1979; World Bank, 1980b; World Bank, 1983a, 1; World Bank, 1986b

(a) Based on purchasing power adjustment

(b) Includes Southeast Asia (e.g., Indonesia and Malaysia)

the relative economic gap narrowed slightly, 1950–75. The LDCs' annual real economic growth of 3.4% was unprecedented, faster than that of DCs in any comparable period before 1950. Indeed LDC *total* economic growth during DDI exceeded the target. Later figures from table 2 show LDC annual growth, 1965–84, 2.9%, in excess of the DCs' 2.4% growth.

ECONOMIC GROWTH AND DECLINE

The tragedy is that subsaharan Africa, one of the poorest third-world regions, has not shared in these gains, as its economy has been stagnant, and its poverty rates and income concentration have been high. *The Great Ascent* expected in the 1960s (Heilbroner, 1963) has become the great descent. Growth gradually declined from the 1950s to the 1960s (1.3% per annum) to the 1970s (0.8% yearly) (Morawetz, 1977; World Bank, 1981a). Subsaharan Africa's annual growth, 1965–84, 0.6%, was far below that of LDCs generally, 3.2%. If you exclude Nigeria, which grew 2.8% annually mainly because of a 1970s' oil boom, Africa grew only 0.2% yearly, 1965–84. During this period, Madagascar, Uganda, Zambia, Zaïre, Ghana, and Niger declined by more than 1% yearly, while Senegal declined 0–1% annually (table 3). Since real growth is overstated as countries modernise, due to the increased proportion of goods and services produced for the market, Africa's overall growth during this period may be zero (Nafziger, 1984).

This trend worsened in the early 1980s, as Africa's real GDP per capita fell 2.3% yearly, 1980–5 (IMF, 1986). ECA (1985) described Africa's economic situation in 1984 as the worst since the 1930s' great depression, and Africa 'the very sick child of the international economy'. Recognising this, the UN devoted its thirteenth special session (1986) to develop a strategy to safeguard Africa's economic survival.

Ghana's decline accelerated, with real annual GDP per capita falling by 0.3%, 1950–60 and 1960–70, but 3.2%, 1970–81. Ghana, whose 1950 GNP per capita ranked first in black Africa and high among LDCs, was overpassed by 1975 by Zambia, Côte d'Ivoire, Congo (Brazzaville), Swaziland, Taiwan, South Korea, Malaysia, Turkey, Iraq, Syria, Colombia, Ecuador, Paraguy, and the Dominican Republic. Investment in Ghana, which increased in the 1950s, declined by 3.1% in the 1960s and 4.3% in the 1970s. Exports, growing faster than population in the 1950s, grew only 0.1% annually in the 1960s, and fell 9.2% in the 1970s (Teal, 1986; Morawetz, 1977).

Table 3. Indicators of African poverty and income inequality

	Popu-lation (ms) 1984	1984 GNP per capita ($)	Annual growth rate, GNP pc (%) 1965–84	% of pop. in poverty 1975 p.p. adj. (a)	Life expec-tancy at birth (years) 1984	Adult (15 yr. or older) literacy (%) late 1970s	Gini index of inc. ineq. (house-holds) 1960s–70s
Low-income countries							
Ethiopia	42.4	110	0.4	68	44	15	
Zaïre	29.7	140	– 1.6	53	51	55	
Mali	7.3	140	1.1		46	10	
Burkina Faso	6.6	160	1.2		45	9	
Malawi	6.8	180	1.7		45	25	0.452
Niger	6.2	190	– 1.3		43	10	
Tanzania	21.5	210	0.6	51	52	79	0.509
Uganda	15.0	230	– 4.4	55	51	52	
Madagascar	9.9	260	– 1.6		52	50	
Kenya	19.6	310	2.1	55	54	47	0.586

Ghana	12.3	350	−1.9	25	53	20	
Mozambique	13.4				46	33	
Sudan	21.3	360	1.2	51	48	32	0.446
Senegal	6.4	380	−0.5	35	46	21	0.513
Lower middle-income countries							
Zambia	6.4	470	−1.3	10	52	44	0.618
Angola	9.9				43	20	
Côte d'Ivoire	9.9	610	0.2	25	52	35	0.415
Nigeria	96.5	730	2.8	35	50	34	0.5
Zimbabwe	8.1	760	1.5		57	69	0.629
Cameroon	9.9	800	2.9		54	41	
Upper middle-income country							
S. Africa	31.6	2,340	1.4		54	65	0.563

Note: Includes only subSaharan countries with 6.0 million or more people

Sources: Aboyade, 1973; Ahluwalia *et al.*, 1979; Diejomaoh and Anusionwu, 1981b; Jain, 1975; Lecaillon *et al.*, 1984; Sewell *et al.*, 1985; Vandemoortele, 1982; World Bank, 1978a; World Bank, 1986b

[a]Based on purchasing power adjustment

Even Kenya, Côte d'Ivoire, Nigeria, and Malawi – all with annual growth rates 2.4% or more, 1960–79 – fell on hard times in the early 1980s. Kenya's real GDP per capita declined 4.1% from 1978 to 1985 (World Bank, 1981a; EIU, 1986).

Côte d'Ivoire, which had an almost negligible manufacturing sector before independence, enjoyed a 3.5% annual growth in real GNP from 1960 to 1974 (World Bank, 1976). But Marxist economist Amin (1973) argued that, for three reasons, the Ivorian economic 'miracle' was transitory. First, fast plantation output growth would be confined to an early period of gains from undeveloped land, cheap Burkinan labour, and improving commodity markets. Second, the rapid industrial growth ensuing from protecting import substitutes at independence in 1960 would soon be exhausted because of restricted domestic markets, declining foreign investment opportunities, and increasing fund expatriation by foreigners. Third, slower growth would exacerbate the strains from inequalities between regions, ethnic groups, Ivorians and immigrants, and employers and workers. Indeed, Côte d'Ivoire suffered from a slowdown in the late 1970s, and negative growth in the early 1980s. Commodity terms of trade fell in the three years after 1980 from decreasing cocoa and coffee export prices. Concurrently, real growth in GDP, 5.2% in 1980, declined to 0.2% in 1981, −2.9% in 1982, −4.1% in 1983, and −3.6% in 1984 (N'Guessan, 1985; Kouadio, 1985).

Even in the midst of Nigeria's oil boom, the ILO (1981) warned that the economy was fundamentally weak:

Large numbers [of Nigerians] are worse off in numerous respects, especially in the rural areas but also in the big new slums of the cities. Even those whose buying power has increased speak frequently of what they have lost – regular supplies of water, continuous electricity, telephones that worked, uncorrugated roads with good surfaces and, above all, the ability to walk or drive around without an ever-present fear of road accidents and armed robbery.

The ILO believes that even a total economic growth of 6% yearly for Nigeria for the next twenty years could be disastrous, if nutritional and social development continue to receive so little emphasis.

In many African countries people do without public services, as governments concentrate on sheer economic and political survival. Features of modernisation to which many Africans have been exposed are withering: trucks no longer run because there are no spare parts and roads are impassable; airplanes no longer land at night in some places because there is no electricity to light the runway. Africa seems to lack the means to generate the resources needed for growth and reducing poverty (World Bank, 1984a).

COMPARATIVE ECONOMIC WELFARE

Africa is among the poorest regions in the developing world. The UN has designated 36 countries – 26 in Africa – with a low per capita income, low share of manufacturing in gross product, and low literacy rates as least developed countries. The UN and other international agencies have tried to get donor countries to increase economic aid to these countries. World Bank data indicate that 1984 GNP per capita in subsaharan Africa was $382, substantially less than other LDC regions except China's $310 and South Asia's $258 (table 2). However, without Nigeria's $730 per capita income, Africa's average is only $274.

Per capita GNP figures have a substantial margin of error – perhaps $100–200 among low-income countries – and should not be used for relative rankings when differences are small. Using market prices valued at official exchange rates distorts international comparisons of GNP per capita (Nafziger, 1984).

Africa's GNP per capita is higher than Kenya's, which is at about the same level as China's, when adjusted for purchasing power. China's adjusted GNP per capita is substantially in excess of India, whose figure is about the same as the South Asia average. Thus, while Africa's average income is among the lowest in the world, it may be no lower than that of China and South Asia (World Bank, 1983a, 1).

INTERTEMPORAL AND CROSSNATIONAL INEQUALITY COMPARISONS

Estimates of LDC income distribution are approximations of what we wish to measure. Frequently, statistical sources understate income not only for subsistence farmers but also for the rich, who often understate income for tax purposes.

Next to Latin America, subsaharan Africa has the highest income inequality (rich/poor income shares) of any LDC region (table 2). Regional income inequality depends on both inequality *between* and *within* nation-states. While subsaharan Africa's *inter*-country differences do not vary much from other LDC regions, Africa's *intra*-country inequalities are substantial.[1] All ten of Africa's *intra*-country Gini indices of household income inequality exceed 0.4, while only six of seventeen of Asia's *inter*-country Gini indices exceed 0.4 (Grosh and Nafziger, 1986).

The few data over time indicate that inequality in Zambia, Ghana, Malawi, Tanzania, and Kenya increased from the 1960s to the 1970s. From 1963–4 to 1970, while Ghana's economic growth was negative, the share of the poorest 50%'s earnings from cocoa (the dominant export) remained at 12%, while the richest 10% increased its share from 40% to 45%. During Zambia's mineral-fuelled growth, 1959–72, as urban formal sector wages increased rapidly, the income share of the bottom 60% fell from 27.2% to 19.5%, while the top 10%'s share increased from 45.2% to 46.5% (ILO, 1977a; Bequele and Van der Hoeven, 1980; Hunt, 1984).

Nyerere admitted that Tanzania had fallen short of the Arusha Declaration's tenth anniversary (1977) goals. Tanzania, he indicated, was neither socialist nor self-reliant, and had substantial poverty and inequality. Indeed, from 1969 to 1975–76, the mainland's poverty rates and cash income concentration increased substantially for rural areas, urban areas, and overall (with the Gini rising from 0.45 to 0.57) (Bukuku, 1985). However, tax-expenditure policies partly ameliorated these trends (chapter 8).

Nigeria has no comprehensive income-distribution estimates over time. From 1960 to 1978, rural poverty remained constant though its rate declined, while urban poverty roughly doubled though its rate probably declined. Federal civil-service studies indicating a substantial increase in income concentration from 1969 to 1976 (roughly a year after the inflationary Udoji Commission salary awards especially increased high-ranking administrative salaries) may reflect the trend in overall income inequality. But this inequality probably declined from 1976 to the end of the decade, with increased salaries for low-income workers, the abolition of subsidised car allowances to high-income groups, the poor performance of the oil and other modern sectors, and the faster growth of agricultural production (Nafziger, 1983; Diejomaoh and Anusionwu, 1981b).

The ILO (1981), based on labour-force surveys and sectoral income estimates, indicates the following 1973 Nigerian average household income: ₦ 329 (about $540) among the 73.6% of households in agriculture, ₦ 727 among the 14.7% with earners in the informal sector, ₦ 1,260 among the 9.4% with formal-sector wage-earners, and ₦ 8,130 among the 2.2% with formal-sector owners and managers.

The World Bank's international comparisons (1978a) indicate that 1973–4 income inequality in Côte d'Ivoire was low (Gini = 0.42), not high (Gini = 0.49) as Ahluwalia's less complete 1970 estimates (1974) suggest. This low inequality was despite top incomes going to expensive expatriates, and low wages to a million immigrant African labourers (from Burkina Faso, Mali, and other neighbouring countries), who are the bulk of the agrarian wage force and are usually paid below the minimum wage. A major contributor to even distribution was the small discrepancy between average farm and urban salary incomes, a contrast to most African countries (chapter 11).

COMPARATIVE POVERTY RATES

Income inequality and absolute poverty are different concepts. Absolute poverty is below the income that secures the bare essentials of food, clothing, and shelter. Determining this level is a matter of judgement, making crossnational comparisons difficult. Moreover, what is considered poverty varies according to the living standards of the time and region. For example, some Americans now classified as poor are materially better off than many Americans of the 1950s or Africans of today who are not considered poor.

Still, despite measurement problems, Ahluwalia *et al.* (1979) designate an international line below which people are assumed to be in poverty. They propose a poverty line based on a standard set in India, the country with the most extensive literature on the subject.

The poverty line is defined as the income needed to ensure a daily supply of 2,250 calories per day, a figure of 200 adjusted dollars (I$200) per person in 1975, adjusted upward by a Kravis coefficient (chapter 3) to reflect purchasing power measured in 1970 US dollars. They find the poverty line in another LDC by finding the equivalency in purchasing power to the Indian standard. Using existing income distribution data, they calculate what percentage of the population of that LDC falls below that poverty line.

The 2,250 calories would be met by the following diet: 5 grams leafy vegetables, 110 grams other vegetables (potatoes, root vegetables, gourds, and so on), 90 grams milk, 35 grams oil, 35 grams sugar, 10 grams flesh foods (fish and meats), 45 grams pulses (peas or other legumes), and 395 grams cereals (rice, maize, millet, or wheat) (e.g., about two cups of hot prepared rice, equivalent in weight to 54% of the total diet) (Rajalakshmi, 1975).

Data on income distribution for 1975 indicate that 46% of the Indian population was below the poverty line (or potentially undernourished). Given information on income distribution, Ahluwalia *et al.*, determine poverty in other countries by finding the percentage of the population from households with an income of less than I$200. About 38% (1.4 billion) of the 1986 LDC population was poor.[2]

The highest 1975 poverty rates by world region were Africa's (51%), Southeast Asia's (49%), and South Asia's (47%) (table 2). Yet a small margin of error for the largest country of each regional grouping – Nigeria, Indonesia, and India – could change the ranking.

We can surmise, however, that subsaharan Africa's poverty rate is among the highest of any region of the world.

In Uganda, Ghana, Zambia, Zaïre, Niger, Madagascar, and Senegal, where income per head declined, 1965–83 (table 3), poverty undoubtably increased. Ghana's cocoa producer real income declined by 41% from 1952 to 1967, while real urban minimum wages in 1973 were almost half those of 1963. In Ethiopia and Kenya, the real incomes of the poor declined even though growth was positive from the 1960s to the 1970s (ILO, 1977; Griffin, 1978).

Poverty rates, highly correlated with malnutrition rates, vary among the population. The ILO's study (1981) of energy and protein intake in Nigeria in 1965 indicated that senior-staff government employees had more than required, junior clerks 90% of that required, urban labourers 60%, coastal, rural farm families 83%, and northern, rural farm families 58%.

Many other LDCs (including China, India, Malaysia, and the Philippines) increased their rural and overall poverty rates even while experiencing economic growth from the 1960s to the 1970s (ILO, 1979; Nafziger, 1985a). African data on economic stagnation and rising inequality suggest added pressure on ruling elites, who often faced declining benefits for upper classes together with increasing poverty rates.

LIFE EXPECTANCY AND INFANT MORTALITY

PQLI (Physical Quality of Life) is a widely-used composite index of social welfare combining literacy rates, life expectancy at birth, and infant mortality rates. The latter two variables represent the effects of nutrition, public health, income, and the general environment. Infant mortality reflects the availability of clean water, the condition of the home environment, and the mother's health. Literacy is a measure of well-being and a requirement for economic development. While PQLI and GNP per capita are highly correlated, rankings do diverge as China's PQLI ranking is high and the Middle East's low. On a scale of 0 (the most unfavourable performance in 1950) to 100 (the most favourable expected in 2000) Japan scores 99, North America 97, Europe and the Soviet Union 93, East Asia 91, Oceania 88, Latin America 77, China 75, Southeast Asia 66, the Middle East 55, Subsaharan Africa 44, and South Asia 44 (Sewell *et al.*, 1985).

The best single indicator of health and nutrition is probably life expectancy, an alternative measure of (the lack of) poverty. Nigeria's poverty rate of 35% is below Africa's 51%, and the LDCs' 38%, ranking close to the Philippines's and Thailand's. But Nigeria's 1984 life expectancy, 50 years, is almost the same as Africa's, which is far below the Philippines's 63 and Thailand's 64, and even the LDC average of 60. Although Nigeria's 1984 GNP per capita ($730) exceeds Ghana's $350, Kenya's $310, and India's $260, their life expectancies (53, 54, and 56, respectively) are higher than Nigeria's. The UN Family Planning Association (1979) indicates that Nigeria's 'health status is... very poor with the prevalence of largely preventable and communicable conditions with high levels of infant and general mortality and morbidity'. Infant mortality rates, 133 per thousand for Nigeria, 125 for Côte d'Ivoire, and 121 for subsaharan Africa, compare to 92 for LDCs generally. Mortality among Nigerian children aged 1–4 is about 60 times as high as Western Europe. Life expectancy did not increase much in the 1970s, despite the rapid oil-led growth (*ibid.*; World Bank, 1986b). In general, Africa's life expectancy (49) is much lower than the next lowest, South Asia (54).

In Africa, infectious and parasitic diseases (malaria, intestinal parasites, dysentery, diarrhoea, and pneumonia) are the major causes of death, with trypanosomiasis (spread by the tsetse fly), bilharzia (carried by a parasitic worm), malnutrition, complications of pregnancy and childbirth, anaemias, measles, tetanus, and tuberculosis also important contributors. Lagos's compulsory vital registration indicates that gastro-enteritis, pneumonia, and measles (nearly all in young children) accounted for one-third of deaths in 1973. In Cross River state, Nigeria (1979), only 18% of all children under six years old had measles vaccination, 5% triple antigen (whooping cough, tetanus, and diphtheria), 5% polio, and 3% BCG (tuberculosis), rates about one-half to one-fourth those of Lagos.

Piped water serves one in four Africans (including Nigerians). Nigeria's water supply, especially in urban areas, did not grow as fast as population in the 1970s. Urban people without piped water (which often fails) rely on illegal connections or on street stand-pipes (often distant from home), and lorries selling water by the bucket (up to a half naira, about $0.70, per litre in 1981). Few rural Nigerians have easy access to plentiful and pure water. Their typical practice is to draw (often) polluted water from wells or streams, in cans or rubber bags, and to carry it home, sometimes for several kilometres (ILO, 1981; ECA, 1983b).

In 1981, no Nigerian town had a modern, central sewerage system. About half the urban population empties pails into the street or on waste ground. People litter garbage on city streets, often flooded because of inadequate drainage.

The falling height-for-age ratios in northern Zambia for all ages under 15 years between the 1950s and early 1980s are signs of declining health and nutrition. African child mortality rates, 50% higher than the LDC average in the 1950s, were double that average in the mid 1980s (World Bank, 1984a). While the population per doctor in Africa dropped from 10,000 in 1970 to 6,500 in 1980, health facilities are concentrated in urban areas. Most rural people have had only limited access to health care. The vast majority of mortal illnesses in rural areas (and many in urban areas) go undiagnosed.

GROWTH OF AVERAGE FOOD PRODUCTION

Annual food output growth per capita, 1963–83, was 0.5% in LDCs generally, 0.9% in Latin America, 1.4% in East Asia (except Japan and China), 0.3% in South and Southeast Asia, and − 0.8% in subsaharan Africa (fig. 3). To avoid distortions due to weather fluctuations, I use a five-year moving average, in which food output in the year 1983 is computed as an average of the outputs of 1981 through 1985. Furthermore, the World Bank (1984a) and the US Department of

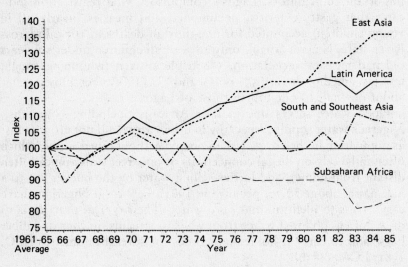

Fig. 3   Index of per capita food production, 1961–5 to 1985
(1961–5 average = 100)
Note: East Asia excludes Japan and China
Source: US Department of Agriculture, 1986

Agriculture (USDA, 1980) expect Africa's food output per person to decline from 1980 through 1990.

African daily calorie consumption per capita – 2,115 in the early 1960s and 2,197 in the mid 1970s – was 20% below the ECA's critical minimum (1983b). Only Côte d'Ivoire's, the Congo's, Liberia's, Senegal's, and Madagascar's 1983 daily consumption was no less than the minimum required (World Bank, 1986b). An American Association for the Advancement of Science symposium argued (Abelson, 1975) annual food production would be enough to feed everyone on earth adequately if distribution were more equal. While *intra*-regional distribution would be adequate for Asia and Latin America, sub-Saharan Africa is the only world region where caloric intake, even if equally distributed, is below minimal nutritional standards (USDA, 1980).

Africa's deteriorating food position began before the Sahel's, Sudan's, and Ethiopia's 1968–74 and 1984–5 droughts. While the roots of Africa's food crisis began during colonialism, the continuing crisis is due to African governments' neglect of agriculture (chapters 6 and 11).

Africa's food self-sufficiency, 98% in the 1960s, dropped to 86% in the 1980s. And food demand growth, dependent more on population growth than average income growth, is growing fast. Projecting Africa's 1986 population of 583 million forward at a 3.2% annual growth rate means 906 million people by 2000. The food deficit (consumption minus production), 3.7% of consumption in 1975, is expected to increase to 25.2% in 1990 (ECA, 1983b; IFPRI, 1977).

For Africa which, unlike Britain, West Germany, and Japan, has no industrial surplus, the deficit means undernourishment. And growing food import demand and rising grain prices exacerbate many African states' balance-of-payments crises.

African food insecurity is high (and increasing since the 1960s) not only because of large food deficits but also due to insecurity from domestic output and foreign-exchange reserve fluctuations, and foreign food-aid reductions. Cereals consumption per capita has had a high coefficient of variation since 1965 (Kirkpatrick and Diakosavvas, 1985).

Percentage food deficits are most serious in Kenya, Mozambique, Senegal, Madagascar, Burkina Faso, Central African Republic, Chad, Guinea, Guinea-Bissau, Mali, Mauritania, Niger, and Somalia. But Nigeria, with a fourth of the population, has subsaharan Africa's largest food deficit. The 'Nigerian disease' (an overvalued domestic currency) reduces food output and increases food import (chapter 12).

From the mid 1960s to the late 1970s, despite the oil boom, Nigeria's per capita food consumption did not increase perceptibly. Based on the small margin between food availability and requirements, the ILO (1981) estimates that the bottom third of the population was undernourished. In the 1960s, tropical medical scholars indicated three-fourths of Ilesh (Western) village's children fell below the 25th percentile by world nutritional standards. However, severe malnutrition was rare except in northern villages (and wartime Biafra).

IMMISERISATION

Africa's lack of economic growth and no improvement in income equality means growing poverty and undernourishment rates, or immiserisation. This immiserising development contrasts to LDCs generally, which experienced growth and a falling poverty rate. Africa's experience is unique, as there is no evidence of any other major world region experiencing immiserisation for any decade since World War II.

§ 5 §

THE COLONIAL ROOTS

Inequalities [in precolonial Africa] existed, but they were tempered by comparable family or social responsibilities, and they could never become gross and offensive to the social equality which was at the basis of the communal life. (Nyerere, 1968)

It is evident that decolonization is not, cannot ever be, a honey-smooth process. (Henissart, 1973)

Despite romantic flights of imagination by writers like Nyerere, idealising Africa's past, castes, classes, and serious inequalities in wealth and power existed before colonial rule. Caste is a hierarchically organised system of occupations, in which entrance into an occupation is determined by birth. Low castes like the Twa in Rwanda, who believed in the rightness of caste and their place in it, posed little threat to powerful and wealthy rulers that used oppression and terror when essential. Only elders and regional notables were in a position to undermine the privileged position of African ruling groups (Bequele and Van der Hoeven, 1980; Markovitz, 1977). Indeed precolonial elites could more easily transmit wealth, opportunity, power, and privilege to their children than elites today.

The next two chapters deal with imperialism, the extension of economic and political power by one state over another, resulting not only from formal conquest and empire, but also from informal controls before and after colonialism.

The European struggle to establish forts and trading-posts on African shores from the mid-seventeenth century to the mid-eighteenth century was part of the wider competition for trade and empire. By the 1880s, European states directly intervened to assure stable conditions for trade and investment. The 1884–5 Berlin Conference clarified European spheres of influence, so Africa was divided on paper by 1900 and was generally under European administration two decades later. European technology was superior in the late nineteenth century, so Africa entered the colonial era concentrating on the export of primary products and the import of manufactured and processed goods (Rodney, 1982; Curtin *et al.*, 1978).

THE COLONIAL ECONOMIC IMPACT

One myth of African history is that the 'primitive' continent had been gradually enlightened by 'civilisation's' spread through greater Western contact. A less value-laden interpretation emphasises Africa's benefit from a broad interchange of culture. Indeed Africans welcomed the exchange of ideas, inventions, cultures, and commodities, but denied imperialism was necessary for this exchange. The poet Cesaire, who fought against French colonialism, spoke of 'societies emptied of themselves, of trampled cultures, undermined institutions, confiscated lands, of assassinated religions, annihilated artistic masterpieces, of extraordinary possibilities suppressed'. Africa would doubtless have continued its precolonial trade, technical borrowing, and internal innovations without colonial restrictions (Curtin *et al.*, 1978; Markovitz, 1977; Cesaire, 1970).

Most of the colonial powers' little investment was in infrastructure (transport and communication) oriented toward opening the country to trade with the mother country, not toward integration within the country or with neighbouring African countries. French West African railroad lines created virtually no internal links but brought goods to the port for export to France. And telephoning from Accra, Gold Coast to Abidjan, Côte d'Ivoire, required connection with an operator in London, then Paris, and finally a line to Abidjan. Estimated foreign investment in subsaharan Africa up to World War II was about $6,000 million at 1978 prices, half government and half private (although investment increased in the postwar period through 1964). Most private investment was in mineral-related industries heavily concentrated in southern Africa. Foreign investors invested their funds overwhelmingly in exports, resulting in lopsided development. All governments expected African colonies to pay their own way. But most new colonies could *not* support the bureaucratic superstructure on top of whatever government existed in precolonial times and a modern military establishment to guard against rebellion (Curtin *et al.*, 1978; Rodney, 1982).

For substantial periods the colonies even made loans to the colonial powers. For example, nearly all of Nigeria's foreign-exchange assests before the 1970s were sterling. British sterling was a key international currency under the post-World War II modified gold-exchange standard. In essence, a country that accumulates sterling, as Nigeria did in the 20 years before 1955, extends credit to Britain, facilitating her long-run investments in underdeveloped countries.

During the period of restrictions on converting sterling from World War II to 1958, Nigeria contributed more dollar earnings to the common sterling pool than she withdrew, and she restricted non-sterling imports in a way to increase the importance of imports from Britain. That strengthened both the balance-of-payments position of the sterling area and the international financial position of the UK (Nafziger, 1983). France had a similar arrangement with its West African colonies.

In most of Africa, colonial expenditure policies were as niggardly as Britain's in Nigeria. According to Nicolson (1969), between 1918 and 1948 British administration in Nigeria

was administration on a shoestring. There was no more than 5s per head of population, for all the current needs of central government, for many of the purposes of local government, and for heavy interest charges on loan capital, mostly used to improve the transportation services in which the whole prospect of prosperity and increasing revenues depended... [During] the upheaval of a second World War... the over-stretched administrative machinery came very near to collapse.

Colonial policy also contributed to today's agricultural underdevelopment. (1) Africans were systematically excluded from participation in colonial development schemes and in producing export crops and improved cattle. British agricultural policy in Eastern Africa benefited European settlers, and ignored and discriminated against African farmers, prohibiting Kenyans from growing coffee. (2) Colonial governments compelled farmers to grow selected crops and work to maintain roads. (3) Colonialism often changed traditional land-tenure systems from communal or clan to individual control. This created greater inequalities from new classes of affluent farmers and ranchers, and less secure tenants, sharecroppers, and landless workers. (4) The colonialists failed to train African agricultural scientists and managers. (5) Research and development concentrated on export crops, plantations, and land settlement schemes, neglecting food production and small farmers and herders. (6) Europeans gained most from colonial land grants and agricultural export surpluses (Eicher and Baker, 1982; Ghai and Radwan, 1983).

Moreover, European penetration resulted in epidemiological disaster. A third of Buganda's (and a higher share of the lower Congo's) population died in the sleeping sickness epidemic beginning in 1902.

At about the same time smallpox epidemics ravaged scattered populations from Kenya to Nigeria. People moved by the colonialists into strange disease environments often lacked the immunities protecting the local population. Kenyan highland workers moved to the coast were not protected from malaria by either immunity or resistance through childhood infection. Then too, many migratory or forced mining, construction, or plantation workers faced appalling working conditions or housing, or a bad diet at the workplace – factors increasing death rates (Curtin *et al.*, 1978).

EUROPEAN – AFRICAN DISCREPANCIES

Differentials in income and social services between Europeans and Africans were substantial, as illustrated by Kenya and Zimbabwe, areas of major white settlement.

In Kenya, the first European settlers arrived in the 1890s when some lands normally cultivated or grazed were temporarily unoccupied due to smallpox and rinderpest epidemics decimating the human and livestock populations. Brooke Bond, James Findlay and Son, and other MNCs establishing coffee and tea plantations, and permanent European settlers (many with little farming experience) imitating Africans in growing crops and livestock took over fertile land appropriated by the colonial government and hired African labour.

Before the Europeans arrived, Kenyan farmers enjoyed use-rights for cultivable and grazing land, while larger kinship groups held the right to lease or sell land. Europeans acquired land without regard for existing occupancy rights. Some Africans mistakenly thought they were leasing land to Europeans, while other Africans sold land they had no right to alienate without kinship or elder approval.

Europeans needed cheap labour to succeed in farming. Although the Kenyan government set aside native reserves, their boundaries were pushed back until the late 1920s, when they were stabilised. Growing population pressures and increasing land acquisition by affluent Africans exacerbated reserve land shortage. The reserve and tax policies ensured a labour supply. While African production accounted for more than 70% of exports in 1912–3, it comprised less than 20% by 1928, as Africans lapsed into subsistence farming to support their increasing population but were forced to work for the Europeans to raise money to pay taxes (Hunt, 1984; Leys, 1974).

In Kenya during the late 1950s, the average European farm size was about 130 times that in the African area. Less than 4,000 Europeans owned 3 million hectares of the best land, four-fifths of Kenya's cultivable land with reasonable rainfall. At the same time in Zimbabwe, the nearly 7,000 European farms had roughly 100 times the average size of the 700,000 holdings in the African area. Only 21% of the European-held land in Zimbabwe and 15% in Kenya were utilised. Moreover, tariffs, the Land Bank, research institutions, and road and railroad construction supported European agriculture, especially in Kenya (Hazlewood, 1985; ILO, 1972).

Zimbabwe's segregation was as firm as many parts of South Africa. Zimbabwe (especially), Kenya, and other colonies with substantial white settlers restricted African migration to the town. In most parts of Africa, Europeans excluded Africans from the most remunerative jobs in government and companies, and European banks did not extend credit for African commerce or real estate (Curtin *et al.*, 1978).

ASIAN – AFRICAN DISCREPANCIES

In the nineteenth and early twentieth centuries, the British imported Indian indentured labour to work on the plantations and railway construction in East Africa. About 1900, the British and French encouraged European, Lebanese, Syrian, Greek, and Indian agents and business people in West Africa and Europeans and Indians in the East, while discouraging (or prohibiting) African intermediaries, industrialists, and large traders. Moreover, banks and trading firms dealt with Asians but distrusted Africans. By the 1930s, Indians, prohibited from buying land, captured much of British East Africa's trade, linking export–import with domestic trade. The few African business people who emerged were involved in small-scale, non-export business, depending on European and Asian capital. African entrepreneurs, denied opportunities they regarded as rightly theirs, constituted a major force in the post-World War II rise of nationalism. After independence, many (especially East) African states nationalised Asian businesses, distributing them at concessionary rates to Africans (*ibid.*; Rodney, 1982; Mamdani, 1976; Markovitz, 1977).

COLONIALISM AND SOCIAL STRUCTURE

African social stratification and political power show some continuity from the precolonial to the (British and French) colonial to the contemporary period. Inter-African politics often explain patterns of collaboration with, and resistance to, the Europeans in the nineteenth and early twentieth centuries. Europeans frequently did not enter battle on their own, but made alliances with local groups needing help fighting one another.

Inequality in Africa was thus fossilised as colonial regimes protected cooperative native rulers against revolt from rivals or masses. Most traditional leaders had to retrain to continue leadership as expertise became more important. But although some newly educated men arose from humble backgrounds, it was usually the powerful and wealthy who better availed themselves of Western (especially overseas) education and training essential for positions in the administration, commerce, and foreign firms. In the 1970s, many political innovations were by Nigerian military rulers with close ties with the Northern traditional aristocracy (Markovitz, 1977; Curtin *et al.*, 1978; Nafziger, 1983).

To be sure, sometimes the colonialists used superior military force to topple unyielding African rulers, pare down local chiefs (in the Belgian Congo, from 6,000 in 1917 to 460 by 1953), or create new authorities. Moreover, European companies tended to exclude competing African business-people. Yet many African rulers, merchants, and landowners maintained their high-class standing through colonialism by timely surrender to, and collaboration with, the colonial power. African traders survived or even enriched themselves as apprentices and compradors. Other Africans preserved control by resisting, negotiating, ignoring, or misunderstanding colonial requirements. European rulers usually had to use African intermediaries to rule. Indeed some African rulers increased their authority under colonial protection, receiving a freer hand against political rivals within their kingdoms. In Western Nigeria, the British, disregarding customary limitations, vested excess power in paramount chiefs, causing tension between them and Yoruba communities.

Differences in education, life styles, and mastery of European languages were indicative of social class differences by the early nineteenth century. And with colonialism, new educational, commercial, and governmental employment opportunities even created new classes. But most European officials preferred dealing with the traditional African authorities and the 'unspoiled, bush African' than the members of the new educated elites (clerks, journalists, lawyers, and intellectuals) who did not 'know their places' (Curtin *et al.*, 1978).

During most of colonialism, Europeans made the fundamental decisions. Africans negotiated and debated in European languages, but rarely competed successfully for expatriate jobs. But colonial territory comparatively cheap to conquer became expensive to hold by the post-World War II period. By the 1950s, some farsighted British and French colonial administrators were seeking ways to maintain future influence without incurring the substantial costs of colonialism. The British and French colonialists began emphasising policies to meet what they considered the reasonable demands of the elite-led nationalist movements, steps that eased the colonial burden and helped shape a postcolonial elite favourable to metropolitan interests. Thus, the British and French accelerated Africanisation of the civil service, the armed forces, and police, and introduced equal pay for equal work, so African salaries were brought into line with foreign salaries.

In most (British and French) colonies, nationalist leaders did not engage in direct action or violence, but formed a coalition to reach an agreement with the colonial establishment for political independence (Markovitz, 1977).

In the Buganda Agreement of 1900, the British parcelled out half the land to the entire hierarchy from king to lowest parish chief, creating a parasitic landlord class. This Baganda ruling class became 'sub-imperialists' within the colony of Uganda.[1] Soon after the colonialists and landlord-chiefs forced peasants to produce cotton for export to Britain. Before World War II, the British appointed educated landlord-chiefs leaders of the Buganda parliament. By 1960, the Ugandan colonial government individualised land ownership, making it available primarily to the affluent. Kulaks, rich peasants who regularly supplement family labour with hired labour, dominated the parliament. Most influential kulaks were also traders, who filled the vacuum when Asian traders were driven from rural areas in 1959 (Mamdani, 1976; Barongo, 1984).

In Northern Nigeria (1912–8), Governor-General Frederick Lugard established 'indirect rule', where compliant Fulani emirs maintained day-to-day administrative responsibility. Indirect rule was mutually advantageous; the British economised on officers and used a well-developed tax collection system and the existing emirate states, and at the same time, the Fulani rulers achieved a secure hegemony by eliminating important sources of both internal and external opposition. Moreover, the British later supported the Northern ruling class's opposition to Nigerian independence where southerners – not sympathetic to maintaining the authority of the traditional aristocracy – were dominant. This support led to an agreement in the 1950s to leave the Northern Region intact at independence (1960) with a majority in the federal legislature.

The Harragin Salaries Commission of 1951 (consisting of British officials) established a basis for Nigerian senior civil servants to retain many of the privileges the colonial administrators had enjoyed, such as high salaries, automobiles, educational allowances, and lengthy vacations. These and other benefits to national leaders made them more compliant (excluding radical anti-British spokesmen) and helped prepare a neo-colonial relationship to Nigerian leaders after independence.

But civil service and university graduate salaries were way out of line relative to those of other Africans. In Western Nigeria just before independence, an unskilled labourer earned about £75 a year, a skilled craftsman £300, and government salaries to university graduates £750–3,000. While previously the bright son of a poor, illiterate farmer could receive lineage financial support for university education leading to a top job, by 1960 or so class lines began to solidify as the educated first generation read books and provided travel and experience to their children, made sure they attended good schools, and provided tutors to prepare them for entrance examinations. In Ghana, after independence, the son of a secondary-school graduate had 17 times the chance of attending secondary school as the son of an illiterate (Nafziger, 1983; Curtin *et al.*, 1978).

French policy of the 1920s, 1930s, 1940s, and 1950s allowed Africans meeting certain educational and cultural standards to attain full French citizenship. These *évolués*, as well as the *assimilados* in Portuguese Africa, were a tiny minority, but important in social and political life. Likewise British officials in West Africa made appropriate allowances for English-trained lawyers, medical men, and other 'gentlemen'. By the 1920s, European colonialists began working with African intermediaries, if only at the lowest levels (Curtin *et al.*, 1978).

A 1950 French law, together with subsequent legislation, provided African higher civil servants with the same fringe benefits as their French counterparts, including family allowances and trips to France. Later African civil servants' standards of living created heavy burdens on the new states' budgets. The colonialists provided the power, perquisites, and patronage base to assist the African bourgeoisie in maintaining its position. Yet government elites in French Africa, like Nigeria, were cut off from the masses. In 1958 when General Charles de Gaulle gave France's African territories the option of their own independence, the African bourgeoisie chose it with continuing links to France (Markovitz, 1977).

In Côte d'Ivoire in the 1950s, indigenous planter capitalists, under a nationalist organisation which eventually became the Parti Démocratique de Côte d'Ivoire (PDCI), challenged and gradually replaced French planters as the dominant political force in rural areas. By the mid 1950s, Europeans were no longer competitive with Ivorians in agriculture, but were engaged in complementary processing and commerce. Ivorian planters, whose incomes came from exports, collaborated with French capital, now in commerce and industry, especially in timber. Colonial state policies favoured French over indigenous capital. When the French timber industry faced increasing competition and depressed prices, the French government reduced export duties and guaranteed sizeable loans.

The Ivorian last colonial and first independence development plans supported the domestic planters and foreign timber industry in several ways. In 1960, the newly-independent Ivorian government provided major help when its agreement to trade union demands for a minimum wage excluded plantation and forestry workers, and when it allowed open immigration from neighbouring countries to ensure a plentiful supply of labour at these low wages (Mytelka, 1984).

Thus, British and French colonialism, especially near their end, built up the African intelligentsia, bourgeoisie, and skilled labourers at the expense of the peasant and worker majority, whose economic position improved little. Many economic inequalities and class divisions discussed in chapters 7 and 8 originated during the precolonial period, but were exacerbated during the colonial and postcolonial eras.

Belgium, however, did not prepare Zaïre for a gradual transition to independence. Until the last two years of Belgian rule, Zaïre's urban, Westernised *évoloués*, employees of the administration, private enterprise, and some self-employed, diverted energies into ethnic organisations not political parties. The struggle for control of the postcolonial state erupted into armed confrontation, secessions, and assassinations. And because the US, Britain, France, West Germany, and Belgium wanted to continue relying on Zaïre's strategic raw materials, the international scramble for postcolonial influence was destabilising (Kannyo, 1979).

EDUCATION

Education in the British, French, and Belgian colonies provided the intellectual skills necessary for clerks, administrative assistants, noncommissioned officers, and operatives for the colonial government, army, or European firms but not for scientists or more productive farmers. Few girls were educated, as the cash-crop, mineral export, and colonial administrative economy made little provision for educated women.

Education was for the subordination of Africans to the European colonialists and enterprises. This was especially true in Kenya during the early twentieth century where the government, in response to white-settler demands for separate education for their children, trained the European and Asian populations, while providing education for few Africans. In 1936, the government spent 5 times as much per pupil for the European as for the Asian, and 33 times as for the African. By 1951, the European–Asian ratio increased to 6 and the European–African ratio to 44 (Curtin *et al.*, 1978; Bigsten, 1984).

Indeed, settlers made clear that an uneducated African was better than an educated one. The 1949 Beecher report on education in Kenya stated frankly:

Illiterates with the right attitude to manual employment are preferable to products of the schools who are not readily disposed to enter manual employment.

(Rodney, 1982)

Yet education to serve colonial aims eventually boomeranged. Not only were many educated Africans estranged from African conditions, but they demanded educational expansion and control, and complained about European–African civil service discrepancies. In the 1930s, the Nigerian press and Nigerian Legislative Council members campaigned for compulsory, universal free education. A 1933 East African Catholic mission report warned that African control of schools was 'causing difficulties in Kenya. Such schools may easily become hot-beds of sedition.' Indeed, during Kenya's Mau Mau rebellion, the British closed 180 independent (mostly Kikuyu) schools.

As discussed below, educated Africans denied economic and civil service opportunities were leaders in the nationalist movements. By the 1940s, the British colonies educated more people than the colonial economy could absorb. The shock troops in Nkrumah's nationalist youth brigade in the 1950s were primary school leavers disaffected because of the lack of skilled jobs in government and the cocoa monoculture. Also in the late 1950s, *évolués* in the Belgian Congo challenged the colonial order when they realised they could not achieve full advancement (*ibid.*; Coleman, 1958; Kannyo, 1979).

Yet the British and French provided excellent education for children of elites (especially chiefs and aristocrats) that had a longstanding, cooperative relationship with the colonial power. Nkrumah (1970) argues that the counterpart of English 'public' (private) schools, which reproduced the class system, was the colonies' elite schools, which choose 'pupils primarily from among the children of chiefs and aristocrats'. In the Gold Coast, for example, in 1953, 12% of the

students had an annual family income of more than £600, 38%
£250–600, and 50% about £250, when the country's average was
substantially below £100. Moreover, the products of anglophone
African schools 'try to be more British than the British, and . . . imitate
the dress, manners and even the voices of the British public school and
Oxbridge elite'. This educated class tended to lead the nationalist
movement in its early stages.

Yet Western education did not always maintain class, but sometimes provided a new base for social stratification. In Nigeria, from the
1840s until 1898 all education was under the control of Christian
missions. As late as 1942, more than 97% of the students were enrolled
in mission schools. Schools were a powerful instrument of Eu-
ropeanisation. The handful of educated, English-speaking Christian
youths became members of a new class. Many Western-educated
Nigerians originated from the lower strata (frequently the slave class).
Indeed many of Nigeria's most prominent nationalist and post-
independence political leaders were but a generation removed from
the most humble status. The status reversal and upward mobility
attributed to Western education in English (as well as French) West
African colonies have few historical parallels (Coleman, 1958).

THE ROLE OF WOMEN

In most precolonial African societies, patriarchal authority severely
limited the power of women, who were protected if they paid
obeisance to the patriarchs. Yet some societies gave women clearly-
defined economic roles, allowing wealth accumulation and limited
economic authority.

Most African women lost this limited power under colonialism.
Men received land titles, extension assistance, technical training, and
education. When men had to leave farms to seek employment, as in
South Africa, women remained burdened with responsibility for the
family's food. A few women, especially West African market women,
became wealthy but the majority worked long hours to survive. In the
late 1930s the colonial authorities colluded with patriarchal African
leaders to increase control over women. In some instances, where they
had an independent economic base, women used traditional female
organisations and methods, not confrontation to male authority, to
oppose both white and black authorities. Women played a prominent
role in many of the early nationalist struggles. In 1929, for example,
illiterate Aba, Nigerian market women rioted spontaneously in
reaction to rumours of taxes on women and dissatisfaction over the

abuses of native chiefs and courts by attacking chiefs and Europeans indiscriminately and destroying trading firms' property. The police only quelled the riot with an overwhelming show of force that killed fifty women and injured numerous others (Parpart, 1986; Coleman, 1958).

REGIONAL AND ETHNIC DIFFERENCES

The differential impact of European commerce and colonialism created inequalities between ethnic groups, including those between Europeans, Asians, and Africans, which have already been discussed, and those among African ethnic communities, now being discussed. The European influence differed substantially from region to region. For example, the coastal southern Nigeria, eastern Tanganyika, Gabon near Libreville, and the Asante areas of the southern Gold Coast, where European intrusion was of longer and more intense duration, had more experience in parliamentary government, a greater political consciousness, higher literacy, and more developed capitalist institutions than inland regions or interior colonies like Uganda.

In Nigeria, British administration was not formally established until 1900, but coastal groups, especially in the Niger Delta region, had already traded with the West for more than two centuries. Africans were represented in the Legislative Council in Southern Nigeria after 1923, but not in the North (under indirect rule) until 1946 (Nafziger, 1983). Indirect rule, like South Africa's 'homelands' policy, reinforced ethnic feelings (Curtin *et al.*, 1978).

Before World War II, the British supported separate institutions and identities for different ethnic and religious communities, a system of 'native administration' to reflect communal loyalty, and an educational system aimed at cultivating a 'love of tribe'. In the early 1920s, Governor Hugh Clifford clearly emphasised that the idea of a Nigerian nation was both inconceivable and dangerous. Even the nationalist leaders before 1934 thought of nationalism in terms of ethnic community (Coleman, 1958).

Before colonialism, the Kikuyu of central Kenya had no common identity or unified political leadership. But their feeling of ethnicity was enhanced after the expropriation of their land for the white highlands, their transformation from independent peasants to working for Europeans, the building of Nairobi in their midst, the concentrated assault of mission Christianity, the new intercommunication in urban areas, and the 1952–6 'Mau Mau' guerrilla rebellion against the British.

In the early 1960s just prior to independence (1963), Kenyan African leaders agreed to a land-transfer scheme where incoming African settlers purchased land from Europeans with funds lent by the new Kenyan government, borrowing money from the British government and the World Bank. A major reason why subsequent President Jomo Kenyatta, other Kikuyu, and Luo leaders no longer demanded free land distribution was that their ethnic communities would be able to do better by purchases of private property than by transfers based on traditional claims.

Colonialism split apart people who were culturally similar. In the early twentieth century, the Lubu Kasai of the Belgian Congo surpassed the Lulua, who shared the same language and similar culture. The Lubu Kasai, who were uprooted during the early European intrusion, subsequently received more Western education, got better jobs in the Katangan mines, and became more prosperous farmers than the Lulua, who united in an ethnic association to improve their competitive position and fought a bloody, urban guerrilla war which drove the Lubu Kasai from Lubumbashi in the early 1960s (Curtin *et al.*, 1978; Leys, 1974).

One of the last major African elites to emerge under colonialism was the military. The British, by recruiting soldiers from loyal ethnic groups regarded as 'martial races', unwittingly influenced post-colonial power and conflict. Many of the soldiers were from the colonial fringes who had little economic opportunity and education – from Northern (not Yoruba) Nigeria, southern Uganda, and non-Kikuyu Kenyans.

NATIONALISM

In British and French colonies, the nationalist movement, spearheaded by a new elite, was promoted mainly by persons who expected to gain economically and politically. The interests of the African bourgeoisie who failed to get positions in the civil service or who were denied private economic opportunities because of colonial discrimination and restrictions conflicted with the British and French. Nationalist movements, especially before World War II, had little mass support, and were divided by class and community. Following this war, lower- and middle-classes, squeezed by falling incomes and alienated from the concerns of the upper stratum, vented a more militant nationalism.

They demanded educational expansion and political representation. Yet most attempts to ally with the quiescent, but periodically erupting, long-discontented peasantry were failures.

Mass nationalism grew after World War II as an increasing number of city dwellers, commercial farmers, wage-earners, radio listeners, and literates were becoming politically relevant. But subsistence farmers were overlooked by policymakers, wage-earners were increasingly discontented, and many primary-school leavers could not find jobs. Above all, the war revealed to the masses of Africans that the European colonialists could not function without their participation (Markovitz, 1977).

In Nigeria, the nationalist movement first became multi-ethnic between 1930 and 1944 in the South, when the real incomes of many participants in Nigeria's money economy declined from a falling trend in the commodity terms of trade. The world depression and war disruption adversely affected Britain's investment, imports, and government spending (Hopkins, 1973).

Additionally, the colonial government, assuming complete control of the economy during the war, issued trade licences only to established firms, thus freezing the superior competitive position of foreign firms. Besides that, peasants received lower than world prices from marketing boards, workers faced wage ceilings, traders encountered price controls, consumers sustained import shortages, and troops experienced racial discrimination.

Labour organisational activity grew during the war in reaction to several policies of the colonial government: the Colonial Development and Welfare Act of 1940 encouraging the establishment of trade unions in the colonies, the defence regulation of October 1942, which made strikes and lockouts illegal for the duration of the war, and denying African workers the cost-of-living allowances that European civil servants received. In addition, the government increased wages only modestly, while the cost of living rose 74% from September 1939 through October 1943. In June to July 1945, 43,000 workers, most of whom were performing services indispensable to the country's economic and administrative life, went on strike for more than 40 days. Aspiring entrepreneurs, deprived of new economic opportunities, and trade union leaders, politicised by the strike's success, channelled their grievances into nationalist agitation. Educated persons, whose primary economic opportunities were limited to private business and professional activity, demanded more participation in the colonial government.

Traditionally, except for some aristocratic groups among the

Hausa, Fulani, and Kanuri, ethnic identity was weak among Nigerians. However, the struggle to obtain the benefits of modernisation strengthened ethnic nationalism, especially around the mid-twentieth century. The heightening of Yoruba nationalism in the West after 1948 was partly in response to the Nigerian national movement in the 1940s, led by the Ibos, an overpopulated Eastern ethnic community with many emigrants to other parts of Nigeria. Hausa–Fulani nationalism was aroused about the same time in response to rival leadership in the drive for independence, and the threat of southern economic supremacy. The elite used traditional identities to transfer potential hostility from class discrepancies to other ethnic communities.

Since 1949, when the Nigerian new elites were first consulted by the British in a constitutional review, peoples of Nigeria have engaged in a continual regional, communal, and class struggle for a share in the economic benefits of decolonisation and modernisation. Between the first regional elections of 1951 and the overthrow of parliamentary rule in 1966, the elite consisted primarily of high-ranking politicians, indigenous rulers, senior civil servants, leading businessmen, and professionals. Most came to prominence after World War II, when the British handed positions, patronage, and economic benefits to Nigerians favourably placed to rule after independence in 1960.

During 1951–60, each of the three major political parties, the Northern Peoples' Congress (NPC), the National Council of Nigeria and the Cameroons (NCNC), and the Action Group (AG), all played leading roles in unifying and locally mobilising the socio-economic elite, and each achieved security and hegemony in one region only, the Northern, Eastern, and Western, respectively. Elites from majority parties in the regional assemblies who also cooperated with the ruling federal coalition dispensed a wide range of political rewards and sanctions, thus retaining their own positions and power, and keeping the masses subordinated. Positions and employment in government service and public corporations, licences for market stalls, permits for agricultural export production, land rights to establish enterprises, and roads, electricity, running water, and scholarships were allocated by the governing elite to its supporters. Each major party was backed by a bank, which assisted in the transfer of substantial public funds in the party (Nafziger, 1983).

The British colonialists in Nigeria, like the French in their West African colonies, helped shape those receiving and excluded from power after independence. Nigerian national leaders who received benefits by cooperating with the British after 1948 became more compliant and barred radical anti-British factions, like the NCNC's radical wing, the Zikist Movement, the National Church of Nigeria, and the Nigerian Labour Congress, whose vision of a free Nigeria included socialism, anti-imperialism, and income redistribution. In Cameroon, the French prevented the socialist, non-aligned Union des Populations du Cameroun (UPC) from participating in the 1956 election, thus setting the stage for negotiating a favourable independence agreement with the pro-French Union Camerounaise party, amenable to continuing a mixed capitalist system (*ibid.*; M. DeLancey, 1986).

In Zaïre, the *évoloués*, those with the intellectual and technical skills to challenge colonialism, were crucial in the genesis of nationalism. They included clerks, school teachers, non-commissioned officers in the Force Publique, ex-seminarians, and other minor cogs in the Belgian system, and were products of Christian mission schools and colonial enterprise needs. For a long time, the *évoloués* accommodated themselves to colonialism, seeking to advance within its system. But as they continued to be blocked from full advancement due to the low pay, racial discrimination, lack of political control, and general subordination within colonialism, they began challenging the colonial order (Kannyo, 1979).

CONCLUSION

Colonialism generally reinforced the inequalities in the precolonial social structure and contributed to postcolonial discrepancies. The European powers supported cooperating native elites, while helping to create partially overlapping educated elites for jobs in the government service and foreign firms. These elites, though often divided by ethnic community, spearheaded the nationalist movement that culminated in independence. In the terminal colonial period, the British and French eased their burden by providing economic benefits to these elites and their allies, and helped pave the way for the neo-colonial relationship discussed in chapter 6.

§ 6 §

TRANSNATIONAL
RELATIONSHIPS

Most anglophone and francophone subsaharan black African countries received their independence between the late 1950s and the late 1960s, while Portuguese colonies won independence in the mid 1970s. Yet Western economic dominance continued long after the independence of most African states, and contributed to their inequality.

Neo-colonialism is the economic, political, and military process by which (mainly capitalist) DCs maintain the former colony as a controlled source of raw materials, markets, and investment after the granting of formal political independence (Callaway, 1975). In Africa, the US, which comprises 26% of world output, and France are major powers, while Britain, Belgium, South Africa, and the Soviet Union are also important.

EXAMPLES OF NEO-COLONIALISM

While neo-colonialism is widespread in subsaharan Africa, in this section I will focus on only a few examples: South Africa's imperialism in Southern Africa with the support of Western capital, France's neo-colonial relations with francophone Africa, and Western neo-colonialism in Zaïre, Mozambique, Angola, and Nigeria.

In South Africa, the colonialists appropriated the most fertile lands located near the transport hub for white settlers while dividing the periphery into small mini-economies with little viability. As indicated earlier, colonial taxation, and credit and marketing geared to European agriculture thwarted African efforts to develop modern farms.

Between 1960 and 1985, almost half the Western MNC investment in Africa was in South Africa, supporting not only apartheid there but also contributing to neighbouring countries' underdevelopment. MNCs and the Pretoria government viewed South Africa as the regional core for their expanding activities throughout the regional periphery, whose role was a labour reserve, a market, and a source of raw materials. MNCs with subsidiaries also in South Africa's neighbouring countries controlled their banking systems, invested much of these countries' surplus in South Africa, shipped raw materials for processing from them to South Africa, and neglected their manufacturing and (sometimes) mining industries. These neighbours bought capital goods, some consumer goods, and even foodstuffs from South African MNCs. Until the 1980s, the international copper companies in Zambia, Zaïre, Botswana, and Namibia built most fabricating factories in South Africa or the West (Seidman and Makgetla, 1980).

South Africa tried to destabilise its neighbours economically and militarily when they attempted to undermine the white-minority government or (in 1982) to establish SADCC (Southern African Development Coordination Conference), a regional economic cooperation arrangement. Destabilisation included delaying or taxing shipments of food and vital inputs, failing to renew migrant-worker contracts, and supporting guerrillas against the neighbours. During the early to mid 1980s, efforts by black-ruled Southern African states to reduce dependence on South Africa were hurt by the Reagan administration's and Thatcher government's 'constructive engagement' with Pretoria.

French colonies have been more closely linked with France than have most British colonies with Britain. The French signed wide-ranging *accords de cooperation* with each new francophone state (expect for renegade Guinea) to ensure that France would provide most of the services it had provided before independence. Research institutions serving the colonies within France continued almost unchanged. Many former colonial officials remaining as employees of the independent governments were responsible for early development plans. In 1972, more than 11,000 French citizens were under cooperation agreements – 2,000 teachers in universities and institutes, and many employed by international organisations and private companies – in francophone Africa.

French colonies were linked to France by preferential tariffs, quotas, and guaranteed export prices. Within a decade after France joined the EEC in 1957, francophone Africa lost some subsidies, but increased overall trade by entering all EEC markets on preferential terms. Francophone countries (except Guinea and Mali, 1962–7) tied their currencies to the French franc, which restricted monetary independence and industrial import substitution, but attracted foreign capital and avoided serious domestic currency overvaluation. But generally these ties encouraged long-established specialisation in primary product exports rather than economic structural change (Fieldhouse, 1986).

Belgium, perhaps the most ruthless of European colonisers, did little to prepare Zaïre for self-government. At independence (1960), the Zaïrian political leaders' struggle for control of the state erupted into armed confrontation, secessions, and assassinations, with foreign governments providing political and military support to domestic factions protecting their interests. The US, Britain, France, West Germany, and Belgium regarded Prime Minister Patrice Lumumba and his followers as an opening for 'international communism' and a threat to Western investment and access to strategic raw materials. The West supported Mobutu Sese Seko's overthrow of Lumumba's government in 1960 and of President Joseph Kasavubu in 1965. Major Zaïrian interests behind Mobutu were the bureaucratic members of the African colonial elite who moved into top political and administrative posts in 1960. Mobutu grew increasingly dependent on American economic and military assistance for the survival of his regime, and welcomed US and other Western investment. The US supported Mobutu and his associates, despite their repression, enormous corruption, and wealth accumulation that immiserised the majority, as it saw no other alternative for safeguarding its economic and strategic interests (Kannyo, 1979; Jackson, 1982).

The US and its NATO allies (especially West Germany and France) generally provided economic, diplomatic, and military support to Portuguese colonial rule against nationalist struggles by the Movimento Popular de Libertação de Angola (MPLA), organised in 1956, and the Frente de Libertação de Moçambique (FRELIMO), founded in 1962, until both achieved independence in 1975. While the US reached a *rapprochement* with Mozambique, providing it with economic aid after 1983, the Reagan administration refused to recognise Angola, joining with South Africa in 1983 to support the effort by Jonas Savimbi's UNITA (the União Nacional para a Indêpendencia Total de Angola) to overthrow the MPLA government.

In the 1970s, Nigeria took several steps that, prima facie, should have reduced its neo-colonial dependence. It cut substantially the share of its trade with Britain; acquired majority equity holdings in the local petroleum extracting, refining, and distribution; and promulgated an indigenisation decree shifting the majority of ownership in manufacturing from foreign to indigenous hands. But these measures did not greatly reduce the neo-colonial nexus. Nigeria's trade was still virtually all with capitalist DCs (with the US replacing Britain as the chief trading partner). In contrast to more diversified exports in the 1960s, petroleum comprised more than 80% of export value for the 1970s. Moreover, only 15–20% of the petroleum industry's total expenditure on goods and services was spent on locally produced items, which do not include most basic requirements like drilling rigs, platforms, heavy structures, underwater engineering systems, and other advanced technologies. Furthermore, MNC ownership was replaced by MNC–state joint enterprises, which enriched private middlemen and enlarged the patronage base for state officials, but did little to develop Nigerian administrative and technological skills for subsequent industrialisation. As I indicate later, Kenya, Tanzania, Zaïre, Malawi, and Côte d'Ivoire made even less progress than Nigeria in using indigenisation requirements to reduce neo-colonial dependency.

GHANA: THE INADEQUACY OF A NEO-COLONIALIST EXPLANATION

Aidoo (1983) attributes Ghana's negative economic growth, hyperinflation, low capacity utilisation, huge national debt, and severe food and foreign-exchange shortages to a neo-colonial crisis consisting of 'direct control of resources and key sectors of the economy by foreign capital; covert and overt interventions by imperialist intelligence agencies; and ideological hegemony achieved mainly through the agency of educational institutions and the mass media'. But Ghana's real economic growth was stagnant in the 1950s, when foreign firms accounted for 60% of manufacturing output, and in the 1960s, when Nkrumah's economic nationalism reduced the foreign contribution to manufacturing to 40%, but highly negative in the 1970s when the foreign share declined even more. Foreign capital, which has shown little interest in Ghana since the 1960s, can hardly be seen as waiting to exploit her resources. Indeed Ghana had more autonomy in monetary and fiscal policy, more state control over international economic transactions, and more deterioration in economic performance since the 1970s than the more neo-colonial neighbouring countries, Côte d'Ivoire, Togo, and Burkina Faso. According to Price (1984), neo-colonialism as an explanation for Ghana's demise is a 'paper tiger'. We should not blame neo-colonialism for all Africa's problems.

INTERNATIONAL TRADE

Neo-colonialism, economic domination without direct colonialism, requires ruling class interests allied to foreign capitalists and governments upholding their joint interests in economic policy and political strategies. But neo-colonialism is unstable, leading to growing class polarisation as inequality becomes more apparent. Income redistribution to avert class conflict is usually at the expense of the domestic ruling classes or foreign capitalists, threatening the benefits of the alliance (Leys, 1974). However, fast growth, as in South Korea and Taiwan, makes benefits possible for foreign capital, domestic capital, workers, and small farmers.

Lardner (1985), ECA's former Policy and Programme Coordination Officer director, argues that independent African states retained neo-colonial policies including: maintaining monoproduct and other export dependence; relying on external initiative for changing this pattern; and intensifying monoproduct export production to secure foreign exchange to get needed inputs.

The overwhelming majority of African international trade was with DCs and only a small fraction with other African countries. In 1983, 83.3% of exports was to DCs, 4.8% to developed socialist countries, 11.3% to LDCs (of which 3.4% was to other African countries), and 0.6% not specified. The same year, 74.2% of imports was from DCs, 7.8% to socialist, and 18.0% to LDCs (3.0% to other African countries) (ECA, 1985).

Each 1% change in the DCs' business cycle index is associated with a 2.2% change in primary commodity prices, influencing African countries substantially. The OECD's quantity index of imports has a major impact on Africa's economic growth (Goreux, 1980; Wheeler, 1984). When the West sneezes (as in 1980–2), Africa catches pneumonia.

Francophone countries, with EEC associate status, have maintained especially strong trade ties with the colonial power. In 1984, some countries' imports from France as a share of the total were Cameroon 47%, Central African Republic 35%, Côte d'Ivoire 33%, Mali 29%, Senegal 26%, Mauritania 19%, and Chad 18%, while export shares to France were Senegal 31%, Cameroon 28%, Central African Republic 26%, Mali 19%, and Côte d'Ivoire 17% (EIU, 1986).

Africa's vulnerability is worsened because of high export commodity concentration. The summation of all subsaharan African countries' three principal exports as a share of total export earnings was 79.1% in 1976–8, an increase from 60.6% in 1961. In eight countries, the 1976–8 share was more than 90%. Indeed in 1985, six primary commodities accounted for more than 70% of subsharan Africa's exports earnings. High commodity concentration is associated with fluctuating export earnings as prices change (Lancaster and Williamson, 1986; Wangwe, 1980). The fall in the price of copper in the 1970s hurt Zambia and Zaïre, and the 1984–5 drought reduced the volume of some of Africa's major exports.

Thus African countries are vulnerable to relative international price instability not only because of greater dependence on more volatile primary product exports but also because of a high concentration of exports in a few commodities and to a few countries.

The predominantly (non-oil) primary products Africa exports and the predominantly manufactured products exported by DCs and a few newly-industrialising countries are not priced in comparable ways. Although global marketing for most primary products is oligopolistic, the African farmer is a price taker, having no influence on market price, so that productivity gains result in lower prices. On the other hand, most industrial production and marketing are relatively monopolistic, with productivity gains leading to higher prices.

For these reasons, Africa's long-run primary-product export prices have deteriorated relative to prices of industrial imports. In a shorter run, from 1977 to 1986, subsaharan Africa's net commodity terms of trade declined 23.4% (Spraos, 1983; IMF, 1986; ECA, 1983a). Thus African countries specialising in primary products suffer from both *fluctuating* and declining terms of trade.

Africa's balance on current account (table 4), like LDCs as a whole, was negative every year from 1977 through 1986. In 1986, this balance was −$11.6 billion, which was −16.2% of exports of goods and services. The 1985 debt service ratio, the ratio of interest and principal payments due on long-term debt as a percentage of exports of goods and services, was 32.3% (IMF, 1986). Moreover, external financial flows to Africa declined from the late 1970s to the 1980s. The debt–GDP ratio exceeded 4 for Zambia, 2 for Chad, Mauritania, Somalia, and Zaïre, and 1 for Gambia, Guinea-Bissau, Côte d'Ivoire, Liberia, Madagascar, Mali, Mozambique, the Sudan, and Togo. The decline in export earnings and resources flows forced a sharp drop in Africa's import volume – by nearly 20% between 1980 and 1985. This has had a major impact on imports of consumer goods, spare parts, investment goods, and inputs needed for domestic and export production, and has curtailed potential economic growth (Lancaster and Williamson, 1986). While much of the external borrowing was for projects to benefit or build patronage for a small elite, the debt crisis has limited overall economic growth, and especially the state's ability to continue meagre anti-poverty programmes.

Table 4. *Nigeria's international balance of payments, 1983*
(₦ million)

	Goods and Services Account (− Debits or Payments)	Current Account	Capital Account (+ Increases in Foreign Liabilities)
Merchandise Exports	+7,612		
Merchandise Imports	−8,847		
Service Exports Minus Service Imports (Net Travel, Transport, Investment Income, and Other Services)	−2,013		
Balance on Goods and Services		−3,248	
Net Grants, Remittances, and Unilateral Transfers		−188	
Balance on Current Account		−3,436	
Net Capital Inflows			+3,162
Net Official Reserve Asset Change			+274
		−3,436	+3,436

Source: Central Bank, 1983.

FOREIGN INVESTMENT

Roughly four-fifths of Africa's commodity trade is handled by MNCs. While their ownership shares in African primary production have declined, their control of processing, marketing, distribution, and services has expanded. For vertically integrated goods like bananas and tea, MNCs exercise much control over pricing and contract specifications, buying from their own plantations and selling to their own processors. But with commodities MNCs buy from independent producers and sell to independent processors, market power is less strong. However, control over global marketing and financing still gives MNCs much power to determine supply and price. For example, three conglomerates account for 70–75% of the global banana market, six corporations 70% of cocoa trade, and six MNCs 85–90% of leaf tobacco trade (ECA, 1983a).

Moreover, MNCs can distort intra-firm transfer prices by over-stating investment, management, and patents costs, overpricing inputs transferred from another subsidiary, and underpricing outputs sold within the MNC to another country, thus understating earnings and tax liabilities, transferring funds extralegally, or circumventing foreign exchange controls in Africa. And most African countries lack the personnel and political strength to challenge MNC price fixing.

The World Bank's report on Africa (1981a) criticises Africa's high tariff rates. Indeed my summary (1984) of the extensive economic arguments for and against free trade argues that tariffs to protect infant industry sometimes promote growth but that their adverse effects on resource efficiency mean their value is more limited than many African policymakers suppose. But African governments often design tariffs to compete against each other to attract MNCs. In Nigeria in the 1960s, the prime motive for establishing foreign manufacturing enterprises was to change a highly competitive market in international trade to one with competition virtually eliminated. Ironically, the greatest pressure for increased protection for manu-facturing was not from government, or even domestic producers, but from foreign capitalists and their local collaborators (Kilby, 1969).

MNCs in Africa contribute to inequality in several ways. Foreign capital usually enters Africa only if political leaders, civil servants, and private middlemen are rewarded for facilitating the joint venture. Much of this reward is for economically unproductive activity, and is paid for by tariff and quota protection, higher consumer prices, or by subsidies from tax revenue. In Africa, where direct taxes like income taxes are not well-developed because of low literacy, poor accounting records, poor administration, and tax avoidance and evasion, the tax structure is usually regressive, meaning that people with lower incomes pay a higher percentage of income in taxes. Any subsidy to inefficiency falls disproportionately on the shoulders of low- to middle-income workers and farmers.

Moreover, MNC-associated enterprises tend to use technology designed for DCs, which have high wages and relatively abundant capital. Estimates based on capital resources available indicate that the appropriate capital stock per person in the US is 45 times that of Nigeria (Stewart, 1974). Additionally, African capital, foreign-exchange, and labour cost distortions that make the actual price of capital cheaper than its market rate encourage MNC high-technology, capital-intensive processes rather than local modification or adapt-ation. Apart from the potential for patronage and corruption for political and bureaucratic elites, there are other reasons for increased inequality. Those who control capital resources (private capitalists or government officials) receive a lion's share of the income from these processes. Even much of the labour share goes to the relatively affluent, high-level personnel and skilled workers. And foreigners constitute a reference for salary and consumption levels for elite Africans, who want to keep up with the Joneses. Moreover, as I point out in chapter 9, capital-intensive technology increases unemployment. In Kenya, the emphasis on an inefficient, highly-protected capital-intensive industrial sector has resulted in 'explosive inequalities' (Langdon, 1980).

When Kenya stressed joint ventures between foreign capital and the government, 1964–70, manufacturing grew no faster than the economy as a whole, partly because Kenya preferred Western capital (allied with African elites) to the indigenous Asian bourgeoisie. Ironically, at the same time that the government, the UN, and Development Finance Corporation of Kenya were identifying new industrial projects, the government pressured local Asians to withdraw capital from trade and even industry. Most Asian manufacturing firms were small-scale, labour-intensive, and had survived (with little protection) in the early 1960s. In contrast, MNCs were usually capital-intensive, used substantial imported inputs, increased external economic dependence, and required high protection (Leys, 1974).

Although Kenya's policy of joint ventures increased government ownership and income, it had only limited success in the goal of Africanising staff, decisions, and control. The Economist Intelligence Unit (1985) indicates that although foreigners owned only 42% of the 1976 total issued capital of large-scale manufacturing and service firms, they controlled about 75% of these firms through majorities on the boards of directors. But because it views society as a whole, government should use an efficiency criterion balancing wages and profits, and savings and consumption, rather than the profit maximisation of private enterprise (Nove, 1983). Yet the Kenyan government, despite overall majority ownership, acquiesced in foreign goals to maximise profits by keeping wages for ordinary workers low.

Inequalities in Kenya created by neo-colonialism have not been limited to industry. Kenya's concentration of land holdings in 1960 were comparable to Latin American inequalities, much higher than the Afro-Asian average. And in the 1960s the newly-emerging large African capitalist farmers (generally politicians, bureaucrats, or their clients) depended on state-administered foreign capital for credit to buy property in the old 'white highlands', while using political pressure to influence public agencies setting agricultural prices. Thus

Kenya maintained its high concentration ratio. In the 1970s, the largest 0.1% of the farm owners held 14% of the arable land, while the largest 2.4% held 32%. While 30% of the smallholdings were under 0.6 hectares, the largest farms exceed 1000 hectares (Squire, 1981; Leys, 1974; Holtham and Hazlewood, 1976).

Chapter 5 indicated that the collaboration between Ivorian petty capital and French industrial capital in the late colonial period continued after independence. State ownership in Côte d'Ivoire, the most industrialised francophone African country, rose from 18.2% of industrial capital in 1971 to 30.4% in 1979, but most was joint ownership with foreign capital. Europeans constituted 6.8% of the 1971 urban wage and salary earners, but received 32.2% of the total wage bill. Ivorian supervisors and managers in industry comprised 5% of the total in 1968 and 28% in 1974. Foreigners held 56.3% of the 1979 total industrial investment, despite limited new foreign investment in the 1970s. But this foreign-led industrialisation provided few new jobs, especially for unskilled and semiskilled workers, since manufacturing's capital intensity was high and increasing in the 1970s (Mytelka, 1984; Young, 1982).

FOREIGN AID

Wheeler's 1984 study of determinants of subsaharan African growth during the 1970s shows no significant association between aid per capita, 1960–80, and growth in the 1970s. This evidence, while not conclusive, raises questions about the value of aid.

Leys (1974) feels aid to Kenya helped harmonise the interests of a dependent bureaucratic and commercial bourgeoisie with foreign capital. Indeed intermediaries in Kenya, Malawi, and many other African recipient countries depend critically on external assistance for income, patronage, and state power. Many high-level government officials depend on aid for control of parastatal activities, dispensing favours to suppliers and contractors, and bribery and kickbacks.

The effectiveness of aid appears to have declined after 1970. In the 1950s and 1960s, most aid to Africa was programme support, e.g., to infrastructure or agriculture. In the 1970s, donors increasingly favoured project assistance, which entailed more specific statements of objectives and means to attain them, more precise monitoring and evaluation, more foreign control over funds, and more local personnel and resources committed to projects. Furthermore, each of the 82 major bilateral, multilateral, and non-governmental organisations in Africa in 1980 had competing requirements.

Where donors underwrite most of the development budget they insist on continual, extensive project supervision and review, so that recipient government agencies become more answerable to them than to their own senior policy officials (Morss, 1984). Donors frequently recommend and supervise poorly conceived projects. But even when well conceived, African officials fail to learn how to do something until they have the power to make their own decisions. Morss argues that the proliferation of donors and requirements has resulted in weakened institutions and reduced management capacity. For example, in 1981, Malawi, lacking the indigenous capacity to manage 188 projects from 50 different donors, hired donor-country personnel (sometimes with donor salary supplements) to take government line positions to manage projects. However, Malawi has not been able to increase its capacity to run its own affairs and establish its own policies.

In many countries, aid is biased against the poor. In Kenya (1963–76), only 11% of development assistance reached the very poor, only a third was directly concerned with rural development, and most of this went to relatively well-off farmers (Ghai, Godfrey, and Lisk, 1979).

DEBT

Africa's external debt crisis has forced many countries to curtail poverty programmes, even though few of these programmes had been funded from foreign borrowing. Nigeria's and Zaïre's government elites sometimes expanded the patronage for intermediaries and contractors so fast that they lost track of millions of dollars borrowed from abroad. During Nigeria's second republic, 1979–83, the ports sometimes lacked the capacity for imports like cement going to government agencies controlled by politicians providing patronage for intermediaries and contractors.

After independence, Africa borrowed heavily for development. It increased borrowing substantially just after the 1973–4 fourfold oil price rise and the subsequent export-earnings reduction from the world recession. Additionally, the grant element of loans declined steadily, from 46% in 1970 to 17% in 1979. From 1982 to 1984, however, total medium- and long-term external financial flows to subsaharan Africa fell from $11,000 million to $3,500 million (and net flows from $3,000 million to negative). Also, average interest rates for new public debt commitments increased from 5.6% to 9.3% (while the grace period shortened by 30%) from 1975 to 1981. Moreover, African countries sometimes borrowed more than absorptive capacity, lacking because of a shortage of skilled civil servants, entrepreneurs, managers, technicians, and educated workers. Finally, the Nigerian, Ghanaian, and Zaïrian ruling classes used foreign borrowing to expand patronage for projects of dubious viability. Subsaharan Africa's outstanding medium- and long-term debt more than quadrupled from $17 thousand million in 1975 to $68 thousand million in 1985. Debt service (the interest and principal payments due in a given year) increased from 18% to 32% of export earnings from 1980 to 1985 (Lancaster and Williamson, 1986; Wangwe, 1980; Nafziger, 1984; World Bank, 1986a).

Who are the major subsaharan African debtors? At the end of 1985, the rank order was Nigeria ($16,600 million, primarily from commercial loans), the Sudan ($8,300 million), Côte d'Ivoire ($8,000 million, mostly commercial), Zaïre ($5,300 million), Zambia ($4,200 million), Kenya ($3,500 million), Tanzania ($3,400 million), Mozambique ($2,600 million), Zimbabwe ($2,400 million, mostly commercial), Madagascar ($2,300 million), Senegal ($2,300) million), Ghana ($2,200 million), Ethiopia ($1,900 million), Cameroon ($1,800 million), Somalia ($1,500 million), and Mauritania ($1,400 million) (Lancaster and Williamson, 1986). Ten of the 16 listed were low-income countries compared to only 3 of the 19 major Asian and Latin American debtors. While 12 listed African countries were IDA-eligible, none of the Asian–Latin 19 were. Since most of the latter were middle-income countries, they generally had higher credit ratings among commercial banks than African countries. Thus, even though only 4 of the top 20 LDC debtors are from subsaharan Africa, its debt is probably more burdensome than that for any other world region.

THE IMF

From 1981 through 1984, 26 (a majority) subsaharan African countries borrowed from the IMF, which seeks the 'restoration and maintenance of viability to the balance of payments in an environment of price stability and sustainable rates of growth'. Other subsaharan countries have drawn structural adjustment loans from the World Bank, complying with its conditions for this balance-of-payments assistance.

IMF-sponsored stabilisation programmes usually include government reducing budget deficits through increasing tax revenues and cutting back social spending, limiting credit creation, achieving market-clearing prices, liberalising trade, devaluing currency, eliminating price controls, and restraining public-sector employment and wage rates. The Fund monitors domestic credit, the exchange rate, and debt targets closely for compliance. Policies generally shift the internal relative prices away from non-tradable goods to tradable goods, promoting exports and 'efficient' import substitution. In effect, these policies shift purchasing power from the urban to rural areas, from consumption to investment, and from labour to capital.

Loxley finds little evidence that IMF programmes restore growth and external balance to low-income African countries. In the 1970s, 5 of 23 African countries reached growth targets, 13 of 18 inflation targets, and 11 of 28 trade targets. Nor have IMF programmes led to bank credit inflows.

In low-income subsaharan Africa, demand restrictions and price and exchange-rate adjustments do not switch expenditures to exports and domestic production or expand primary product production quickly enough to have the desired effect on prices and trade balance. After 1981, the IMF emphasised shock treatment for demand restraint, rarely provided financing for external adjustment, and cut pro-grammes from three years to one year, applying Reaganomics internationally. One year is not enough to begin the adjustment processes. As indicated in chapter 12, the average trade-balance adjustment takes three to five years, usually (like the US in 1985–6) beginning with a worsening trade balance in the first year.

Many African governments feel the IMF focuses only on demand, while ignoring productive capacity and long-term structural change. Additionally, these governments object to the Fund's market ideology and neglect of external determinants of stagnation and instability. Moreover, IMF austerity curtails programmes to reduce poverty and stimulate long-run development. But the Fund perceives its role as international monetary stability and liquidity, not development.

Yet IMF leverage to persuade African governments to undertake austerity in the face of internal political opposition was less in the 1980s than in the 1970s, partly because of the drying up of special funding beyond direct IMF credits. But in the 1980s, the World Bank's adjustment loans consolidated IMF conditionality. Moreover, the Bank leads donor coordination, increasing the power of external leverage. Many African recipients, lacking personnel, have abdicated responsibility for coordinating external aid, increasing World Bank and donor influence (Loxley, 1986; ECA, 1985).

CONCLUSION

Neo-colonial economic relations in Africa usually involve alliances between foreign capital and domestic political leaders, bureaucrats, and intermediaries. These domestic elites usually benefit from invitations to MNCs, which often use high technology inappropriate to Africa's resource endowment. Some of the same elites depend on foreign aid for expanding state power. Yet even if foreign resource flows increase growth, little 'trickles down' to the poor.

When growth or foreign flows fall, disadvantaged classes are usually hurt the most severely. While Africa's rulers incurred debt partly to expand patronage, they respond to external pressures on debt crises by reducing social programmes, especially those for small farmers, workers, the unemployed, the sick, and the elderly.

ৡ 7 ৡ

CAPITALISM, SOCIALISM, DEVELOPMENT, AND INEQUALITY

Capitalism refers to an economic system where the means of production – lands, mines, factories, and other capital – are privately held, and where legally free but capital-less workers sell their labour to employers. Under capitalism, production decisions are made by private individuals operating for profit (Dillard, 1972). Under Western concepts of socialism, the state or community owns the means of production on behalf of the workers. The surplus (capitalist profit, interest, and rent) not invested is distributed to workers or community members.

CROSSNATIONAL COMPARATIVE DATA

Ahluwalia (1974) indicates that the average income share of the poorest 40% in socialist DCs is 24%, compared to 16% for non-socialist DCs, and 12.5% for non-socialist LDCs. High socialist income equality is to be expected since people do not own land and capital. Moreover, socialist countries' faster progress in expanding mass education and reducing population growth also contributes to greater income equality. Socialist income inequality is due mainly to wage discrepancies between sectors and skill classes.

Yet while socialist countries generally have lower income inequality, enough non-socialist countries have attained success to serve as examples. A wide variety of LDC governments have succeeded in reducing poverty, increasing equality, and meeting basic human needs of nutrition, education, health, sanitation, water supply, and housing for the overwhelming majority of their populations: from capitalist-oriented economies like South Korea and Taiwan to mixed economies like pre-1977 Sri Lanka to decentralised socialist economies like Yugoslavia to centrally planned economies like Cuba and pre-1978 China (see chapter 1).

65

SOCIALIST IDEOLOGIES FOR NEW STATES

Many African intellectuals, nationalist leaders, and politicians believed that *laissez-faire* capitalism rigidly adhered to during the colonial period was responsible for slow economic growth. Once independence was won, most African leaders pushed for systematic, state economic planning to remove these deep-seated, capitalist obstacles. Such sentiments were expressed in a statist (usually called socialist) ideology that stressed government's role in assuring minimum economic welfare for all citizens.

Many African leaders agreed with Nkrumah (1965), who wrote that 'the vicious circle of poverty, which keeps us in our rut of impoverishment, can only be broken by a massively planned industrial undertaking'. He was sceptical of the market mechanism's effectiveness, argued for the 'uncounted advantages of planning', and contended that government interference in the economic growth of developing countries is 'universally accepted'. Vigorous state planning would remove the distorting effects of colonialism, and free third-world countries from dependence on primary exports. Other key charismatic leaders, Tanzania's Nyerere, Zambia's Kenneth Kaunda, Guinea's Sekou Toure, and Senegal's Leopold Senghor emphasised 'African socialism'.

Since most African business classes were weak at independence, the argument for the state spearheading economic development was strengthened. Yet decisions concerning government size were usually based less on economic reasoning than on ruling elites' interests. Most elites were politicians, professional administrators, and bureaucrats, and wanted to protect their interests from business people. Elites perceived an anarchy of the market which, reinforced by their lack of control, produced a statist ideology.

AFRICAN SOCIALISM

African socialism did not necessarily coincide with the Western socialist concept of the ownership of most capital and land by the state. Instead the African variety usually included the following: a high level of state ownership in modern sector industry, agriculture, transport, and commerce; a penchant for public control of resource allocation in key sectors; a de-emphasis on foreign trade and investment; a priority on inward-looking production; and a rapid Africanisation of high-level jobs (Acharya, 1981a).

Early proponents stressed that socialism was in harmony with

Africa's communal traditions. Land was held by the community, and work was organised on a group basis. Kinship was strong, individualism was weak, and class struggle and distinction were alien to Africa, especially in the traditional village (Berg, 1964). Yet while African socialism and egalitarianism appealed to the populace, most political leaders were vague concerning their programmes.

CLASS CONFLICT UNDER SOCIALISM

Socialism in Africa was not introduced by revolutionary struggle, but by a state bourgeoisie coping with the instability of modernising under capitalism. Indeed Nkrumah (1970) branded African socialism a myth, arguing that its supporters neglected the fierce class 'struggle between the oppressors and the oppressed in Africa'. While class divisions were temporarily submerged during the struggle to eject the colonial power, they returned with increased intensity, Nkrumah contended, 'particularly in those states where the newly independent government embarked on socialist policies'. Perhaps in retrospect he would have included as an oppressor his Minister of Communications and Transport, Krobo Edusei, who imported a gold bed for his wife costing £84,000, indicating: 'Socialism does not mean that if you have made a lot of money, you cannot keep it' (Aidoo, 1983).

African leaders are not unusual in calling statism or state capitalism socialism, and claiming it free from class antagonism. Bettelheim (1976, 1978) argues that the Russian Revolution of 1917 did not erase divergent class interests. The Soviet Union created a new ruling class – the 'state bourgeoisie' – in place of the old bourgeoisie of Tsarist Russia. The economic interests of this new bourgeoisie – made up of the Communist party, the *Praesidium*, and the bureaucracy – are antagonistic to those of Soviet workers. Soviet workers and peasants do not control individually or collectively their means of production, their work processes, and the distribution of goods and services they produce (Sweezy, 1976).

Self-proclaimed 'socialist' governments – Nkrumah's Ghana (1957–66), Toure's Guinea (1958–84), Modibe Keita's Mali (1960–8), Nyerere's Tanzania (1961–85), Kaunda's Zambia (1964–   ), Marien Ngouabi's Congo-Brazzaville (1968–77), Siyad Barre's Somalia (1969–   ), Thomas Sankara's Burkina Faso (1983–87), and the radical regimes of Ethiopia, Benin, Guinea-Bissau, Cape Verde, Sao Tome, Madagascar, Mozambique, and Angola – tried to eliminate class privilege and prevent bourgeois rule. Nearly all produced domination by a state or managerial bourgeoisie, so labelled by critics sympathetic to socialism (Sklar, 1979).

Calling countries Marxist–Leninist and moderate socialist states has little value in differentiating economic structure. Often these labels are related to identification in the East–West conflict, reaction to corruption, or rhetoric for internal consumption, rather than internal differences. Thus Congo–Brazzaville, the first self-proclaimed Marxist–Leninist African state in 1963, was relaxed and moderate when conversing with foreign business people (Young, 1982).

In Africa it is the state, rather than private ownership of the means of production, that is the focus for class struggle. Thus, we need to go beyond an analysis of the bourgeoisie that includes the middle and business class to a broader concept, the managerial bourgeoisie, which also includes the state or bureaucratic bourgeoisie.

THE LIMITS OF SOCIALIST PLANNING

While African countries have a state bourgeoisie, they do not have the centralised control over planning that the Soviet ruling class does. Since 1928, the Soviet controlling plan has authorised what each key-sector enterprise produces and how much it invests. Even Soviet planning, more comprehensive than in any other country, has not been as totally planned and rigidly controlled as most think. Soviet planning began modestly. During the civil war of 1918–21, enterprises ignored planning directives. Not until 1925–6 did Gosplan, the State Planning Committee of the USSR, which consults with ministries, republics, and enterprises, have the personnel and authority to plan detailed input–output relationships.

Even today in the centrally planned key sectors (heavy industry, much of light industry, and a small part of agriculture), there is much local, extraplan discretion – government simply cannot control all operations details. For example, bad weather or shortages sometimes prevent the delivery of essential materials so that enterprise managers adjust by hoarding, bartering, and other informal arrangements. Presently, over half of Soviet GNP remains out of the purview of planners and under the control of local officials, enterprises, and even private markets. These activities, however, are generally dependent on state policies for financial controls, purchasing, pricing, wage schedules, labour mobility, education and training, turnover taxes, foreign trade, and so forth (Gregory and Stuart, 1986).

While African planning is less likely to represent a binding commitment by a public department to spend funds than Soviet

planning, African state policymakers and planners do control channels of access to production and distribution, and usually have the
power of 'life and death' over an enterprise through tariffs, taxes,
subsidies, licences, access to foreign exchange and essential inputs.

Except for Algeria, most African socialist regimes (e.g., Tanzania,
Guinea, and Mali) lack the strong state and capable administration
needed to implement socialism.

SOCIALISM: A FOCUS ON TANZANIA

In 1962, a year after independence, Nyerere instituted ujamaa
socialism (encouraging collective efforts and avoiding wide wealth
disparities) and land nationalisation. He expanded the traditional
concept of ujamaa from household to the community, emphasising
respect for each member, common property, and obligation to work.
The ruling party, TANU (the Tanganyika African National Union,
now the Chama Cha Mapinduzi), subsequently pressed for a major
state role to establish ujamaa villages, which would use existing
technology but benefit from economies of scale from organising a
larger labour force (Hyden, 1980). From 1967 to 1976, the percentage
of the rural population living in ujamaa villages increased from 0%
to 91.3%.

Outside government officials started the ujamaa villages, and
planned and executed their activities, but achieved few break-
throughs, as many villages were completely mismanaged. In many
instances, ujamaas were just front organisations for capitalist farm
operations (Mapolu, 1984).

For some Tanzanian party cadres, ujamaa politics meant neglecting efficiency, leading a Hungarian consultant to caution in a public
speech:

Very often can be heard declarations, that during the building of socialism we have to
throw away every idea of capitalist origin, or every idea which does not derive from
Africa. This is a grave mistake. Socialism doesn't reject capitalism in total. It takes
useful ideas from it. The motive of the development of all societies is to preserve the
useful ideas of the previous system, and to cast away only the unuseful ones. (Hyden,
1980, citing F. Nagy)

The 1964–69 Five-year Plan for Economic and Social Development
committed the country to egalitarianism and African socialism.
Nyerere's 1967 Arusha Declaration on behalf on TANU was in response
to low foreign aid, drastically falling sisal export prices, agricultural
settlement failures, few benefits to the rural population, increasing

inequality, and growing unemployment. TANU emphasised local self-reliance, with foreign aid just a supplement.

Foreign capital usually penetrated Tanzania through Nairobi headquarters, so Tanzania had even less control over this capital than most African countries. After 1967, the public sector replaced the private sector as the major modernising vehicle. The 1971 Mwongozo (party guidelines) signalled the end of capitalist management, and stressed workers' rights but not duties, thus undermining the moral underpinnings of the government sector. After Mwongozo, many workers used party authority to intimidate management. Managers became increasingly concerned about labour unrest and indiscipline, as the following feature article illustrates:

We have dismantled and demoralised the disciplinary machinery and the terminal focus of loyalty in institutions, offices and other work-places. Management no longer has control over labour and workers' misinterpretation of political speeches and documents... As a result in some work-places there is technically no management, no foreman, no leaders of operations, no organisation. Workers have neither motivation nor incentive because management has crumbled down and is not in a position to reprimand and reward. .... In effect, these days no government officers in a ministry, no manager in a para-statal organisation, no foreman in a work unit and no person technically responsible to direct public operations or a piece of work dare insist on work standards or better job performance of his colleagues without risking to be disastrously unpopular or appear eccentric. In most cases he will be stigmatized as a 'colonialist' by both his coworkers and the immediate associates (before his expulsion is demanded).
(A. N. Nderingo, 'Which Way Workers', *The Standard*, 11 November 1971, cited by Hyden, 1980)

The precedence of political over management decisions meant many commodities were produced with little knowledge of existing demands. Tanganyika Packers, which lost its overseas sales agent in 1974, still produced canned meat with no assurance of markets, resulting in a huge pile-up of meat, some of which had to be destroyed. After 1974, the party tried to subordinate political relations to production relations, and reintroduce discipline into the work force (Hyden, 1980).

Other development landmarks were the 1972 decentralisation measure to bring mass participation in decisionmaking, and the 1974–6 villagisation, a resettling of peasants into larger villages, which facilitated rural collectivisation, government authoritarian control, and the extension of bureaucratic patron–client relationships into the village. Resettled peasants saw themselves as government employees rather than independent farmers. Government took the harvest and paid settler peasants what remained after deducting costs. Some settlers were more prosperous, employing labour almost like rural capitalists (*ibid.*; Mapolu, 1984).

By 1978, 90% of rural dwellers were living in these new 'development' villages, facilitating government providing schools, dispensaries, water facilities, and other social services to the population. But opposition grew as government implemented the exercise too hurriedly, sometimes using violence, choosing unsuitable sites, or settling too many people in one village. Villagisation enabled the state bourgeoisie to control settlers without providing wage employment directly. In tobacco production, government and the companies decided how much land should be under tobacco leaf, when and how to plant, weed, harvest, and cure, who supplied the seeds, fertilisers, and insecticides, who graded the tobacco, and who marketed it, with the villager supplying only his labour (Mapolu, 1984).

Nyerere (1977), ten years after the Arusha Declaration, observed that most Tanzanians were poor, many had lower standards of living than in 1967, inequality was high, and the country was neither socialist nor self-reliant. He pointed out:

> I am a very poor prophet. In 1956 I was asked how long it would take Tanganyika to become independent. I thought 10 to 12 years. We became independent 6 years later! In 1967 a group of the youth who were marching in support of the Arusha Declaration asked me how long it would take Tanzania to become socialist. I thought 30 years. I was wrong again: I am now sure it will take us much longer.

Tanzania failed in building socialism partly because it could not cut the government servants' ties to the rural economy. Selflessness and incorruption were difficult to instil in party leaders, when most had large numbers of extended family members and clients to support, especially in peasant agriculture. Moreover, communal farming's reduced peasant inducements and efficiency resulted in production shortfalls (Hyden, 1980).

In Tanzania, the state bourgeoisie rose at the expense of the private middle and capitalist classes. The Arusha Declaration resulted in widespread nationalisations (especially sisal estates) and expropriation (with large grain farms becoming state farms or operated by ujamaa villages), increasing the bureaucracy's control of the state and power relative to local capitalists. While the state's involvement in export–import and wholesale trade, milling, and other light industries hurt indigenous capitalists, the nationalisation of foreign firms hurt the comprador managerial and capitalist class dependent on them (Shivji, 1976).

In Tanzania, salaries, perquisites, and amenities to the higher rungs of the state bureaucracy have appropriated much of the surplus. The middle and upper rungs of the civil service expanded from 4,500 posts (1961) to 12,000 (1971) to 16,200 (1974) and to more than 20,000 (1980).

Government spokesmen stressed the modest living standards of upper and middle civil servants. Yet their wages relative to earnings of ordinary workers and peasants are closer to Nigeria's and Kenya's substantial discrepancies than the more egalitarian Western differences. The lack of automobiles for most university graduates in government service in Tanzania, like Ghana, is not the result of egalitarian policy, but low average GNP.

Since Arusha, state officials have controlled channels of access and distribution in the economy, giving officials from the national to village level many opportunities for capricious and corrupt behaviour, ranging from dealing with large MNCs to petty traders. Corruption especially damages socialist regimes like Tanzania by undermining their egalitarian principles of income redistribution, poverty reduction, and majority rule (Freund, 1981; Markovitz, 1977).

Even more than in Tanzania, a substantial proportion of the government budgets of Ghana, Guinea, and Mali, countries labelled socialist, have included bureaucratic expense and conspicuous urban expense. Thus, Marxist economist Amin (1965) laments that 'Austerity, the revolutionary effort to use new and less costly methods, has not resisted the appetites of the new bureaucracy.' More recently, Jeffries (1982) thinks that economic liberalisation in Ghana would do more than anything to recreate values of honesty and accountability, as making market and official prices coincide would mean less scope for corruption and embezzlement.

NKRUMAH'S AND HOUPHOUET-BOIGNEY'S WAGER: GHANA AND CÔTE D'IVOIRE

In 1957, Nkrumah wagered Felix Houphouet-Boigney of Côte d'Ivoire, similar in resource endowment to Ghana, that in ten years history would judge statist Ghana more successful economically than market-oriented Côte d'Ivoire. But Côte d'Ivoire grew faster and reduced poverty much more than Ghana since 1957.

Since the 1950s, Côte d'Ivoire's economy dramatically outperformed the Ghanaian economy. From 1950 to 1960, Côte d'Ivoire's annual real GDP per capita growth was 1.5% compared to Ghana's −0.3%, from 1960 to 1970 4.2% compared to Ghana's −0.3%, and from 1970 to 1981 1.4% to Ghana's − 3.2%. While investment grew for both in the 1950s, Ivorian investment grew 12.7% annually in the 1960s compared to Ghana's 3.1% decline, and in the 1970s increased 12.1% while Ghana's fell 4.3% yearly. Yet ironically, for all three decades, Ghana's net barter terms of trade moved more favourably than Côte d'Ivoire's.

Why did Côte d'Ivoire grow faster? Ghana's large public investments in the first half of the 1960s were so inefficient that an unparalleled growth in investment–income ratios contributed to little increase in income. Moreover, Ghana faced a continuing balance-of-payments problem during the 1960s and 1970s, largely because of an increasingly overvalued cedi that discouraged export volume expansion, especially in cocoa. In contrast, the Ivorian CFA franc was maintained much closer to market-clearing rates, thus providing incentives to supply increased exports (Teal, 1986).

Birmingham, Neustadt, and Omaboe (1966) considered Ghana, at its independence in 1957, the most prosperous and least impoverished country in black Africa. But Ghana's increased income inequality, together with a continuing decline in GNP per capita, meant steadily increasing poverty rates (see chapter 4). While Côte d'Ivoire has no comparable data, its positive growth suggests no increasing poverty rates among Ivorian citizens since the late 1950s and early 1960s (though foreign plantation workers may have increased poverty). Indeed Côte d'Ivoire's declining poverty rate matched Ghana's by 1975 (table 3). But while Ivorian growth has decelerated but remained positive since then, Ghana has continued its economic decline, suggesting that Ivorian poverty rates in the mid 1980s were probably lower than Ghana's.

Ironically both countries' growth and poverty rate trends could reverse in the late 1980s. Before 1983, Ghana's highest price distortion index among non-communist LDCs (World Bank, 1983b) reduced productivity, protected inefficiency, and discouraged resource mobility, thus diminishing growth and savings, and creating product and resource shortages. In 1983 the Ghanian government devalued the cedi on most transactions closer to a market rate, increased farm producer prices, removed price distortions on oil and other goods, and reduced deficit financing. Beginning in 1984, growth accelerated, the balance-of-payments improved, inflation fell (ECA, 1985), and poverty rates probably declined. On the other hand, Côte d'Ivoire's growth rate decelerated (turning negative in the early to mid 1980s), suggesting that Amin (1973) correctly anticipated exhaustion of previous gains from a strategy based on plantation agriculture and import-substitution industry (chapter 4). While data are lacking, Ivorian poverty rates and income inequality have probably been increasing during the 1980s.

Côte d'Ivoire's pre-1980 success and Ghana's pre-1983 failure and post-1983 turnaround suggest the importance of the market in stimulating growth and efficiency, especially in early stages of development, where countries lack the administrative resources for detailed programmes for public-sector enterprises and comprehensive physical controls of production and investment.

MIXED CAPITALISM: CAMEROON, NIGERIA, KENYA, AND MALAWI

Cameroon, Nigeria, Kenya, Malawi, and Côte d'Ivoire, like virtually all subsaharan African states, include a considerable public component in manufacturing, mining, construction, and public utilities, but they also have a substantial private sector, so can be classified as mixed capitalist economies.

Cameroon's mixed capitalist economy's annual 2.9% growth rate (1965–84) has been among subsaharan Africa's fastest. While the ruling Cameroon National Union (CNU) government promoted private initiative through tariff rebates and tax holidays, it intervened to form parastatals for public utilities and other enterprises essential for national sovereignty. The state regulated oligopolistic industry, provided credit for small business enterprises, and retained price incentives for small private farmers, who dominated agriculture. But most of Cameroon's parastatal National Investment Corporation's (SNI's) joint industrial ventures in the 1970s ran at a loss, as local administration lacked the experience to manage rapid public investment growth (Ndongko, 1986; Willame, 1986).

Nigeria has adhered to an ideology of nurture capitalism with the directly productive sector dominated by private enterprise, the state investing in infrastructure as a foundation for private activity, and government providing programmes and policies to stimulate private (especially indigenous) enterprise (Schatz, 1984).

In his 1965 budget speech, Finance Minister Festus Sam Okotie-Eboh argued against socialism in these words:

The basic principle of socialism, the principle from which nationalisation springs, is the complete subordination of individual freedom to the supposed interests of the State... Let there be no mistake about this: there can only be one kind of socialism, and this... is by its basic denial of personal freedom un-Nigerian and a violation of entrenched clauses of our Constitution.

Nigeria's need to-day is... for men of initiative, men with new ideals, planners and thinkers, the kind of men whose pioneering vision, allied to faith and plain hard work, built the United States, the Great Britain, the Canada that we know to-day. We need men with practical ability who will preach what they truly believe – and practise what they preach. A nation cannot be built on theories, but on the effort, the enterprise, the initiative and the peculiar genius of every individual citizen.

None of the major Nigerian political parties controlling national or regional governments from 1951 through 1966 were socialist parties or parties strongly committed to egalitarian issues. Even the Action Group (AG), led by Chief Obafemi Awolowo, who criticised capitalism, had as its backbone the rising new class of professionals, business people, and traders. The AG, the Western region's ruling party, 1951-62, did not redistribute wealth, except to party leaders. Populist leaders defined themselves as socialist but, like Adegoke Adelabu, in local and regional politics were too astute and ambitious not to appear conservative and traditionalist (Bienen, 1981; Sklar, 1963).

After Nigeria's civil war, 1967–70, with rapidly increasing petroleum output and prices, and government's control of oil extracting, refining, and distribution, the state became the predominant source of economic surplus. By the mid 1970s, petroleum revenue accounted for more than three-fourths of total federal revenue. For the most vigorous, resourceful, and well-connected venture capitalists (usually politicians, bureaucrats, army officers, and their clients), productive economic activity had faded in appeal. Manipulating government spending had 'become the golden gateway to fortune'. The managerial bourgeoisie used the state, not to support capitalist production, but to further their own private interests, labelled pirate capitalism by Schatz (1984).

In 1964, one year after independence, Kenya's ruling class merged in the Kenya African National Union (KANU) under President Jomo Kenyatta's leadership. The rulers soon represented themselves not only as African socialists, but also nationalists and pragmatists, putting Kenyan interests first, and driving out radical socialists aligned with socialist countries. The government ideology was embodied in *African Socialism and its Application to Planning in Kenya*, Sessional Paper No. 10 of 1965, a statement not excluding private ownership, but requiring capital to be used for the 'general welfare'; emphasising rapid economic growth through large inflows of foreign capital; indicating nationalisation as undesirable; stating a lack of class divisions among Africans; promising equitably (but not equally) distributed incomes through political democracy and some government controls, including landholding limitations and progressive taxation; and stressing Africanisation of the management and capital of foreign firms and assistance to African private enterprise. The document was encouraging to the US ambassador and representatives of other capitalist countries. In 1964–6, radicals within the Kenya People's Union (KPU) criticised KANU's African socialism as a 'meaningless phrase', a 'cloak for the practice of total capitalism'. According to the radicals, the government was promoting the 'development of a small privileged class of Africans' in the name of socialism. But even KPU's promises were limited to distributing white settler land only to the landless, and providing free primary education for all. KANU's response was to harass the KPU, detain its activists without trial, and refuse most KPU nomination papers (Leys, 1974).

The World Bank (1983b) and its economist Acharya (1981b) view Malawi as one of Africa's greatest economic successes due largely to low price distortions (based on an index of agricultural and energy product prices, wages, interest rates, foreign-exchange rates, trade restrictions, and inflation). Yet while Acharya is correct in indicating the benefits of price incentives, Kydd and Christiansen (1982) argue that Malawi's agricultural policy has not been very market-oriented, and that its agricultural development has lacked success. In fact, the majority of Malawi's population has had declining real living standards from the mid 1960s to the late 1970s. The massive emphasis on government spending on infrastructure has been at the expense of health and education. Peasant agricultural productivity declined during the period. While Malawi's development strategy had a low degree of bias against agriculture generally, a policy of promoting large-scale estate agriculture damaged the peasant sector. Indeed Malawian national-income data vastly overstate growth in the peasant agriculture sector. From 1965 to 1982, real output per land resident in Malawian peasant farming declined 1.3% annually. Peasant maize output per land resident declined 2.0% yearly during the 1970s, a figure close to subsaharan Africa's general experience (Kydd, 1984).

Although Malawi's life president Hastings Kamuzu Banda promised not to nationalise the private sector, he has, according to Hirschmann (1987), 'presidentialised' it. In the 1970s, Banda controlled the country's two commercial banking groups and owned over 99% of Press (Holding) Ltd, which grew extraordinarily fast through new investment, mainly in estate agriculture, takeovers of existing commercial and industrial concerns, and in partnership with foreign equity capital. He ordered all Asians out of rural areas, and then moved his retail company to replace businesses vacated by Asians. Moreover, 45% of ADMARC's (a Ministry of Agriculture parastatal with monopsony buying power over peasant cash crop sales) loans and investments were extended to companies wholly controlled by Press. Finally, Banda instructed banks to lend money to local senior politicians, civil servants, and military personnel who became a stable bourgeoisie dependent on him. Growing private African control of the economy was concentrated with a few individuals, primarily Banda's associates, supported by Western development agencies (*ibid.*; Kydd, 1984).

Nigeria's income inequality is probably no higher than Tanzania's which is higher than Malawi's and lower than Kenya's and Cameroon's (table 3; Willame, 1986). While the composition of Nigeria's and Tanzania's managerial bourgeoisie differ, the relative discrepancies between their average incomes and those of workers and peasants are likely to be similar. Chapter 4 indicates that the income inequalities of socialist Tanzania and capitalist Nigeria, Kenya, and Malawi probably increased from the 1960s to the mid 1970s, although Tanzania probably redistributed income to the poor slightly through taxes and government spending.

MARKET INTERVENTION

Since independence, African politicians have tried to replace the market with a political market-place, with little emphasis on efficiency.

African countries with no more than 15% price discrimination against farmers were Chad, Malawi, Burkina Faso, Rwanda, Somalia, Central African Republic, Kenya, Lesotho, Zimbabwe, Cameroon, Botswana, Congo, and Côte d'Ivoire. Those with no more than 40% discrimination were Zaïre, Ethiopia, Uganda, Tanzania, Guinea, Benin, Sierra Leone, Madagascar, Togo, and Ghana. Countries in between were Mali, Burundi, Niger, Sudan, Senegal, Liberia, Zambia, and Nigeria. Government intervention in pricing inputs and outputs and replacing private with state trading was negatively correlated to output growth in (especially smallholder) agriculture during the 1970s and early 1980s (Vengroff and Farah, 1985; Cleaver, 1985; Acharya, 1981b).

The World Bank's (1983b) ranking of overall price distortions indicates Ghana (first), Nigeria (second), and Tanzania (third) high, Kenya, Ethiopia, Côte d'Ivoire, and Senegal medium, and Malawi and Cameroon low among 31 LDCs.

As an example of these distortions, Kenya's widespread price controls on food and basic consumer items are expensive, using considerable skilled personnel and financial resources that could be used for more productive purposes. Additionally, controls have distorted the economy, misallocating resources. Most importantly, price controls increased poverty and inequality, and reduced basic-needs fulfilment. For instance, effective price controls on necessities result in low rates of returns relative to luxury-good production with no controls. Investment moves from price-controlled industries to non-controlled ones, and reduces production of necessities in the long run. In Kenya, between the mid 1970s and mid 1980s rent control affected low-income housing, so housing developers stressed middle- and upper-income housing, largely uncontrolled and booming. Price controls on maize reduced the amount planted, adversely affecting availability and costs for poor rural and urban consumers in the long run. Small farmers, lacking access to storage, not only faced price controls, but had to sell at a time of maximum supply, receiving an even lower price. Price controls resulted in chronic shortages of goods and services, frequently compelling low-income consumers to buy on the black market or do without (*African Business*, Feb. 1986, pp. 23–4; *Africa*, Apr. 1986, p. 78).

PUBLIC-SECTOR INEFFICIENCY

Many of Africa's parastatal enterprises are wasteful, with low capacity utilisation and substantial losses, indicating inefficient resources allocation and an erosion of available capital resources. Compared to capitalist countries like Côte d'Ivoire and Cameroon, African socialist countries were more tolerant of losses and more resistant to bankruptcy to eliminate inefficient enterprises. Yet even Nkrumah (1973, from a 1964 speech) thinks there are few reasons to justify these losses:

I must make it clear that these State Enterprises were not set up to lose money at the expense of the tax payers. Like all business undertakings, they are expected to maintain themselves efficiently, and to show profits. Such profits should be sufficient to build up capital for further investment as well as to finance a large proportion of the public services which it is the responsibility of the state to provide.

Some African political leaders have reassessed the role of the public sector. Tanzania's President Ali Hassan Mwinyi, when installed in 1985, set deadlines for efficiency, sound management, and profitability in parastatals. In 1986, the Tanzania Sisal Authority sold nine of its

estates while planning to run others jointly with foreign capital
(*Africa*, Apr. 1986, pp. 14–15).

CONCLUSION

Class conflict and income inequality do not vary much between
African socialism and mixed capitalism. In both systems, the managerial bourgeoisie use the economic levers of the state to enlarge their
size and prosperity. Indeed even state intervention in the market tends
to increase poverty and inequality, as chapter 11 indicates further
when discussing price policies biased toward urban areas.

§ 8 §

THE RULING CLASS AND THE PEOPLE: CONFLICT AND DISCREPANCIES

Those who take the meat from the table
Teach contentment.
Those for whom the contribution is destined
Demand sacrifice.
Those who eat their fill speak to the hungry
Of wonderful times to come.
Those who lead the country into the abyss
Call ruling too difficult
For ordinary men.

Bertolt Brecht, *From a German War Primer*, 1937

As chapters 5 and 6 indicate, the nationalist leaders in the struggle for independence neglected class differences among the African population. Indeed nationalist movements before the 1940s had little mass support, and were divided by class and community. After World War II, the British and French eased colonial administration by policies enabling a cooperative African ruling class to live in privilege analogous to colonialists and settlers.

The bourgeoisie comprising the African ruling class is much broader than the private capitalist class, including high-ranking politicians and military officers, senior civil servants and government administrators, managers of parastatal corporations, top professionals, and traditional authorities (e.g., chiefs and emirs). This class rules primarily through its power over the means of production controlled by the state (Sklar, 1979). Although income and occupation do not correspond one to one, in nearly all African countries you find this top class followed by clerical and sales staffs and skilled workers and then by unskilled workers, farmers, and seasonal workers.

Classes are based on ownership or control of land, physical capital, and human capital. The African ruling classes – both urban and rural – use the accumulated advantages of wealth and power to reproduce their class standing in subsequent generations through education, training, experience, and other human investment, as well as investment in physical property.

Changing productive modes create new class configurations. While colonialism's demand for educated clerks and business collaborators gave rise to new classes, the most crucial years for Africa's new class formation and re-formation have been the 1950s through the 1980s. Class formation varies widely between and within African countries. Nigeria's, the Congo's, and Ghana's bourgeois and working classes are more developed than those of Malawi, Niger, and Chad, in initial stages of class formation. But within Nigeria, known for its cultural diversity, formation in the North took place within the traditional emirate order structured by feudal principles of aristocratic rank, while in the south, which lacked rigid class stratification, the rise of the dominant class was a product of modern social change – Western education, modern communication, urbanisation, and the growth of capitalism.

Before Ethiopia's 1974 revolution, its modern ruling class arose from within the feudal traditional order. The educated administrative elite came from the families of landowners, officials, and merchants. While the revolution blocked enrichment by inherited land holdings, it did reinforce modern education and public employment as the source of the Ethiopian ruling class (*ibid*).

Is class determined by power or production relations? In reality, the two interact. Controlling political power is essential for, yet dependent on, controlling productive relations. Fusing elites is critical in dominant-class formation. While the sources of power of business, government, political, military, professional, and traditional elites varied, they united and acted in concert in the terminal colonial and early independence period to control the state. Political parties and government agencies were agents of class formation. Parties and regimes created elaborate systems of administrative and commercial patronage, not only with the bureaucracy and parastatals, but also by liberally using public funds to promote indigenous private enterprise (*ibid.*). Yet the struggle for power by coalitions of classes, subclasses, and communities never ends, as regimes are forced to modify policies, include new interests, or are even overthrown.

Ruling classes vary in size, expanding as the economic pie grows, and contracting as it gets smaller. When growth becomes negative, as in parts of Africa, 1965–86, it becomes more difficult to support as large a ruling class. Contradictions and disunity can grow among a previously dominant class.

Sklar believes the authoritarian government is the most common political device for dominant-class consolidation in Africa. Authoritarian regimes infringe liberty by not allowing citizens the right to freely form political associations to compete for control of the state. When the dominant class cannot organise state power effectively, military intervention becomes probable. Military regimes usually represent the dominant class, enabling it to establish itself as a well-integrated hegemonic group.

Authoritarian regimes consolidate the power of the dominant classes, sometimes contributing to Huntington's goal (1968), political order and stability. Critics ask: should we 'value the stability of a concentration camp or torture chamber? Stability for whom and in whose interest? These questions must accompany any premium [on] maintaining systems and power structures. Conflict, dissent, revolution [like the eighteenth-century French Revolution] – the politics of the oppressed and of struggle – sometimes move men and weigh more heavily in balancing desirable social goals' (Markovitz, 1977). Indeed, as in Nigeria and Pakistan in the late 1960s and early 1970s, authoritarianism contributed to increased income inequality and political decay (Nafziger, 1983).

Moreover, people widely resent the oppression of authoritarian regimes, which do not provide for orderly governmental change. Because of the possibility of political change being eruptive and costly to bourgeois classes, some try to introduce or restore liberal and limited government (Sklar, 1979).

The military in Africa has not produced any answers to the long-run problems of economic growth, income redistribution, and the development of political culture and long-term political viability. Suspending activity by political parties does not develop an indigenous political system. Most military regimes lack the two-way communication with the masses provided by effective political parties. Nigeria's General Olusegun Obasanjo's claim before handing over the civilian leadership on 6 September 1979 that his government had 'laid down the basic infrastructure of stable political order' is in doubt in light of subsequent military coups (Gutteridge, 1985).

Countries whose economies grew (and reduced poverty rates) most rapidly experienced less military interventions in politics than did the slow performers. But causation does not run only one way since coups may have hindered African economic development (McGowan and Johnson, 1984).

Control of the means of production is highly, but not perfectly, correlated with income and class. The line between capital owners and controllers and their agents, and workers is not clear-cut. Thus, many African professionals, technicians, and other white-collar workers do not initially own or control substantial property. But they are not only leading investors in human capital, but also make enough income to accumulate some wealth (including housing). Moreover, they identify with the social order of the ruling class which has created and protected their privileges. Chapter 9 discusses the concept of a 'labour aristocracy' further.

Wage and salary differentials in Africa today are among the highest in the world. Lecaillon *et al.* (1984) indicate that among wage and salary earners, the salaried managers, executives, and technicians receive 30 times the income of the unskilled in Côte d'Ivoire, and 10 times in Senegal. And the disparity in average income in the early 1970s between subsistence farmers and executive, supervisory, and technical personnel was 1 to 58 in Zambia (with upper group non-Africans only), 1 to 34 in Senegal, 1 to 32 in Swaziland, and 1 to 27 in Côte d'Ivoire, compared to other LDC ratios of 1 to 20 in Colombia and 1 to 10 in Malaysia.

In Zambia, 1968 average annual earnings were ZK 1,300 for African miners, ZK 640 for non-mining workers, and ZK 145 (including subsistence) for peasant farmers. Among peasants, in the mid 1970s, the 20,000 prosperous Zambian farmers had 10–15 times the per capita incomes of the 850,000 poor subsistence farmers (Good, 1986; Ghai and Radwan, 1983).

In Nigeria, interpersonal income distribution in the modern sector increased from 1960 (Gini = 0.5) to 1975/6 (0.7), declining to 1979 (0.6), with sluggish oil growth. But relative wage and salary differentials narrowed in both public and private sectors from 1965 to the late 1970s, even though these differentials were still much larger than in DCs (Bienen and Diejomaoh, 1981).

Class implies a system characterised by conflict, not simply a hierarchy of inequalities. But African class conflict does not follow Marx's scenario of a united working class overthrowing a capitalist state. Nigeria has the largest private capitalist class in tropical Africa. Yet even the Nigerianists at the Soviet Academy of Science, when I lectured in Moscow on 24 May 1978, admitted that Nigeria's industrial proletariat was too weak for such a revolutionary role.

Classes exist even where people are not conscious of their situation. Officials in the capital, as in Nigeria, may live in isolation from the country's problems. And many of Africa's poor are beyond the gaze of the casual visitor to a village – away from roads, away from markets, or living on the outskirts of the village. Even the working class may not be conscious of class, as ethnic or regional identity, or a common interest in fighting the colonial power or some other enemy can override class divisions and divert class conflict.

THE WORKING CLASS

The working class consists not only of the relatively few employed as industrial and service labourers, but also of many of the Africans on farms, whether small landowners, sharecroppers, tenants, or landless workers. Wage employment and cash crops are alternative ways of responding to commercial encroachment on the traditional way of life. A fall in the demand for labour in the monetised sector increases the emphasis on cash-crop production, whereas a drought or bad harvest forces people on the farms to enter the wage-labour market. MNCs, their subsidiaries, and domestic intermediaries can either purchase or export locally grown farm crops, or organise production themselves on a plantation, using labour in a wage-earning capacity.

The individual wage-earner lacks control over the price of his labour power, just as the farmer lacks control over the prices of his product. Employers can replace workers by others or by machines, and primary-product buyers can shift to new supply sources or find synthetic alternatives (Allen, 1972).

I consider peasants producing crops for the family's subsistence, petty traders (often wives and children of industrial workers), artisans in one- or two-person enterprises, and small farmers members of the working class. The dividing line between farmers producing commercially and for subsistence is not clear, as most farm people are involved in both activities. Petty trading requires little capital and skill and, like wage employment and small farm production, is subject to the whims of the market. Moreover, as I point out elsewhere (1977), Africans may be 'pushed' into petty business because they are unemployed or have few other options in the hired work force.

LINKAGES BETWEEN PEASANTS AND WORKERS

The most obvious link is poor, rural peasants who work (often involuntarily) for wages for commercial farmers either part- or full-time. (See chapter 9's discussion of the preharvest 'hungry season' among the poorest of these peasants.) The other connections are farm migrants to urban areas, their remittances to the rural family, and off-farm employment opportunities.

Migration to the cities is a larger contributor than natural population growth to urbanisation in subsaharan Africa (with 27% of the population urbanised) than in the most urbanised LDC, Latin America (67%), where natural increase is the major source of urban growth. In Nigeria, for example, rural–urban migration accounted for more than 60% of urban population growth, 1952–76. A worker and his family decide whether to migrate to the city on the basis of his farm earnings compared to urban expected income (wages times the probability of finding employment). Small farmer commodity surplus can either curb large-scale urban emigration or cushion the would-be urban unemployed from destitution during the job search (Population Reference Bureau, 1986; Sada, 1981; Harris and Todaro, 1970; Martin, 1984).

Alternatively, the farmer may use off-farm employment to supplement his income. In Kenya and Nigeria, variations in the incomes of farm households are highly correlated with education and the amount of off-farm income, especially urban wages and remittances. Indeed household non-farm income is the key to determining farm productivity and household income in Kenya. Farm families receiving urban wages bought land, hired farm labour, financed innovations, purchased farm inputs, and increased farm income. Most without a regularly employed person earn no more than enough to enjoy the necessities of life. A study of Northern Nigerian villages found that off-farm income accounts for nearly 40% of the total income of the top quintile, but only 22–27% of income of the four bottom quintiles, while a west-central Nigerian survey indicated rural family income and capital per hectare significantly correlated with percentage of income from non-farm sources (Smith, 1978; Collier and Lal, 1986; Kitching, 1980; Matlon, 1981; Olayide and Essang, 1975).

Thus, people and resources flow, not only from rural to urban areas, but also back to rural areas. This is true not only among working people, but also among urban elites who keep close ties to the rural family and village.

THE BOURGEOISIE

After independence, a tiny ruling bourgeoisie devoured most of the new African states' resources. The public sector and its average real salaries grew steadily, even when real per capita growth was slow or negative. In 1964–5, administrative salaries comprised 47.2% of Senegal's budget; not a single dollar was spent on direct investment. At the same time, Cameroon spent 18 times as much money on administration as capital investment. In one year in the 1960s, francophone Africa spent six times as much importing alcoholic beverages as fertiliser, and twice as much on perfume and cosmetics as machine tools (Markovitz, 1977).

Most African countries, under informal imperialism or colonialism during the period when the West and Japan were undergoing rapid industrial growth, lacked a strong indigenous capitalist class. A home-grown capitalist revolution did not take place in Africa because of Western economic and political domination in the colonial and imperial period. Capitalism arose in Africa less through the growth of small competitive firms domestically than through the transfer from abroad of advanced monopolistic business. Even where a fledgling capitalism took hold, the African business and middle classes lacked the strength to spearhead thoroughgoing institutional change for major capital accumulation and technical change, and had to seek allies among other classes.

Africa's meagre economic base and weak bourgeoisie – even in mixed capitalist countries like Côte d'Ivoire, Cameroon, Nigeria, Malawi, Kenya, and Botswana – result in some built-in contradictions. Rapid expansion of output and economic surplus can undermine the hegemony of the existing ruling class. Yet slow growth, with greater ruling class shares of the surplus, threatens foreign capital, provides too few inducements for workers, or increases potential mass rebellion.

The smallness of the economic surplus and the political expectations and poverty of the African masses exert revolutionary pressures. The nationalist movement before independence politicised the African masses. Nationalist leaders had to stress self-determination and equality to win a following to put pressure on the colonial power. Now the demands from this radical consciousness are directed at the African ruling class, who cannot meet expectations by maintaining existing productive relations. Since their stagnating economies give them little room for manœuvring, they resort to increased repression and violence to control the masses. But this increases tensions, and forces the African ruling classes to depend more on foreign economic and political support. While some factions of the ruling class – intellectuals, populist politicians, and benevolent military leaders – stress redistribution and growth, hoping to seek political support from newly active political groups, the contradictions mentioned earlier limit this (Ake, 1981).

In Tanzania (see chapter 7), there has been class conflict between the dominant 'bureaucratic bourgeoisie' (whose power increased with nationalisation and expropriation), and workers and peasants.

In Ghana, officials had few means available to consolidate state power and make their incumbency less precarious, because they lacked a nationalist myth and a legitimising doctrine. As an ever larger portion of the economy was used to generate political support, pressure built up anew to expand further the economic role of the state for fresh economic resources to be converted to political use. Ghana's economy followed this dynamic, as it became increasingly state-centred and 'anti-development' during the 1960s and 1970s. Statist economic policies were not so much ill-conceived as undermind by the priorities imposed on officials by the Ghanaian political system (Price, 1984).

In post-1970 Ghana, Zaïre, and Uganda, the ruling class miscalculated how it could generate resources to keep its ruling coalition together. When threatened by slow economic growth, the ruling class became more coercive and corrupt to maintain its power and level of resources.

CLASS REPRODUCTION

In both precolonial and colonial periods, wealth and privilege were advantageous in transmitting class standing from one generation to another. The sons of African elites were more likely to get jobs and education during colonialism. Yet indigenous classes were still being formed during colonialism, as African elites lacked control of the state for intergenerational class reproduction. But during the late (especially British and French) colonial and early independence periods, as African households gained privileged access to state resources, the African upper and middle classes became more self-conscious and self-perpetuating. I discuss class maintenance here broadly, waiting until chapter 10 to analyse education's role.

Neo-classical economists believe that African mixed and capitalist economies allow substantial upward socio-economic class mobility for those with energy and enterprise. (See my critique of neo-classicism, 1977.) Collier and Lal analyse the mechanism for the upward movement by Kenyan smallholder farm households in 'Why Poor People Get Rich: Kenya, 1960–79' (1984). According to the study, households with urban wage employment are among the poor who have the wherewithal to become rich. However, the authors provide no evidence that the smallholder households who use urban wage employment to become prosperous were poor to begin with. As indicated in chapter 9, smallholder poverty rates are below pastoralist, migrant farmer, and landless farm worker rates. Not surprisingly, those smallholders who have the access and surplus for more education, training, farm inputs, funds, and the luxury of a longer time horizon (and have more affluent urban relatives) are more likely to send household members to the city to get well-paid jobs.

Morrison's (1981) all-Nigerian study of wealth and status inequality shows that father's and son's education are positively correlated, with virtually no intergenerational downward mobility in education. Children born after the late 1940s to early 1950s, when communalism and nationalism became a more conscious vehicle for country-wide high-class formation and consolidation, are more likely to retain their parents' class status.

Most members of Tanzania's modern elites, though of rural origin, described their families as economically 'above average' in their community. Many parents of these elites had high traditional status. The colonial government provided special schools for the traditional nobility's and upper-class's children, who became members of the modern elite. Thus even socialist Tanzania's elite originated predominantly from families with an above average to high socio-economic status (Hopkins, 1971; Markovitz, 1977).

INDIGENISATION

Immediately after independence, African governments relentlessly pursued Africanisation of their civil services, catapulting Africans overnight from relatively junior posts to positions of high responsibilities. Hastily established institutes of administration provided crash training programmes for African bureaucrats. In Nigeria, the number of federal public service posts occupied by Nigerian citizens increased from 85 (15%) of 568 on independence day, 1 October 1960, to virtually all 4,066 by 1962. In all of tropical Africa, an estimated 100,000–200,000 foreign-held posts were Africanised between 1958 and 1968. Standards fell and efficiency suffered. But today the majority of African administrations are in African hands (Adedeji, 1981; Ogbuagu, 1983).

After civil services were Africanised, governments turned to Africanise their national economies (in the 1960s and 1970s), especially as they became disillusioned with poor economic performance. Except for Côte d'Ivoire, Liberia, and Gabon, each African country nationalised at least one foreign enterprise during the period, concentrating in banking, insurance, and petroleum distribution.

African states felt it necessary to go beyond nationalisation to indigenisation of ownership, control, personnel, and technology, strengthening indigenous private and public enterprise at the expense of foreign-controlled enterprise. The primary objectives of Africanisation are greater self-reliance and self-sustaining growth (Adedeji, 1981).

Ake (1981) believes indigenisation's prospects are poor, since if complete it means doing without international aid, capital, imported technology, and imported consumer goods, and making international capitalism an implacable enemy. But if indigenisation means a partnership between the African ruling class and international capitalism, it could mean continued capture of social resources by the state in the name of the people but for the primary benefit of the state bourgeoisie.

Africanisation often increased indigenous inequalities. In Kenya land resettlement and Kenyanisation of jobs and businesses in the 1960s, while reducing racial discrepancies between African and higher-income non-Africans, increased the spread between the top and bottom Africans. Those Kenyans who benefited included the small group filling high-level positions previously held by non-Africans, the group of employees in the modern urban sector, the small minority of those receiving land transfers from European farmers, and the small bourgeoisie – traders, builders, transporters, small industrialists, and service and repair business people (ILO, 1972).

Zaïre nationalised its largest copper-producing firm, a Belgian concern, GECAMINES (General de Carrieres et des Mines du Zaïre), in 1967. While its dominant position and privileged access to inputs make it financially profitable, the firm uses more foreign exchange than it generates, is highly capital intensive, has large excess capacity, and is not well-integrated with other Zaïrian sectors.

Zaïre's 1973 nationalisation of palm oil changed it from a leading export to a net import by 1977. Government-appointed Zaïrian plantation managers, most of whom lacked interest and competence, systematically depleted the plantations' working capital to rescue their own financial position, hedging against future loss of power (Gran, 1979).

The Nigerian Enterprises Promotion Decrees of 1972, 1977, and 1981, shifted the manufacturing sector from foreign majority ownership in the 1960s to indigenous majority ownership in the mid and late 1970s, even though some foreigners naturalised, converted equity to debt holdings, or used other loopholes to continue ownership or control. Business people like Chief Henry Fajemironkun, former president of the Lagos Chambers of Commerce and Industry, participated in government economic policymaking, influencing the implementation of indigenisation, which became an instrument for a few civil servants,

military rulers, business people, and professionals to amass considerable wealth through manipulating state power. Several top bureaucrats
and military men benefiting from fraud resigned to join business or were
forced from government because of conflicts of interest (Ogbuagu,
1983).

To finance indigenous acquisitions, the government established the
Bank for Commerce and Industry, and directed commercial banks to
allocate at least 40% of their loans to Nigerian businesses. Ironically, an
indigenisation policy designed partly to reduce foreign concentration
created Nigerian monopolies and oligopolies, especially among those
with the wealth and influence to obtain capital and government loans to
purchase foreign shares. Additionally, access was concentrated geographically, as five of the merchant banks selling shares publicly were
located in Lagos, and the sixth was in Kaduna. Aboyade (1974) shows
that because of government assistance to elites, Nigeria's 1972–4
indigenisation increased inequality.

Egalitarianism was more of an issue when Nigeria amended the
indigenisation decree in January 1977, requiring additional transfers
to Nigerians. Under this amendment, an individual Nigerian could not
acquire or own more than 5% or ₦ 50,000 of the *public issue* of equity
share capital of any one company. But it is widely believed that most of
the private placings of shares went to only a handful of influential
buyers who had privileged access to the necessary information and
finance (Teriba, 1981).

Additionally, Nigerian entrepreneurs still lacked the capital, and
management and technical skills to effectively replace foreigners in
most industries reserved for them by law. As a result, some industries
covered under the 1977 indigenisation act were reclassified under the
1981 law to permit more foreign participation. Many Nigerians
acquiring shares in indigenised companies were content with divi-
dends paid to them by foreign managers. So most Nigerians increased
shares of foreign industries without the enterprising zeal and managerial or technical know-how to take on higher responsibility of
running the economy (Ogbuagu, 1983).

CLIENTALISM

Nation-building involves extending the discrete hierarchical solidarities existing locally or regionally to the national level. Clientalism, the
dominant pattern in Africa, is a personalised relationship between
patrons and clients, commanding unequal wealth, status, or influence,
based on conditional loyalties and involving mutual benefits. Cliental-

ism overlaps with, but reaches beyond, ethnicity. The ethnic identity of the client may be amalgamated with, widened, or subordinated to the identity of the patron, who exchanges patronage, economic security, and protection for the client's personal loyalty and obedience. Clientalism often operates within a political party, as in the case of the *Parti Démocratique de la Côte d'Ivoire* (PDCI), or the Northern People's Congress, 1960–6, an instrument of Northern Nigeria's traditional aristocracy (Lemarchand, 1972).

THE STATE BOURGEOISIE AND THE MARKET

The World Bank (1981a) criticises African states for overextending parastatal operations, suggesting the state should allow market forces to direct its economic destinies. But it is unrealistic to expect the state bourgeoisie to implement a decentralised market approach. Dispersing decisionmaking power to the numerous petty traders, artisans, and small industrialists without a quid pro quo would threaten the economic interests of the ruling class, whose patronage base is enhanced by the viability and monopoly returns of large, private business allies and public corporations. Inefficient and wasteful industrial policy and parastatal management serve specific class interests. The question is not just what policies but which class alliances would increase efficiency.

Moreover, as chapter 11 contends, African governments prefer project-based to price-based policies to increase agricultural supplies because projects help to build and reinforce a political patron–client system. Government leaders profit more by subsidising farm implement, fertiliser, and seed costs than by spurring prices to produce farm goods. The state bourgeoisie can manipulate farmers better through market intervention than with a free market (Nyongo, 1984; Bates, 1981).

Most official marketing boards buy crops from farmers to sell on the world market. While these monopsony boards insure financial success and raise funds to transfer from agriculture to industry, they also often divert funds to members and clients of the state bourgeoisie, who may ally with processors to keep crop prices low.

Most African states try to keep food prices low to satisfy urban workers and their employers (MNCs and government). Urban unrest from increasing living costs sometimes contributes to governments losing power or even being overthrown. Insecure African ruling classes forgo policies promoting rural innovation and reduced urban-rural income gaps to insure political survival.

General Ignatius Acheampong, Ghana's leader, 1972–8, ruled Ghana when world cocoa prices were at record heights. But Acheampong and his collaborators skimmed public resources at an extraordinary pace. *West Africa* (11 Sept. 1978, p. 1775) indicated a discrepancy of $300 million in 1977–8 between reported state cocoa sales proceeds and prevailing world prices. Acheampong is reported to have accumulated a personal fortune of $100 million in six years of rule, while hyperinflation and massive shortages destroyed the wealth and livelihoods of most citizens (Young, 1982).

THE STATE BUREAUCRACY IN FAST-GROWING ASIAN COUNTRIES

African bureaucracies have been much less development-minded than those of three newly industrialising countries (NICs), Japan, Korea, and Taiwan. These NICs not only have much higher per capita GNPs than Africa, but also enjoy low household income inequality (all three Ginis less than 0.3) compared to Africa's high inequality (all ten Ginis available more than 0.4). A key to the NICs' successes is the freedom the state gives to economic agency bureaucrats and leaders, who are relatively insulated from societal demands for distribution of resources. Key state actors can perform as economic entrepreneurs – setting output goals, designing economic strategies, accumulating savings, redirecting resources to high-growth sectors, and choosing technologies based on economic criteria. The NICs' remarkable economic direction and rationality results from the flexibility given state economic decisionmakers by insulating them from immediate political pressures. While African states are permeated by ethnic, regional, family, and class interests, the NIC state bureaucracy is relatively autonomous (Price, 1984).

TANZANIA'S STATE BOURGEOISIE

In Tanzania, the state stressed ujamaa socialism and economic development, thus justifying economic intervention to extract a surplus. While Nyerere and a few government officials originated Tanzania's socialist ideology in the early 1960s to improve worker and peasant living standards, the state bourgeoisie later adopted socialist slogans more widely in an attempt to legitimise its coercive policies (Stein, 1985).

Tanzania's bureaucracy grew rapidly after the 1967 Arusha Declaration and 1972 'decentralisation' (with increased central government personnel in the regions). The total established posts in the Tanzania civil service rose from 65,708 to 295,353 (a 349% increase), 1966–80. From 1966 to 1976, *total* economic growth increased 4% yearly, wage employment 3%, and civil service employment 13%. During the same period, government expanded upper parastatal salaries and lower bureaucratic salaries while freezing salaries and reducing housing, car and domestic appliance benefits for upper bureaucrats. Post-tax differentials between the highest and lowest salaries paid to civil servants declined from 33:1 in 1967 to 15:1 in 1974 to 5:1 in 1981.

Yet real (inflation-adjusted) differentials did not decline as much as these nominal figures suggest, since low-income classes were hurt worse by the more than 10% yearly inflation rates between the early 1970s and early 1980s. Food prices increased faster than other prices during that period. Between 1971 and 1975, the amount of maize meal that could be bought with a day's earnings (at minimum wage) dropped from 15.1 to 5.7 kilograms. Inflation, together with only modest wage increases, reduced real minimum wages 41% from 1963 to 1981. Moreover, consumer-goods output declined, especially for low-income groups. Finally inflation redistributed income from those holding money (e.g., wage earners) to the issuers of money (the state) through the central bank (Bukuku, 1985).

Still high-level government servants argued they could not support relatives (to say nothing of clients) on these incomes. Lower income and perquisites, together with shortages of vehicles, operational supplies, and other physical support, contributed to the increased embezzlement of public funds, unaccounted cash, nepotism, inefficiency, irresponsibility, and negligence of civil servants during the 1970s. The constant reorganisation, restructuring, and launching of new operations without proper evaluation contributed to uncertainty, adding to ineffectiveness. Grievances and shortcomings in the civil service undercut the national commitment to socialism (Mukandala, 1983).

Officials resented successful ujamaa villages (over which they had no control) in their area of operation. So after 1967, the central bureaucracy established regional development programmes, enabling it to compete with local authorities in developing patron–client relations in rural areas. Since state officials believed price incentives had only limited effects, virtually all turned to an authoritarian, managerial approach. The most common way out of farmer antagonism for the bureaucracy was for it to develop patron–client relations with individual ujamaa villages. Yet central bureaucrats had only limited patronage to offer in exchange for increased production, as the peasants received many social amenities free of charge.

Tanzania's compulsory villagisation, 1973–6, a massive centralised resettlement campaign, moved five million rural people. Many peasants forced to abandon their previous residence were relocated in villages that could not support them, or where they had to walk kilometres to obtain cultivable plots. In 1975, the government replaced the marketing cooperative movement with government agricultural export monopolies, in which peasants had no voice. Payments were frequently delayed or not paid at all. The government's concurrent effort to replace middlemen with ujamaa shops to reduce capitalist individualism had to be delayed due to shortages of essential items. Cooperatives, serving as middlemen, were closed down, as the bureaucracy could not control them. After 1973, the state bourgeoisie siphoned off an increasing amount of peasant surplus. In 1974–5, for example, the official cotton agency took 40.5% of cotton export receipts, the export tax 7.1%, the cooperative margin 11.9%, and the producer only 40.5%. Beginning in 1974–5, the rural economy declined, as peasants resisted by growing subsistence crops and selling cash crops on the black market. Most peasants refused to use fertilisers, because they had little effect on production and increased villagers' debt. Food production per capita declined 13.6% from 1966 to 1981, while food imports increased rapidly. Moreover, after the mid 1970s, crime and unrest increased (Hyden, 1980; Mapolu, 1984).

Although world agricultural prices generally increased after 1970, Tanzania's severe output cutbacks were spurred by low official producer prices, heavy taxes, and increasing parastatal marketing and administrative costs. Farmers diverted some crops like coffee into unofficial channels, neglected and abandoned some coffee, sisal, and cashews, and shifted resources from cash crops (cotton and tobacco) into subsistence production (World Bank, 1981a).

From 1967 to 1974 in Tanzania, the number of large manufacturing establishments increased rapidly as a result of nationalisation, the subsequent introduction and expansion of large parastatals, and the adverse effect of socialist policies on small private establishments. Because government policies favoured large firms, growth took place despite low commercial efficiency.

Beginning in 1967, the Tanzanian government acquired a majority shareholding of 57–60% in six large manufacturing firms in brewing, tobacco, shoes, metal boxes, and cement, and a 49% holding in another large industrial enterprise. From 1967 to 1974, employment in parastatal manufacturing increased from 5,302 to 34,778 (30.8%

yearly) compared to 2.8% for nonparastatal manufacturing. Average employment size in parastatal industry expanded from 204 to 740 from 1967 to 1974, while the non-parastatal size increased from 72 to 79 over the same period. Moreover, the total number of large establishments (with 100 or more employed) rose from 80 to 149 over the period, increasing or remaining roughly constant in the major industrial regions, Dar es Salaam–Coast, Tanga, Arusha–Kilimanjaro, and Mwanza–Mara–Shinyanga–West Lake, while small establishments (with 10–99 employed) declined, especially in the four major regions (Silver, 1985).

After 1967, all nationalised enterprises in manufacturing were under the control of the National Development Corporation (NDC), a holding company for state-owned industries. NDC's surpluses, as well as the gains of the nationalised banking and financial institutions, increased substantially beginning in 1967. In the first few years, industrial enterprise management and organisation did not change, as NDC had management agreements with foreign firms, often former owners.

In the early 1970s, public-sector employment increased rapidly with local government reform, while government collected dues less effectively and parastatal overhead costs rose and profits declined quickly. The Hirfindahl index of manufacturing employment concentration increased from 0.55 in 1967 to 0.74 in 1974. At the same time, Barry's diversification index indicates a 132.1% increase in aggregate manufacturing employment concentration, of which 59.0% was due to parastatal expansion (*ibid.*; Hyden, 1980).

KENYA'S MANAGERIAL BOURGEOISIE[1]

Kenya's post-independence bureaucracy also grew rapidly, especially from 1965 to 1969. Although pay scales increased slowly, this did not matter as promotions resulting from Africanisation and expansion were rapid. But by 1970, expansion was slow, private sector pay was rising, political corruption was steadily increasing, and morale was falling. The 1971 Ndegwa public-sector pay commission responded by awarding a non-inflationary pay increase, but lifting most restrictions on civil servants engaging in private enterprise (Leys, 1974).

Kenya's African capitalist class originated in the 1920s and 1930s. After independence it received the support of the state in appropriating land to create new African large-scale capitalist farms, and for licences, credit, preference schemes, and distribution rights to expand commercial capital. Indeed good contacts in the bureaucracy became as important to Kenyan capitalists as knowledge about production and marketing. Public office often became the main road to private-sector wealth accumulation. African capitalists grew stronger after 1963, despite their declining efficiency, because of their symbiotic relationship to the bureaucracy and foreign capital (Swainson, 1977; Bigsten, 1984).

Could we expect this government and capitalist elite to forgo gains and implement the ILO recommendation (1972) to redistribute from growth? A dissident member of parliament responds:

It is difficult to change when the people who are supposed to change it are involved... We have sung this song long enough because we started in 1963. Let us not blame anybody now because has the Cabinet sat down and drafted a policy on land ceiling... No! Because they are the biggest grabbers of land in this country. We must not just talk in this House. We must be able to lay the blame where it belongs and the Cabinet is the precise place where it belongs... however, are we to sacrifice the interests of 12 million people on the altar of twenty-three people?

Our economy is capitalist and any country which bases its economy on capitalism is bound to have troubles... There are always troubles because the idea of capitalism is to grab and run... What can prevent us from owning all the property in this country? We should have a land ceiling so that no man can own vast tracts of land.

(Ng'ethe, 1980, citing *Proceedings of the National Assembly*)

For Marcussen and Torp (1982), The Kenyan ruling class

embraces the type of conspicuous consumption which is the hallmark of the feudal ruling caste, where the patron has to impress his dependent clients with the hollow pomp and lavish signs of wealth and influence. They respect the big belly squeezed under the steering wheel of the Mercedes far more than they respect talent, quality and productivity. Perpetual parasites, they are simply not good enough to be truly bourgeois.

In 1986, the annual salaries for the top civil-service scale, K£9,330–10,986 ($11,000–13,000), were roughly 30 times as high as the minimum, K£339, a widening of the ratio during the previous five years, and among the highest ratios in the world (EIU, 1986).

UGANDA'S MANAGERIAL BOURGEOISIE

Uganda's leading African bourgeoisie just before independence (1962) included the capitalist farmers (kulaks), traders, and bureaucrats. In the decade before 1962, colonial policies subsidised tractor hire (only economical for the large farmer with 8 hectares or more); provided a promotional corporation, credit guarantees, and hire purchase for African traders; and retained colonial benefits and salaries for African civil servants. Kulaks gained control of the parliament (*Lukiko*), as

African traders were subordinate to Indian traders, and bureaucrats to the foreign members of the civil service.

Indian capital, allied with the state (especially Bagandans) and multinational capital, moved into manufacturing after independence with tariff and other protection. By 1966–7, the state ceased its support to Indian businesses, trying to replace them with parastatals. But the state gained little more than formal ownership, as control was still in the hands of private foreign or Indian capital. Additionally, the Trade Licensing Act of 1969, with its annual licence fee of shs. 500, adversely affected African business.

Unlike Tanzania, which had one ruling bourgeoisie, Uganda had two separate bourgeoisies – Baganda (with kulaks at the core) and non-Baganda (dominated by a governing bureaucracy). Struggles between these bourgeoisies occupied the political stage until 1971.

Ruling-class factions combined to grant the demands of mutinous soldiers for Africanisation and higher pay in 1964, but split by allying with different groups of army officers, thus politicising conflicts within the army. President Milton Obote's government's 1970 redistribution programme was a threat to the closely-knit privileged elements – business people, professionals, civil servants, and landowners – in wealthier Buganda and the south. When civil servants opposed the programme, Obote tried to rely on the military establishment. But high average military incomes (at $1,275, more than 42 times income per capita) had created a self-consciously privileged military establishment determined to protect its status. The 1971 coup, which made it possible for soldiers to continue personal accumulation, took place before Obote could implement his announcement to grant Asians citizenship (and thus increased importance in trading) (Mamdani, 1976; Sklar, 1979; Lofchie, 1974).

Field Marshal Idi Amin, head of state following the coup, expelled Asian business people from Uganda in November 1972 and subsequently nationalised British and US industries and agricultural estates, creating economic chaos in the short run. Imports and domestic distribution came to a virtual standstill. The major capitalist countries, the World Bank, and the IMF cut off loans and technical assistance to Uganda. The Amin government either created parastatals from the formerly Western and Asian establishments, or distributed them free to influential groups in the military and civil service. From 1972 through the time of Amin's overthrow, 1979, Africans dominated the economy, but at the expense of workers. However, some Ugandan private or parastatal firms cut output substantially for lack of inputs and spare parts, forcing some workers back to rural subsistence, and weakening the trade union movement. And as exports to capitalist countries declined, peasants diverted their energies from cash crops to food production (Barongo, 1984).

ZAMBIA'S MANAGERIAL BOURGEOISIE

In the first five years after Zambia's 1964 independence, half the white, large-scale farmers departed. Members of the new bureaucratic bourgeoisie and other urban elites invested in farms vacated by departing whites. Farm holdings continued to be highly concentrated, but in the hands of African elites.

Zambian industrial parastatals have been very inefficient. Kaunda was appalled at thefts, wastage, indolence, and inflated overheads in parastatals representing corruption of 'alarming proportions'. He believed the Zambia Industrial and Mining Corporation (ZIMCO), which he chaired, was potentially 'a con-man's dream world' where any travelling salesman might sell anything at any price, and where state managers buy only where they get kickbacks.

High-level personnel in government and the parastatals receive car and entertainment allowances, free electricity and water, servants and security guards, overseas travel allowances, and housing subsidies. Earnings disparities between non-Zambian and Zambian employees, public–parastatal and private sectors, highest and lowest wage-earners, and urban and rural workers are wide. Salary increases in the 1970s widened the income gap between public–parastatal employees and common people. The Zambian parastatal and government bourgeoisie has redistributed income from the majority of the population to itself (Good, 1986; ILO, 1977b).

ZAÏRE'S MANAGERIAL BOURGEOISIE

When the Mobutu regime seized power in 1965, it consolidated the emerging managerial bourgeoisie. The post-1965 political and admini-strative classes originated from the African bureaucratic elites who formed political parties and occupied posts as ministers, members of Parliament, diplomats, and administrators at independence, and the many Zaïrians who moved into state administration with the flight of Belgians in the wake of the July 1960 Force Publique mutiny (Kannyo, 1979).

The Mobutu government promulgated an ideology of conservative anti-colonial nationalism, emphasising Zaïre's political and commer-cial elite owning equity capital. Since this elite previously had no capital, it had to be obtained from the state. This was either done openly or more frequently through rents extracted from facilitating foreign capital's entry (Young, 1982).

The Zaïrian regime sustained itself in power by investing to build up bonds of personal loyalty to Mobutu. In the 1970s and 1980s, much of the money used to sustain these ties came from state funds. Controlling the state administration and its access to corruption was vital for the Mobutu regime's survival (Hyden, 1980).

In 1972 in Kinshasa, 6.6% of the Zaïrians who held high managerial positions in the public sector earned 29.2% of all government wages and salaries. In the private sector, high-level managers, 2.8% of private wage earners, earned 30.8% of total wages. About 30% of total demand for consumer goods was concentrated in 5% of the wage earners, the top-level managers (Makala-Lizumu and Elas, 1979).

The Mobutu government's continuing political crisis began soon after the 1973 Zaïrianisation measures, coinciding with a decline in the price of copper from $3,370 per metric ton in April 1974 to $1,350 in December 1974 to $1,280 per metric ton in December 1975. Inflation increased rapidly at the same time. The beginning of the Angolan civil war in 1975 cut off the Benguela railroad, a vital lifeline for Shaba (Katangan) mining and industry (Kannyo, 1979).

Zaïrianised businesses were distributed as benefits to Mobutu and political and bureaucratic elites, with no provision for compensating former owners. Many indigenised businesses soon became bankrupt because Zaïrian acquirers either simply stripped their assets and abandoned them or lacked capital, technical knowledge, and commercial skill. After these failures and the sharp copper price drop in 1974, Mobutu placed many of the larger businesses with the state. But with the 1975 external capital crisis, most Zaïrians had to surrender their newly-acquired businesses to their former foreign owners. Unbridled private capitalism, unrestrained by a public ethic, perverted the Zaïrian polity (Young, 1982).

Since 1965, the state has served as the arena or object for struggle for distribution and extraction control. The ruling class has broadened its clientage, putting more Zaïrians on government payroll. And the rich and powerful have obtained legal title over large tracts of land by physically removing cultivators from the land or expropriating their few resources through taxes or state power (Newbury, 1984; Gran, 1979).

In 1977, President Mobutu denounced *le mal zaïrois* (the Zaïrian disease), stating:

Everything is for sale, everything is bought in our country. And in this traffic, holding any slice of public power constitutes a veritable exchange instrument, convertible into illicit acquisition of money or other goods.   (Lemarchand, 1979)

For Young (1984), Zaïre is a decaying irrational state, with reduced competence to relate material means to policy ends. State agencies become solely preoccupied with their own reproduction. Even the most dedicated individual efforts are defeated by pervasive demoralisation and venality. The Zaïrian armed forces, while dangerous to the unwary and unarmed, are unable to contend with armed challengers unless supported by foreign cadres. Zaïre has systemised state corruption, from petty survival venality at the lower echelons to kleptocracy at the top. Mobutu and his collaborators have become internationally notorious for their extraordinary fortunes. The state accumulates resources and hires labour, but provides little health service, education, transport, infrastructure, and court system. The costs of the presidency, the security forces, and the educational system remain very high in the decayed Zaïrian state. To run it requires continual monetary expansion and endemic hyperinflation. Many seek economic survival outside the public realm in the underground economy. Most Zaïrians, especially peasants, are poor, and appear resigned, wholly absorbed in the precarious quest for daily survival.

NIGERIA'S MANAGERIAL BOURGEOISIE

Government grew rapidly as its expenditures rose from 9% in 1962 to 44% in 1979 as a percentage of GDP (Central Bank; Office of Statistics). Nigeria centralised power during its civil war with the breakup of regions, and in the 1970s, as the oil boom enhanced the centre's fiscal strength and increased political competition for resources.

Individuals with powerful government positions are subject to great pressures over the distribution of patronage. Clientalist patterns of politics are often organised around village, region, or ethnic ties. However, the expansion of the government's share of the economy did not increase political and administrative capability much. Instead the large bureaucracy created a high capacity for obstruction and delay. Government office is personalised, with little delegation of authority and much corruption. Government budgeting and planning is weak, and accounting and auditing often non-existent (Forrest, 1986).

The median salary of a firm's managing director was 6.5 times that of a foreman, a narrowing of relative salary from 1965 to 1972. Within the civil service, wage and salary differentials in the 1970s were wide but declining. The pay ratio of permanent secretary to general unskilled labourer, 17.6:1 in Nigeria in 1975, compares to a ratio of 3.8:1 in Britain. However, the Nigerian top bureaucrat also had generous housing and vehicle allowances (Fajana, 1981).

High-priced housing and automobiles are indicative of upper-class status. Before the late 1970s, an employee with ₦2,500 or more annual income was entitled to a car loan and subsidised housing. In Benin City in 1974, 11% of the heads of households owned cars, 44% motorcycles and bicycles, and 45% no vehicles; 5% of the population lived in independent bungalows, 2% in independent, detached storey buildings, and 15% in semidetached houses or flats, a group roughly approximate to middle- to upper-class housing. Some 73% of the population of Benin occupied only a single room, compared to 72% in Lagos, 68% in Kaduna, 63% in Warri, and 51% in Ibadan. In these cities, about 20–25% of the 1974 population had a water closet (Sada, 1981).

Businessmen formed an important minority in the nationalist movement and the post-independence party leadership, supporting the liberal use of public funds to promote indigenous private enterprise. Nigerians moved into manufacturing partnerships with Lebanese, Indians, or other private foreign investors, but later were in business by themselves. The 1972 and 1977 indigenisation measures expanded the Nigerian (especially industrial) capitalist class, but mainly among a privileged few.

Ibos felt the timing of the first indigenisation decree was an exclusionary measure adopted after a devastating civil war when they were economically incapacitated (compared to Yorubas and Hausa-Fulanis) and restricted from economic opportunities outside Iboland. Moreover, since the 1977 law involved widespread Nigerian 'fronting' for foreign interests, there were few opportunities for newcomers (most Ibos) to indigenisation (Ogbuagu, 1983).

The oil-fuelled increase in public capital expenditure, 1973–7, resulted in 'euphoric planning', overwhelming the administrative machinery and contributing to inefficient resource use. In stepping up spending, the government relaxed its procedures for selecting and executing projects, moderated those for competitive tendering and project appraisal, spent too much on capital relative to current outlays, and sometimes simply handed over 'turnkey' projects to foreign contractors. And the neglect of a maintenance budget relative to new capital resulted in traffic congestion, and water and power failures (ILO, 1981; Schatz, 1978).

Civil servants, who ran the affairs of the military government,

1966–79, were well placed to influence (for a 'commission') the choice of contractors, suppliers, etc. for particular projects. Companies commonly entered bribes and kickbacks in their accounts as 'promotional expenses' (Ohiorhenuan, 1984).

The National Party of Nigeria (NPN), the ruling party from the beginning of the second republic (1979) through the 1983 coup, was held together by a careful distribution of office and rewards to regions and groups. The NPN received support from many wealthy business people building up personal networks. The reason for their political activity at all levels of the state and party was to defend property and business interests against rival predators and the whims of those who exercise state power where private property is not legally secure, state intervention is rife, and a state governor can ruin a business overnight (Forrest, 1986).

In 1981, in the face of Nigeria's oil revenue decline, state expenditures expanded rapidly, and external reserves dropped substantially as imports under the NPN government reached record levels. This expansion included political payoffs and rewards associated with state employment expansion, large salary increases for legislatures, an expanded police force linked closely to the ruling party, large project expenditures (including the poorly planned new federal capital Abuja), and wage pressures. Moreover, in the early 1980s, governors controlled import licences, which they sold to wealthy business people supporting the state's ruling party. By 1981, financial discipline had broken down, with several governors setting aside funds for their and their clients' use outside the state legislatures' scrutiny. A number of states built up large arrears in payments to state employees, and several states could not pay teachers. The result was strikes, absenteeism, and disruption or paralysis of teaching and public services for prolonged periods. Although the NPN favoured foreign investment, its net flow remained low due to high electricity, water, and roads costs, an obstructionist bureaucracy, exchange controls, and inconsistent government policy. The increasing political incompetence and economic mismanagement by Shehu Shagari's NPN government turned business against him by 1982–3, and helped lay the basis for the coup (*ibid.*).

CÔTE D'IVOIRE'S MANAGERIAL BOURGEOISIE

Chapter 5 discusses the origin of the PDCI, the nationalist organisation that became a political party, from which have come most of

Côte d'Ivoire's leaders since 1945. The party, under Houphouet-Boigny's leadership, was pluralist and multipartisan, aiming at unanimity in selecting leaders from diverse political and ethnic backgrounds. This political elite was from the civil service, the professions, or planter or industrial capitalists, well-educated, typically 40–50 years old, and a product of the colonial system, but not from traditional occupations like small farming, hunting, fishing, cattle herding, or crafts. Yet Houphouet-Boigny picked men generally not well-known even within their own regions. This ruling elite remained stable from 1959 to 1980 (Bakary, 1984).

At the end of the 1970s, the monetary income of 400,000–600,000 households and the livelihood of 4 million of 8 million Ivorians depended on coffee and cocoa, which accounted for 78% of exports in 1960 and 58% in 1979. Timber, pineapples, bananas, cotton, rubber, and palm oil provided for increasingly diversified export revenue sources. Land size and improved farm machinery have been strongly correlated with the adoption of export crops. Additionally, the ruling class used credit distribution to regulate who joined the larger export planters.

Ivorian industry depended on increasing tariffs and subsidies, especially in the 1960s. Costs, especially of foreign salaries, royalties, and fees for foreign technical services, equipment, and inputs, were high.

Côte d'Ivoire's planter class supported foreign domination of Ivorian industry to forestall the ascension of a local commercial and industrial bourgeoisie. But the 1970 economic strategy of encouraging foreign capital to move from import-substituting to export industries, increasing investment opportunities for Ivorian capital, and Ivorianisation of managerial and technical personnel in industry had limited success in the 1970s and early 1980s. With the CFA franc overvalued, foreign investment was inadequate to increase export orientation. More than 80% of total foreign investment, 1973–9, was reinvested earnings rather than capital inflows.

Although the state bought share capital in numerous foreign enterprises in the 1970s and 1980s, it did not significantly increase control or develop entrepreneurial talent. And because of insufficient domestic savings and limited new foreign investment, Côte d'Ivoire turned to foreign banks for loans and foreign suppliers for credit. Since the mid 1970s, Côte d'Ivoire has become more vulnerable, with falling export prices and increasing external debt. After 1979, the balance of payments worsened, resulting in austerity measures imposed by the

IMF and repression of domestic demand. Reduced demand hurt Côte d'Ivoire's import-substituting industry.

Efforts to Ivorianise industry since the late 1970s have made little progress. To be sure, the state has been playing a larger role in agricultural processing, and making electricity, water, and other social goods available. Yet although the share of foreign investment declined throughout the 1970s, foreigners still held a majority of total industrial investment in 1979. Moreover, the industrial sector, though it grew rapidly, was so capital-intensive that it provided few new jobs. In 1972–6, industrial output grew by 21.1% annually, while employment increased 8.4%; in 1977–81, annual industrial output growth was 7.0% compared to only 3.8% for industrial employment. Total capital formation per employed person increased 61% from 1970 to 1981. Furthermore, Ivorian manufacturing has a high import content, encouraged by an overvalued CFA franc, which together with subsidised credit, encouraged the use of capital-intensive technology, especially by foreign firms (Campbell, 1985; Mytelka, 1984).

Local investors were increasingly linked to the state. From the 1960s through mid 1980s, at least two-thirds of Ivorian investors or promotors of small industries were members of the civil service or held political positions. In response to a 1971 state decree, 80% of the bakeries were Ivorianised by the mid 1970s, but 66% of the Ivorians were civil servants. Moreover, one-third of the firms with private Ivorian interests had state participation. This reflected the state's policy, similar to that of the Japanese government in the 1880s, of buying shares from foreigners and transferring them to private indigenous investors. Additionally, the state used public funds, services equipment, protected markets, access to credit, influence, and so on to help private Ivorian capital.

From the early 1960s through the early 1980s, Côte d'Ivoire's ruling class used revenue, credit, and employment expansion to shape alliances and stabilise politics. As economic growth and official marketing boards' (Caisses de Stabilisation) surplus declined in the 1970s and 1980s, the state depended more on excess borrowing, especially from foreigners, to maintain the coalition of interests with direct access to the state. Planter-class support for the state remained only through concessions like access to credit and low wages to migrant workers.

Since the late 1970s, Côte d'Ivoire's ruling class has no longer had access to substantial accumulation from agriculture (through the Caisses) to support and enlarge its ruling group. Unlike 1963–4, when the government raised civil servant salary scales after 'plots' against the government, in the early 1980s, the government had less room to manœuvre. In the 1970s and early 1980s, real wages declined in both urban and rural areas. Moreover, there is an excess supply of primary and secondary school leavers relative to appropriate jobs. As a result, the informal sector provides a livelihood for an increasing proportion of the population (Campbell, 1985).

TAXATION AND GOVERNMENT SPENDING

Direct taxes like personal and corporate income, property, wealth, and inheritance taxes are elastic taxes, i.e., the percentage change in taxation exceeds the percentage change in GNP. The largest source of revenue in DCs (10–20% of GNP) is the progressive personal income tax. If well-enforced, it redistributes income from the rich to the poor.

Africa generally relies heavily on indirect (import, export, turn-over, sales, and excise) taxes. Direct taxes as a percentage of total taxes (1969–71) are: DCs 64.7%, Ghana 23.2%, Kenya 42.2%, Tanzania 33.2%, Zaïre 26.4%, and Zambia 61.1% (because of copper MNC corporate taxes). Few African countries rely much on income taxes, because they have trouble administering them.

The following conditions must be met if income tax is to become a major revenue source in Africa: a predominantly money economy; literate taxpayers; widespread accounting records honestly and reliably maintained; much voluntary taxpayer compliance; and honest and efficient administration (Nafziger, 1984; Tanzi, 1966). Even the West, to say nothing of Africa, has trouble fulfilling these conditions.

Africa's public-sector share of total health spending averaged 62% in 1975–80. Health accounted for 5.3% of 1980 public spending in West Africa and 4.7% in East Africa. Yet to take advantage of government spending on health, people have to travel to clinics, wait there (sometimes hours), and perhaps spend money on drugs. These private costs mean poor African families use health services less than rich ones. Still, while Africa's subsidies to transport, electricity, water, post office, telephone (disproportionately benefiting urban popu-lations, especially affluent ones), and education (see chapter 10) substantially increase inequality, health subsidies usually have a less adverse impact on inequality (Jimenez, 1986).

Health services are, however, unequally available in Zaïre. While only 19% of the bottom 55% socio-economic class of Kinshasa's 1975 population had access to medical facilities, all of those of the top 14% socio-economic class had access (Makala-Lizumu and Elas, 1979).

In Tanzania, spending on health, schools, housing, and transport, together with a 1974 progressive personal income tax, redistributed income to low-income classes. Unlike the pre-1974 tax, which includes poll and flat taxes that were regressive at the lower end, the 1974 tax abolished personal taxes at the minimum wage. In 1981, marginal tax rates began at 25% for a monthly income of Tshs. 620 ($31) and rose to 65% at Tshs. 5,000 and 95% at Tshs. 13,980. For salaried people, income was taxed at the source. Yet tax evasion has been very high for business people and non-salaried earners because of the steep marginal rates and the tax department's understaffing and under-equipping (Bukuku, 1985). Realistically, few economies can expect much voluntary taxpayer compliance on non-wage income at marginal rates in excess of 60%.

Bukuku argues that Tanzania's excessive fiscal redistribution contributed to a productivity decline between 1967 and the mid 1980s. Moreover, the government's radical policy changes – villagisation, closing down private shops, abolishing cooperative unions, eliminating local governments, and creating numerous new parastatals – brought about economic uncertainty that reduced growth. Thus, government policy enlarging the poor's disposable-income shares probably also increased absolute poverty by slowing growth.

Kenya's fiscal policies exacerbated income inequalities. Property tax was low, the income tax was roughly proportional, and many potentially liable employees and numerous self-employed evaded taxes. Most public expenditures were in cities, though poor areas had low-quality service; high-income employees had superior medical services, access to better education, and so on; and extension services, loans, inputs, subsidies, and other farm programme benefits went primarily to progressive farmers (ILO, 1972).

The Zambian government provided substantial loans and subsidies to agricultural cooperatives, which often treat funds as income rather than investment. Poorer peasants viewed producer cooperatives as providing assistance for well-to-do farmers. Settlement schemes, also, concentrated state resources on relatively few people in the most prosperous regions. Government devised individual farming units of 60–100 hectares on the settlements, which created a rural capitalist class primarily from members of the ruling United National Independence Party (UNIP) or those well-connected politically (Good, 1986).

Before 1975, Nigeria had no federal (only a state) personal income tax. Evasion and poor enforcement resulted in income tax collection failing to increase as a proportion of income in the 1960s, even in states/regions with a progressive tax. But Nigeria's 1975 uniform tax, as amended in 1977, levies a marginal tax rate of 45% for persons earning ₦ 15,000–20,000, 55% for ₦ 20,000–30,000, and 70% for more than ₦ 30,000. However, professionals on salary (with income taxes withheld) declared much higher incomes and paid much higher taxes than the self-employed, who frequently evaded taxes (Omorogiuwa, 1981). Few tax defaulters have been prosecuted due to cost, delay, and uncertainty in overburdened courts. Reducing evasion today will require separate tax courts, increased spending on tax enforcement, using tax clearance certificates before providing official services to the self-employed, widespread tax compliance by high government officials, and cutting the highest marginal tax rates.

The increased income inequality from the income and employment effects of Nigeria's oil boom in the 1970s, which benefited a small population, was reinforced by inequitable public expenditures. Federal spending on investment and services since 1974, 70–80% derived from petroleum revenues, shows a substantial concentration of benefits toward higher-income recipients. Transportation projects, like highway and flyover expenses, have favoured high-income Nigerians and foreign businesses (Diejomaoh and Anusionwu, 1981b; Odufalu, 1981).

HOUSING

Most Nigerian cities have reserved government housing, primarily for the elite. Zoning by social class makes it politically easy to put pipe-borne water, roads, security, electricity, and waste disposal in elite neighbourhoods. Elites move out of declining neighbourhoods to better ones, concentrating low-income classes in deteriorating slums. In the late 1970s, the federal government located the secretariat close to the elite class supported by car loans and allowances, but further away for low-income workers who spend more time and money getting to work.

Nigeria's cities have serious overcrowding and widespread slums. In Lagos thousands sleep in the streets. Rented accommodation (in 1981) absorbed 30–40% of the incomes of the Lagos poor. Poor housing conditions, with overcrowding and lack of ventilation, increase airborne diseases such as measles, tuberculosis, and other respiratory diseases (Sada, 1981; ILO, 1981).

A sizeable proportion of African urban housing accommodating unemployed migrants, factory workers, clerks, and even skilled workers consists of overcrowded tenements and slums, many unauthorised. These slums and shacks embarrass the ruling elites and interfere with their planning. Slum demolition frequently provides opportunities for elites to broaden patron–client networks through new commercial or housing programmes.

Compulsory rehousing only benefits those who can afford the housing, and re-establish their pattern of life, so they are not too far from kin or work. These conditions are rarely fulfilled. Overly expensive standards hurt low-income families and may lead to spontaneous housing uncontrolled by public authorities. What the poor do for themselves is frequently illegal.

In the early 1970s, the World Bank used a site and services approach in Dakar, which levelled unoccupied areas, divided them into evenly laid-out lots, and provided limited access to water and electricity. The authorities sold lots on hire purchase, allowing each family to construct its own dwelling and make improvements over time. While this allowed more low-income families to afford plots, almost half of Dakar's population was still too poor to qualify (Gugler and Flanagan, 1978).

In Kenya, traditional methods of designing and building usually achieved greater efficiency than imported technology, while the threat of demolition reduced housing standards. So, in the early to mid 1970s, the government used low-cost urban Site and Service Housing Schemes (SSHS) to upgrade infrastructure and communal facilities in existing squatter and slum areas, provide site and service plots, and equip settlement plots with communal services. The plot-owner built the house through his family's or friends' efforts (sometimes with loans and technical assistance), on a cooperative basis, or through subcontracting. SSHS houses not only promoted employment, but cost a fourth to a fifth of a similarly sized conventional house, because of owner initiative and local material use (ILO, 1972; Ghai, 1980).

CONCLUSION

In Africa, the state is the major focus for class struggle between a managerial bourgeoisie (consisting of politicians, administrators, military officers, chiefs, and professionals) and the working class. The ruling bourgeoisie uses taxes, government spending, public programmes, market intervention, and indigenisation policies to maintain its size and stabilise its rule. But Africa's slow economic growth since 1965 has compelled this class to reduce the size of the coalition it supports or use repression to extract a greater share of the majority's tiny surplus, increasing the probability of coups or other regime turnovers. Ironically, heightened insecurity puts pressure on the state class to rely even more on short-run palliatives that benefit the military, civil service, and other privileged groups but increase income concentration.

⸇ 9 ⸇

WORKERS, THE UNEMPLOYED, PEASANTS, AND WOMEN

In chapter 8 I presented a political economy analysis of class conflict between Africa's managerial bourgeoisie and the working class, which I defined to include also peasants and small farmers who have little control over the prices of their products. This chapter looks at inequalities among both wage-earning and farming populations, and how women and the unemployed contribute to income concentration.

THE LABOUR MOVEMENT

The strength of the African wage-earning class exceeds its number (50% of Zambia's 1960s' economically active population, 30% of the Congo's and Gabon's, 20% of Kenya's, Ghana's and Côte d'Ivoire's, 5% of Nigeria's, and less than 5% of Togo's, Burkina Faso's, Niger's, Mali's, and most others'), because of its strategic location in cities and expanding commercial sectors, its organisation, and its conflict with government (both ruler and major employer). African labour's emphasis has not been on political objectives or changing the economic system but on bread-and-butter issues.

Despite difficulties, trade unions organised under British and French colonial rule sometimes struck and resisted elite-led nationalism. The 1945 Nigerian strike tied up the economy for more than 40 days. Also Tanganyikan workers supported Dar es Salaam dock workers in a general strike in February 1947 that triggered a major political crisis.

Strikes protesting the wealth, corruption, capriciousness, and authoritarianism of ruling elites indicate that trade unions have at times been independent of African political leaders. The seventeen-day September 1961 strike against Nkrumah's Convention People's Party's compulsory wage deduction, increased taxes, and party favouritism and corruption reflected a reformist urban populism. Approximately 800,000 workers demonstrated the Nigerian government's fragility when they went on a general strike 1–12 June 1964 to protest about no post-independence worker pay raises but substantial increases for and corruption among senior civil servants and politicians. Workers even repeatedly defied the Lagos government's wartime strike ban (with postwar extension), 1969–73 (Markovitz, 1977; Nafziger 1983; Bienefeld, 1979; Jeffries, 1975b).

Yet careerist and upwardly-mobile trade union leaders, especially in countries where modern-sector firms pay high wages relative to mass average income, have given in to pressures by local politicians, bureaucrats, and capitalists to create 'responsible' unions oriented to wages, working conditions, and length of the work week rather than changing the economic system's inequalities (Bienefeld, 1975).

After Kenya's independence, Labour Minister Tom Mboya, former General Secretary of the Kenya Federation of Registered Trade Unions, expected unions 'to play their part ... to help consolidate independence and economic reconstruction'. Kenyan officials viewed all organised social forces not controlled by government as potential threats (Bigsten, 1984).

In Uganda, worsening worker conditions and union leader opposition to strikes gave progressives within the dominant Uganda Peoples' Congress (UPC) party an opportunity to articulate labour interests. In 1963, UPC's Youth League organised unofficial wage strikes through the country, including a general strike. The state responded by exploiting ethnic divisions among workers, blaming militant Kenyan unionists for sabotage, making strikes illegal without exhausting official disputes procedures, imprisoning four strike leaders, banning the Uganda Federation of Labour (formed before independence), and setting up a new union federation purged of progressive members and autonomy. By 1965, the ruling party had no base among urban workers (Mamdani, 1976).

Independent Tanzania was in a more precarious political and military position than during late colonialism, and could not allow union demands to deter foreign investment. In 1964, the TANU government disbanded the TFL (Tanganyika Federation of Labour, which after 1955 had made advances under colonialism), and established the Minister of Labour as the general secretary of the National Union of Tanganyika Workers (NUTA). Although international trade union federations opposed the move, workers had virtually no reaction, despite TFL leaders' arrests. Ironically, foreign capitalists voiced fear that the government take-over would end 'free labour and free investment'. The government vascillated between providing substantial worker benefits, and appealing to foreign capital by restraining labour and exhorting productivity increases. Yet despite its poor administration and communication, NUTA improved working conditions, while maintaining industrial peace, partly by playing off sectional and other interests against each other (Bienefeld, 1979).

Even though in June 1964 Nigerian trade unions defied the call of the prime minister to return to work, and almost spurred his government's collapse, they could not translate their victory into further political strength. The federal government gave preference to the moderate unions which, realising they could not hold their position against leftists, lost further interest in unified labour action. And the progressive political coalition failed to forge an election alliance with leftist labour leaders. Before the end of 1964, labour unity had disintegrated, because of cross pressures between class identity and ethnically-based political parties.

Nigeria's trade unions lost their independence during the military government, 1973–9. From 1973 to 1976, the government assumed the power to ban any union, cancelled the registration of existing central labour organisations, and appointed an administrator to carry out these organisations' duties. After a 1977 commission report, 11 trade unionists were banned from all further union activity. Under terms of a 1978 decree, the more than 1,000 previously existing unions were reorganised into 70 registered industrial unions under the Nigeria Labour Congress (NLC), the sole central labour organisation. Although the government consolidated the union structure, it also suppressed the most effective advocates for higher wages, improved working conditions, and greater worker control, and weakened the autonomy of union leadership. In the early 1980s, a civilian government could no longer control the numerous shop floor bargaining units and the stronger trade unions that had previously held the workers' loyalty. In May 1981, the NLC mobilised 700,000 of 1,000,000 organised Nigerian workers for a two-day strike, despite the opposition of a government-supported faction (Nafziger, 1983).

IS THERE A LABOUR ARISTOCRACY?

Does the working class share common interests *vis-à-vis* the ruling class? Have the better-off, more skilled labourers been 'bought off' by the ruling class? In 1858 Engels referred to the English proletariat 'becoming more and more bourgeois', and in 1892 to skilled artisans forming a labour aristocracy. More generally, his view, later refined by Lenin, was that the British ruling class used the benefits to workers

from British international economic suzerainty to spur their nationalism at the expense of international worker solidarity (Marx and
Engels, 1953; Waterman, 1975).

Doubtless the advantages the Western and Japanese labour aristocracy receive from the domination by capitalist countries in the
international economic order help explain why most DC workers
support policies benefiting their capitalist elites at the expense of LDC
working people. Thus, the US's largest labour federation, the
American Federation of Labour-Congress for Industrial Organization
(AFL-CIO), supports US military intervention backing third-world
elites at the expense of LDC workers and peasants. Does African
labour also support the ruling class?

Fanon (1963) argues that African

trade unions realise that if their social demands were to be expressed, they would
scandalise the rest of the nation: for the workers are in fact the most favoured section
of the population, and represent the most comfortably off fraction of the people. Any
movement starting off to fight for the bettering of living conditions for the dockers and
workmen would not only be very unpopular, but would also run the risk of provoking
the hostility of the disinherited rural population.

Arrighi and Saul (1968) view the African proletariat (especially
skilled and semiskilled) as joining with elites in expropriating the
economic surplus generated by the rural peasantry. For them

Higher wages and salaries [established during the colonial period] foster the
stabilisation of the better-paid section of the labour force whose high incomes justify
the severence of ties with the traditional economy. Stabilisation, in turn, promotes
specialisation, greater bargaining power, and further increases in the incomes of this
small section of the labour force, which represents the proletariat proper of tropical
Africa. These workers enjoy incomes three or more times higher than those of
unskilled labourers and together with the elites and sub-elites in bureaucratic
employment in the civil service and expatriate concerns, constitute what we call the
labour aristocracy of tropical Africa. It is the discretionary consumption of this class
which absorbs a significant proportion of the surplus produced in the money
economy.

How do those like Fanon, Arrighi and Saul, who contend there is a
'labour aristocracy', view class conflict? The capitalist does not
expropriate surplus created by the worker. Instead the state, representing both the bourgeoisie and privileged workers, transfers resources from peasant agriculture to capitalist industry. Let us examine
whether the labour aristocracy extends to Africa.

For Huntington (1968), 'the industrial worker in most modernizing
countries is almost a member of the elite; he is economically far better

off than the rural population, and he is usually in a favored position from governmental policy'. For Kilby (1969)

Rather than being an exploited group, organized labour is already a highly privileged minority. Whether initiated by modernizing nationalists or the departing colonial benefactor, the full range of welfare measures contained in the ILO conventions (e.g., minimum factory conditions, workmen's compensation, a limited working week, paid holidays, old age and medical insurance, etc.) have now been implemented in the unionized sectors of nearly all the countries of Latin America, Africa, Asia, and the Middle East...Likewise on the wages side, the labourer's earnings considerably exceed his opportunity income outside the organized employment market – in short, he is enjoying a higher standard of living than he has ever before known.

The problems and tensions arising out of the adaptation to the industrial way of life in the less developed areas have proved to be far less significant than nineteenth-century history or twentieth-century sociological theorizing would indicate. Indeed it is difficult to find instances of *industrial* unrest in backward economies. There is much *labour* unrest but it has little to do with the absolute wage or conditions of work; rather it is, as in Nigeria, an expression of relative deprivation by the 'haves' *vis-à-vis* the even smaller minority of the 'have-mores'. [Italics in the original.]

Scholars (e.g., Dudley, 1972) using incomparable categories point out that the average annual wages of workers are much higher than per capita income in most African countries. But while per capita income figures are derived by dividing gross income by both the working and non-working population, average wages are computed by dividing wages *only* by the working population.

Pfefferman's survey (1968) of Dakar wage-earners, biased some-what in the direction of better-off employees, found that the average worker supported 9.6 persons. The non-wage income of these households was negligible. While average disposable income per wage-earner in the sample was 20,000 CFA francs per month, per capita income in wage-earners' households was only 2,075 per month, roughly equal to average monthly per capita income in the groundnut areas of rural Senegal.

The ratio of the average annual wages of daily-paid and semiskilled workers in the public services to GDP per capita in Nigeria in 1963–4 was 3.7:1 (in contrast to rough estimates for comparable ratios of 2:1 in the US and 1.5:1 in Western Europe) (Aluko, 1971). However, as Peace demonstrates (1975), Nigerian wage-earners are the focus of a kinship network including some less fortunate who seriously drain permanent workers' financial accumulation. Indeed, the ratio of Nigeria's labour force to population was 1:3. Thus, the GDP per capita of daily-paid and semiskilled *government*-worker households was only 23% more than that of the total labour force, which consisted of 56% in the low-income agricultural sector (Nigeria, 1968, III). But since government wages were likely to be higher than private-sector wages, worker household GDP per capita may not have been higher than that of the labour force.

Of course, the proportion of privileged workers varies from one part of Africa to another. For example, while in Kenya and Uganda a large majority of skilled workers are employed in capital-intensive manufacturing MNCs, in Ghana most skilled workers are employed in government industries or public corporations that lead MNCs and other private firms in keeping wage rates down. Jeffries (1975a) estimates that whereas the 1970 skilled to unskilled wage ratio in Kenya and Uganda was 3:1, the same ratio in Ghana was less than 2:1.

Perhaps most African workers are in the informal sector of craft, petty trading, and small industrial enterprises with less than ten employed. Production in these firms is labour-intensive, with usually no more than a few simple tools. Wages are low, as government rarely enforces minimum wages and union legislation in these firms. Indeed, in Nigeria in 1975, even the informal-sector self-employed received only 62% of the net annual income that low-income wage earners in the small modern sector received. And these self-employed rarely expand their firm to modern-sector size. The gulf between Africa's modern and informal urban sectors is wide (Fajana, 1981; Nafziger, 1986).

Still, the African informal-sector labour market is closely integrated with both farm and modern sectors. Rural emigrants sometimes start with jobs in the informal sector, or resort to them when they fail to get modern-sector jobs. However, informal-sector wages are often no higher than farm subsistence incomes, and may undercut wage settlements in the formal sector.

With modernisation, wage earners have increased their share of the economically active population, so they are relatively less privileged now than in the 1960s. Additionally, informal-sector employment has probably not declined since 1960, and may still be as large as in the modern sector.

Yet doubtless there are a few wage and salary earners in the upper echelons of government, parastatals, and MNCs, as well as es-tablished trade-union leaders, whose interests are closer to African elites and their foreign allies than to the majority working class. But these upper-echelon workers do not comprise the bulk of Africa's wage-earners, who are unskilled or semiskilled workers with low wages.

THE UNEMPLOYED

The Economic Commission for Africa (1983b) expects Africa's estimated 1975 urban unemployment rate, 10.8% (compared to Asia's 6.9% and Latin America's 6.5%), to increase to 14.6% by 2008. This high and growing unemployment rate is caused by the labour force growing faster than job opportunities. Rapid population and educational growth means 22% of all new entrants in 1983 and 41% in 2008 (projected) are school leavers 15–24 years old.

Assume agricultural employment remains constant, so that growth in employment is limited to industry (non-agriculture). Africa's industrial sector employs 9% of the labour force. Thus, this sector needs to increase its total employment 24% yearly to absorb current labour force growth of 2.2% (i.e., $0.09 \times 0.24 = 0.022$).

Because of the increasing capital intensity of industry, its employment growth is slower than its output growth, only 1.3% annually, 1973–84. For example, Côte d'Ivoire's industrial sector, though it grew rapidly, was so capital-intensive it provided relatively few new jobs. In 1972–6, industrial output grew by 21.1% annually, while employment increased 8.4%; in 1977–81, annual output growth was 7.0% compared to only 3.8% for industrial employment. Total capital formation per employed person increased 61% from 1970 to 1981. After 1981, growing capital intensity, combined with slow capital formation growth, exacerbated Côte d'Ivoire's unemployment problem even more (World Bank, 1986a; World Bank, 1986b; ILO, 1976; Nafziger, 1984; Mytelka, 1984; Campbell, 1985).

Africa's unemployed are usually young (aged 15–24), primary or secondary educated, and urban residents. Illiterate people cannot wait for a better-paid job. They remain on the farm, or become street, shop, or market traders. At the other extreme, highly trained people are scarce enough that university graduates usually get well-paid jobs immediately. But those in between, primary and secondary school leavers, are neither assured of high paying jobs nor completely out of the running for them. Thus, there may be a substantial payoff to a full-time search for a job. The educated unemployed tend to be young, with few dependents, and are supported by their families. Most eventually find work, usually within a year, although some have to lower their job expectations. Except for possible political discontent, the costs associated with this unemployment are not as serious as they appear. The unemployed, usually supported by an extended family in a job search, are less likely to be from the poorest one-fifth of the

population than the Western unemployed. Thus although unemployment increases income inequality among the educated, it does not
increase overall inequality (World Bank, 1980a; Adelman and Robinson, 1978).

In Nigeria, primary school leavers and dropouts account for 78% of
the unemployed who are 8% of the urban labour force. People 15–23
years old, comprising 25% of the population, account for 70% of the
unemployment, while those aged 24–29 have 17% of the unemployment. About 69% of the unemployed have no previous work
experience. Unemployment duration gradually increased after 1960 so
that in 1971, 1% were unemployed less than a month, 6% 1–3 months,
13% 3–6 months, 21% 6–12 months, 20% 12–18 months, 7% 18–24
months, and 32% 24 or more months. Zambia's secondary school
leaver unemployment statistics indicate a similar pattern, albeit a
slightly shorter duration and lower unemployment rate (Falae, 1971;
Sada, 1975; ILO, 1977b).

Many organisational methods and ideas, management systems,
machines, processes, and other technologies Africa imports are not
designed for Africa but for DCs, which have high wages and relatively
abundant capital. Estimates cited in chapter 6 indicate the appropriate
capital stock per person in the US is 45 times that of Nigeria.

The low foreign exchange price and the official preference for
imported capital goods combine to make the actual price of capital
cheaper than its market price. And when this occurs with wages higher
than market rates, African countries end up using more capital-
intensive techniques and employing fewer people than would happen
at market resource prices. Distortions in these prices and inflexible
resource requirements for some production processes result in higher
unemployment, increasing income inequalities between property
owners and workers, and between highly paid workers and the
unemployed (Nafziger, 1984).

When capital–labour ratios in industry are inflexible, the small
amount of capital available in Africa may limit high rates of
employment of the labour force. But the use of more appropriate
technology can be stimulated by the following measures:

1 Encouraging the production of more labour-intensive goods
   within each industry (e.g., sandals instead of fancy leather shoes).
2 Fulfilling the same need by substituting a more labour-intensive
   good. Housing may be more or less fulfilled by the Lagos
   sidewalks, caves, mud huts, multistorey flats, single-family houses,

or palaces. In Northern Nigeria, bamboo-reinforced mud huts with tin roofs are more labour-intensive (and affordable) than Western-style single-family dwellings.

3 Emphasising goods consumed by the poor, which are more labour-intensive than goods the rich consume. Government policies to improve income equality increase the demand for cotton shirts, sandals, mud huts, and ungraded maize, and reduce the demand for more capital-intensive luxury goods, particularly imports. In Kenya, the high income concentration results in demand establishing dual production for the high-income luxury and the low-income markets (ILO, 1972).

4 Removing luxury components from existing goods and services. Poor quality soap produced with labour-intensive techniques can perhaps substitute for Western detergents. Traditional herbal medicine may be used instead of high-income Western medicine.

5 Government influencing employment by directing official purchases toward labour-intensive goods.

6 Planners or entrepreneurs choosing a more labour-intensive existing technology. In 1974, the Kenyan government established the Rural Access Roads Programme (RARP), stressing labour-intensive technology, decentralisation, and local participation in planning and implementation to improve transport to relatively inaccessible rural areas, stimulate the latter's development, and provide employment opportunities to rural low-income groups. In 1977–8, RARP cost per kilometre was only K£2,050 compared to K£7,500 for a conventional programme; and wages comprised 49% of RARP compared to 25–30% of the conventional programme (Ghai, 1980). The UN Industrial Development Organisation (1981) indicates a wide variation in choices of processes, equipment and scale of operation in several industries, including iron and steel. A country can operate semi-integrated (steelmaking plus rolling) plants economically as low as 20,000 tons annually, and pig iron plants as low as 5,000 tons annually. Yet substituting labour for capital may be greatly limited in brick making and other industries if high-quality products are to be produced.

7 Substituting labour in peripheral and ancillary activities such as materials receiving, handling, packaging, and storage (e.g., using people instead of fork lifts and conveyer belts).

8 Using less-modern DC (e.g., pre-computer office) equipment in good condition, if readily available.

9 Generating technology locally, through industry research or through research organisations designed specifically to produce

appropriate technology. However, many such organisations fail if research is not directed by managers, technicians, and marketing specialists familiar with the firm and its work force. But even this labour-intensive technology will not be carried out if factor and product prices are distorted (see below).

10 Scaling down foreign technology to fit African skills and resources.

Where adaptation requires costly use of scarce engineers, managers, and other skilled persons, however, it may be cheaper to transfer the technology outright rather than to spend the resources to modify it.

Appropriate technologies may not always save capital, as engineers, managers, and other skilled persons may be even scarcer, making it cheaper to transfer technology outright than to find manpower to modify it. Thus, capital-intensive, machine-paced, or process-oriented operations, which save on scarce personnel, may sometimes be suitable. For example, modern factory methods for making shoes and wooden furniture use more capital per worker than cottage methods, but save on skilled labour, since each operative needs a narrower range of skills than the shoemaker or carpenter making the whole product. Thus, if skilled people are limitations, using the more modern capital-intensive methods may be appropriate (Morawetz, 1974; Khan, 1974).

In some instances, an African country need not produce a high-technology capital-intensive product but, if some of the product is essential, will import it until local production can compete with it at more modest protection. Kenya's first locally assembled saloon car, the Uhuru, originating with Isuzu Motor Corporation of Japan and launched by General Motors Kenya Ltd in late 1985, had an initial local content of 30%, but at a Ksh 340,000 ($23,000) retail price, it was a luxury car only for the political and managerial top elite, and not competitive with the Volvo and Mercedes. Diseconomies of small-scale production have been too high to produce the car economically (EIU, 1986; *African Business*, Mar. 1986, p. 72).

The million-dollar Bura irrigation and settlement scheme to produce cotton for export and to house previously landless families in an unpopulated semi-arid area in eastern Kenya (financed by the EEC, European governments, and the World Bank) is another capital-intensive project that failed. In 1986, visitors found eroded irrigation canals, abandoned plots, poor crops, tumbledown and insanitary housing, wildlife grazing on irrigated land, high mortality rates, severe protein deficiency and wasting in many young children, and an air of desolation and decay. The project not only increased the poverty and malnutrition of families participating, but also contributed to Kenya's international debt burden that restricted programmes to address poverty and inequality (*African Business*, Apr. 1986, pp. 18–19).

Even when there is a wide choice of capital-labour combinations, African countries may not choose labour-intensive methods because of factor-price distortions that make wages higher and interest rates and foreign exchange costs lower than market rates. Widely-used inducements to investment such as subsidised interest rates, liberal depreciation allowances, and tax rebates make capital costs artificially low without having much effect on investor decisions (ILO, 1972). Also low foreign-exchange prices (discussed in chapters 11 and 12) make capital cheap. These distortions increase unemployment by reducing the demand for labour.

PEASANTS, LANDLESS WORKERS, COMMERCIAL FARMERS, AND GOVERNMENT BUREAUCRATS

Africa has high urban inequality (with an average Gini of roughly 0.50), high urban–rural discrepancies (chapter 11), and low rural inequality (Gini roughly 0.35) compared to LDCs generally (ILO, 1982b). However, the earlier scholarly assumptions of land abundance, widespread customary land-tenure systems, and the widespread prevalence of subsistence family production are no longer valid and overstate rural equality. After independence, government expenditures were biased in favour of large-scale prosperous farmers. Somalia concentrated agricultural spending on ranches and costly irrigation and settlement schemes, Nigeria and Ghana on state plantations and large-scale commercial farmers, and Botswana on programmes to benefit large-scale livestock owners (Ghai and Radwan, 1983). Moreover, in Kenya, Malawi, and Zambia, land concentration increased as indigenous elites used their power to acquire substantial private ownership or government control of land.

Kenya's substantial rural inequality corresponds to large variations in natural endowment (topography, climate, soil types, and vegetation) (House and Killick, 1983). During the colonial period Africans cultivated land little suited for farming, because of settler cultivation of high- and medium-potential land.

Among Kenya's African population, rural inequality and land concentration increased from the late 1960s through the mid 1980s (Collier and Lal, 1986). The Kenyan bourgeoisie, bureaucracy, and their clients used state support to appropriate (usually formerly white settler) land to create new African large-scale capitalist farms, and obtain licences, credit, and inputs. Moreover, government selected relatively well-off experienced farmers, rather than the landless and unemployed, for low-density land resettlement schemes in which credit, inputs, research, and extension assistance were concentrated. As indicated in chapter 6, land in Kenya is almost as unequally distributed as in Latin America (Livingstone, 1981; Hunt, 1984; Hazlewood, 1985).

Government has oriented agricultural research and extension toward large farms (especially cash crops, coffee, tea, pyrethrum, sisal, and wheat) and their mechanisation. Extension officers work primarily with 'progressive' (usually rich) farmers, increasing rural inequality by neglecting the poor farmer (House and Killick, 1983).

Collier and Lal (1986) used a poverty line for Kenya which adjusted for urban–rural differences in cost of living. They found a national poverty rate of 29.4% (a figure useful for inter-class comparisons), compared to low poverty rates among 245,000 landless workers with good occupations (0%), 270,000 gap farmers (0%), 20,000 larger farmers (0%), the 700,000 Nairobi population (2.9%), and the 700,000 non-Nairobi urban population (5.7%); moderate poverty rates among 10,340,000 smallholders (28.9%), 75,000 pastoralists who farm (33.3%), and 600,000 large farm squatters (33.4%); and high poverty rates among 200,000 migrant farmers (55.0%), 725,000 pure pastoralists (84.9%), and 420,000 landless workers with poor occupations (50.0%) (or 31.7% among all 670,000 landless workers).

Poverty rates in Kenya probably increased in the late 1970s and first half of the 1980s among pastoralists (vulnerable to weather fluctuations and confined by encroaching agriculture, wildlife, and environmental destruction to a decreasing area), women (heading about a quarter of rural households), unskilled urban wage earners, those in the informal sector, landless workers, and less prosperous smallholders in areas of drought or high rainfall (EIU, 1985).

Landless squatters are one of the government's major target poverty groups. They occupy state or private land to which they have no title and from which they eke a meagre income. Alternatively, they take low-wage jobs in urban areas or on large farms.

The government is also concerned with traditional pastoralists, like the Masai and Samburu, who occupy large areas of rangeland. This lifestyle cannot continue beyond the turn of the twenty-first century, as the subsistence demands of the rapidly growing population are beginning to outstrip the capacity of the resources available (House and Killick, 1983).

In the 1950s and 1960s, Uganda subsidised about 60% of a private farmer's tractor hire service. While the average farm size in Buganda in the 1960s was two hectares, tractor hire only helped farmers with at least eight hectares. Additionally, large farmers received subsidised loans that often were not paid, and often controlled the cooperative marketing and processing of Arabica coffee and cotton (Mamdani, 1976).

After 1970, the Amin regime ruined capitalist agriculture by default. The government removed some institutions serving the peasants and severely hampered the work of others, thus crippling Uganda's cotton and other cash crops. Peasants withdrew from their previously active economic role. From 1972 to 1975, most responsible for sustaining modern capitalist institutions were forced to leave the country or were killed. The government bureaucracy had little or no experience of managing large-scale agricultural organisations (Hyden, 1980). Many people were malnourished in the 1970s, as the economy collapsed, inflation ran rampant, shortages were endemic, and corruption became a way of life.

Malawi's agricultural land inequality is substantial and increased from the 1960s to the 1980s. Many holdings are too small to meet subsistence requirements. In 1980–1, two-thirds of the peasant households held less than 1.5 hectares.

The ratio of the value of estate agricultural production to officially marketed peasant production increased from 0.79 in 1964 to 2.07 in 1980. Although estates depended on peasants for food, they competed with them for land, labour, and administrative support.

The parastatal ADMARC had monopsony control over the crop sales of peasants, appropriating their surplus and transferring them to the estates. By keeping prices low, ADMARC accrued profits of MK 155,920,000, 1971–8. In 1978, loans and investments from ADMARC were distributed in the following way: 67.7% in estate tobacco, sugar, and related industries; 22.6% in other modern-sector industrial and commercial firms; 5.4% in banks and finance companies; and 4.3% in peasant agriculture. Most of this surplus was loaned to Banda and his clients in politics, the bureaucracy, and the military. While estate agriculture expanded rapidly in the 1970s, it involved considerable waste, as management standards were low, owners were ill-informed concerning farming, and conservation was poor.

As peasant agriculture declined in the 1970s (see chapter 7), more peasants had to seek estate-sector employment to survive, reducing real wages 36% from 1979 to 1980. The already heavy burden on peasant women increased. In 1980–1, 35% of rural children were malnourished just before harvest, 27% soon after harvesting, and 56%

suffered from nutritional stunting (Kydd and Christiansen, 1982; Hirschmann, 1987; Kydd, 1984).

Zambia's policies contributed to a per capita income in the 1970s for 20,000 prosperous Zambian farmers 10–15 times that of 850,000 poor subsistence farmers. Government provided subsidies for the rich rural classes and loans to agricultural producer cooperatives, which treated the funds as income rather than investment funds. Poor peasants viewed cooperatives as providing aid for well-to-do farmers. Settlement schemes in fertile regions concentrated state resources on a relatively few individuals, many of whom were well-connected politically or members of the ruling United National Independence Party. Individual farming units of around 60–100 hectares on the settlement schemes helped create a rural capitalist class. Kaunda publicly reprimanded a Bank of Zambia agronomist who pointed out the heavy subsidies, waste, and theft on state farms and other grandiose agricultural projects (Good, 1986; Ghai and Radwan, 1983).

In Côte d'Ivoire, in the early 1970s the official minimum wage, usually applied among Ivorians in export crop plantations, was higher than Zaïre, Senegal, Togo, and Cameroon. However, from 1970–1 to 1980–1, the *real* minimum wage dropped about 40%. Additionally, the increased sharecropping and annual wages circumvented the minimum hourly wage. All this, together with slow wage growth to immigrant workers, probably meant agricultural inequalities increased between the early 1970s and early 1980s (Young, 1982; Campbell, 1985).

Vielrose (1974) (analysing Nigeria's 1963 rural population) and Malton (1981) (surveying three Kano state villages, 1974–5) indicate the ratio of mean per capita income of the first decile (bottom tenth) of the economically active population to the tenth decile (top tenth) mean was 1:5. Nigeria's rural inequality has increased since 1970 because of land allocated to politically influential people and rural development programmes designed for property owners. Yet income inequality and land concentration are still low compared to urban inequality and other LDC rural inequality. But except for the southwestern cocoa regions, the richest fourth of Nigeria's rural households would be considered relatively poor in urban Nigeria.

Matlon's average household consumed 11% more calories than the required level indicated by the FAO, a standard higher than that set by Ahluwalia *et al.* (1979). Households with incomes in the first decile experienced a calorie deficit of 25%, and in the second decile 15%, while domestic food production met consumption requirements only among households in the ninth and tenth deciles. The poorest 30–40%

of households were seriously impoverished, relying on high-income households for grain during the preharvest hunger period.

A 'hungry season' before the beginning of a new harvest is widespread in West Africa, sometimes seriously affecting the poorest 30–40% of households. These households are caught in a poverty trap, in which selling labour and obtaining credit at high interest rates to ensure survival through the hungry season results in less income and high interest payments in future years. Initially, farmers sacrifice self-sufficiency to produce cash crops, no longer growing early maturing crops that fill the 'hunger gap' between harvest. Thus the poorest Kano state households were less subsistence-oriented than the richest ones. Since staples millet and sorghum were the least profitable crops, the lowest-income households allocated more resources to profitable cash crops like groundnuts, increasing dependence on surplus food producers. Moreover, poor households were more likely to rent land, farm poorer quality soil, and work for wages. Yet time spent in wage labour competed with planting and weeding on their own fields. Because of low working capital positions, poor households planted later, delayed their first weedings, and weeded less intensively later.

Poor farm families are also more vulnerable than in 1960 as a result of individualised consumption replacing community or clan sharing. Furthermore, poor farm families who cannot afford to purchase food just before harvests, when cash resources are lowest and prices are highest, neglect their own farms and sell labour to richer farmers. They accept a lower income from their own farm to guarantee short-term survival. Reduced calorie and protein consumption during a period of more work leads to weight loss and greater chances of contracting diseases. The trap may get worse each year (Nafziger, 1984).

African peasants have traded their dependence on nature for a dependence on the state bourgeoisie. Even peasants that spend most of their time producing directly for their own families and clans are not free of government policies regarding land transfer, cooperative and state agriculture, commodity prices, off-farm employment, and benefits of education, water, electricity, and roads. Hyden's (1980) autonomous ('uncaptured') peasant, free from state machination, has almost vanished in Africa. The peasant who wishes to escape the influence of the state on his livelihood has few places to go.

WOMEN

Authority is the cultural belief that people have a legitimate right to wield power. In Africa, women exert power indirectly through withdrawal, calling on the supernatural, control over food, manipulating men, aligning with powerful men, and collective action, rather than through direct office.

Low female literacy (half that of men), limited economic opportunities, and domestic burdens relegate women to the lowest economic and political rungs, even in socialist countries. Land reform in Ethiopia in the 1970s allocated land to male family heads, while Mozambique's Land Law of 1979 failed to establish women's rights to land. Government agricultural policy favours male heads of households and development plans often ignore women. The Cameroon government directs little extension assistance to women farmers, who grow most food crops. Lt Jerry Rawling's reforms in Ghana in the early 1980s attacked women as symbols of wealth while wealthier male businessmen and bureaucrats escaped. But Africa's contemporary decline may benefit women, as rebuilding weak states can spur new alliances between sexes (Parpart, 1986; V. DeLancey, 1986).

Though women are the backbone of the Kenyan rural economy, they enjoy few advantages. While men seek wage employment in major centres, women play the dominant role in small-scale farming, often on smaller plots and with lower returns than male-headed households. Women's workloads are heavy as a result of childbearing (eight children in the average rural family), water carrying, wood collecting, increased weeding from new crop varieties, and other farm tasks from increasing land pressure (House and Killick, 1983).

A Kenyan woman has the right to land from her husband's estate to fulfil her traditional role of raising food crops. If she provides enough for the family, she can sell the surplus from her garden privately. But when men divert hectarage for cash crops, women do not have adequate maize to feed their families (Kitching, 1980; *West Africa*, 26 May 1986, pp. 1108–9).

Kenyan women get a substantially lower return to training and education (university rates of return are negative) than men, because of discrimination, withdrawal from the labour force, and living in the same place as husbands (Bigsten, 1984).

In precapitalist Nigeria, women tended children, cooked, farmed, and processed and marketed farm products. Younger women and children undertook domestic tasks, leaving older women to concentrate on more specialised occupations. In Yoruba communities, many women were involved in trade. Southern Nigeria has no tradition that women should be excluded from earning income. Yet because female education in Nigeria has lagged behind male education, women have limited opportunities in the modern sector (Dennis, 1983).

In Northern Nigeria's rural villages, average female earnings, 23%

of the male figure, varied from 58% of male earnings (₦ 103) among first-decile households to 8% (₦ 52) in the tenth decile. Indeed female labour force participation and earnings were inversely related to household income status (Matlon, 1981).

In Nigeria (and other African countries), women and children may suffer from undernourishment because of maldistribution of food, even in families with incomes well above the poverty line (ILO, 1981).

Outside of agriculture, 83.5% of Ghanaian women in the labour force in 1970 were self-employed (mostly as traders), 12.8% wage and salary earners, and 3.7% unpaid family workers. Female labour force participation rates generally increased with age up to 55–59. In Accra-Tema, Ghana, female employees shoulder most of the responsibility for cooking, house cleaning, laundry, and other housework, while two-thirds of the male employees did not do any housework.

Ghanaian educated women are primarily in teaching, nursing, and clerical work, with very few in professional, administrative, and managerial jobs. Yet Akan men label a woman not in the labour force *Obaa kwadwofo* (a lazy woman). Moreover, in many ethnic groups, where inheritance is matrilineal, it is essential for the wife to build up capital for herself and her children's support. Women also continue to work to protect against the marriage breaking down (Date-Bah, 1982).

CONCLUSION

Although Africa's main inequalities are between wage earners and property owners, there are also discrepancies among the working class. But despite a few privileged wage earners in the top civil service and the professions, the majority of Africa's hired workers are unskilled or semiskilled workers with low wages.

Africa's unemployment rates are among the highest in the developing world. Including the unemployed, usually young, educated, urban, and supported by the extended family, does not increase Africa's overall inequality.

Agricultural concentration, though low, is increasing as a result of government policies that provide credit, subsidies, inputs, extension, and access to land ownership to the managerial bourgeoisie and their clients. Poor farm families appear to be more vulnerable to hunger and poverty today than in the 1960s. Female farmers' relative position has declined over the decades because of a widening gender gap in education, land rights, extension help, and access to inputs.

§ 10 §

MAINTAINING CLASS
THE ROLE OF EDUCATION

Equal opportunity to compete in a race that necessarily results in a small number of winners and a large number of losers is Orwellian newspeak. It defends inequality in the name of equality... , and helps induce mass acquiescence in the perpetuation of an unequal social order. (Manley, 1983).

African state educational policies are crucial in income distribution. Africa's 1981 primary enrolment rate (as a percentage of children aged 6–11) was 78%, the secondary rate 15% (denominator age 12–17), and the rate for university and higher institutions 1.8% (denominator 18–21 years old). The Economic Commission for Africa (1983b) projects rates in 2008 to be primary 83%, secondary 55%, and 16% higher.

Africa has the lowest primary, secondary, and university enrolment rates of any world region. In 1980 primary enrolment rates were 78% in Eastern Africa and 55% in Western Africa compared to 79% in South Asia, 87% in developing Europe, Middle East, and North Africa, 96% in East Asia and the Pacific (including China), 102% in Latin America and the Caribbean, 83% in LDCs as a whole, and 101% in DCs. Secondary enrolment rates were 10% in Eastern Africa, 14% in Western Africa, 30% in South Asia, 42% in East Asia and the Pacific, 43% in developing Europe, the Middle East, and North Africa, 44% in Latin America and the Caribbean, 26% in LDCs generally, and 88% in DCs.

The public sector plays a major role in financing education. In 1975, 82% of primary students and 70% of secondary students in West Africa, and 57% of primary and 55% of secondary students in East Africa, enrolled in public schools. Additionally, a substantial proportion of African university students enrolled in public universities. And education averaged 21.5% of public spending in West Africa (the highest of any LDC region), 14.1% in East Africa, and 16% in LDCs generally. State subsidies in Africa are large, as fees for public education recover only 5.7% of the cost of primary education, 11.4% of secondary education, and 1.9% of higher education.

The social rates of return to investment in education in Africa are high – 28% for primary education, 17% for secondary education, and 13% for higher education. Private rates, which consider only (direct and forgone) costs borne by individuals, are even higher. The more the state contribution to financing education, the greater the margin by which the private rate exceeds the social rate (Tan, 1985b; Jiminez, 1986).

How do educational level differentials in lifetime earnings vary internationally (assuming a 10% interest rate)? Hinchliffe (1975) indicates that in the late 1960s the ratio of higher educational to primary educational earnings in Nigeria (10.25:1) was higher than Ghana's (9.08) and Kenya's (7.55), and much higher than Asian and Latin American (2.60–5.65), US (2.76), and Canadian (2.89) ratios. (The relative position of Nigeria's university graduates may be even higher than the figures suggest, due to subsidised housing and car loans for high-level public employees, not abolished until April 1979). Nigeria's and Ghana's higher to secondary educational earnings ratios (4.45 and 4.48 respectively) exceeded Kenya's 3.04, Asia's and Latin America's 1.42–3.54, the US's 1.65, and Canada's 1.81. Secondary to primary earnings ratios of Kenya (2.48), Nigeria (2.30), and Ghana (2.03) were higher than Asia's and Latin America's (1.39–1.83, except for Colombia's 2.46), and the US's 1.68 and Canada's 1.59. African earnings ratios for primary education to no education (2.53 for Ghana, 2.32 for Nigeria, and 1.72 for Kenya) were not much different from Asia and Latin America (varying from 1.56 to 3.45).

Africa's premium for university over secondary education is high (even relative to other LDC regions), because of Africa's greater scarcity of university graduates (especially in the 1960s) and higher university educational costs than other LDCs. Indeed in Africa, government wages are frequently based on the cost of acquiring the training essential to meet requirements for the job rather than on labour supply and productivity. And 1976 educational expenditures per pupil in higher education in subsaharan Africa were more expensive than any other world region, and 100.5 times more per pupil than primary education. The same expenditure ratio was only 9.0 in South Asia, 8.7 in East Asia, 8.1 in Latin America, and 2.0 in DCs. Moreover, Africa's premium for secondary over primary education was also relatively high because of Asia's and Latin America's greater secondary educational expansion (World Bank, 1980a). Even though educated wage structures in Africa adjust slowly, we can expect that as university and secondary education expands, its relative premium will fall.

The cost of public education for one student as a percentage of GNP per capita is higher in Africa than in any other world region: in francophone Africa 29% for primary school, 143% for secondary school, and 804% for higher education; in anglophone Africa 18% for primary, 50% for secondary, and 920% for higher. In LDCs generally, unit costs are 14% of GNP per capita for primary education, 41% for secondary, and 370% for higher; in DCs 22% for primary, 24% for secondary, and only 49% for higher.

Africa has high costs despite mediocre educational quality and high student–teacher ratios, especially in francophone Africa. However, teachers' salaries are two to three times higher relative to income per capita than in Asia or Latin America. Additionally, state subsidisation of education is more pronounced in (especially francophone) Africa than other LDC regions, and these subsidies rise with the level of education (Mingat and Psacharopoulos, 1985).

EDUCATION IN REPRODUCING CLASS

Chapter 5 indicates education was a vehicle of upward mobility during colonialism. But as the African ruling classes took form during the terminal colonial and early independence periods, they used their wealth and position to get access to education to transmit their class status to their children. Class lines began to solidify as the educated first generation read books with children, made sure they attended good schools, and provided tutors to prepare them for entrance examinations.

In the Belgian Congo in the 1950s, educated people entered into the lower-ranking bureaucracy, positioning themselves to become part of the political and bureaucratic elite after independence. In Côte d'Ivoire, among 72 government ministers, 1959–80, 68.4% were university graduates and 30.1% secondary graduates. After Ghana's independence, a secondary-school graduate's son had 17 times (and a university graduate's son 34 times) the chance of attending secondary school as an illiterate's son. Some children of the unschooled still get secondary or higher education, but their chances get smaller each year as class lines harden (Bakary, 1984; Jewsiewicki, 1979; Curtin *et al.*, 1978).

As Bowles (1978) argues, capitalist and state capitalist production, characterised by a hierarchical division of labour, requires that a relatively small group of future technicians and managers calculate, decide, and rule, while a much larger group 'learns' to follow instructions accurately. Different amounts and types of schooling to different children bring about this labour-force stratification. School credentials serve as a gatekeeper, even when the 'learning' has little bearing on jobs available. Popular pressure from poorer workers and peasants for schooling to all children often results in creating a dual educational system between urban and rural schools, or between private and public schools.

Education may certify an individual's productive qualities to an employer without enhancing them. Educational requirements serve primarily to ration access to inflated salaries. The signals from this perverse wage-setting mechanism do not provide consistency between educational output and employment opportunities. Furthermore, school leavers may be encouraged to wait for well-paid jobs rather than immediately accept a job that pays much less. If the wage difference is high enough and the probability of obtaining a higher-paid job is sufficiently large, a period of job seeking will yield a higher expected lifetime income. These reasons help explain the high unemployment among the educated in African countries like Nigeria, Kenya, and Côte d'Ivoire.

THE REDISTRIBUTIVE EFFECTS OF EDUCATIONAL SPENDING

Education is a major vehicle to increase inequality. In 1980, African children of white-collar families benefited disproportionately from educational subsidies, receiving 5–10 times as much benefit as farm children. In francophone Africa, white-collar workers comprised 6% of the population but their children received 36% of state educational subsidies, a spending-population ratio (SPR) of 5.9. Manual workers and traders, with 18% of the population, received 21% of the subsidies (a 1.2 SPR), while farmers, with 76% of the population, received 44% of the subsidies (with SPR 0.6). In anglophone Africa, white-collar workers comprised 6% of the population and their children got 23% of subsidies, (a 3.8 SPR); manual workers and traders comprised 18% of the population and received 21% of the subsidies (a 1.2 SPR); and farmers had 76% of the population and 56% of the subsidies (a 0.7 SPR) (Jimenez, 1986). Since taxation is rarely progressive in Africa, free or heavily subsidised education in Africa usually redistributes incomes from the poor to the rich.

Primary education can be an exception, favourably affecting

equality of opportunity. As primary schooling expands, children in rural areas, the poorest urban children, and girls have a greater chance to go to school. In general, public expenditures on primary education redistribute income toward the poor, who have larger families and almost no access to private schooling. Public spending on secondary and higher education, on the other hand, redistributes income to the rich since poor children have little opportunity to benefit from it (World Bank, 1980a).

Yet primary education provided free by African governments is not free to the student's family. To benefit from education, the family has to purchase books, supplies, uniforms, transport, and (sometimes) room and board. For poor people, these costs are major limitations. In Malawi, the average cost of sending a child to primary school (not counting forgone cost) was 19% of per capita GNP in 1983, and more than 100% for secondary school. Even in Tanzania, which tried to curb the inequality associated with rapid secondary school expansion, the average cost for secondary school was 49% of per capita income in 1981. Additionally, the poor, who often live in rural areas or other places far from schools, may have to travel more and pay more for room and board than the rich. Moreover, for poor families, the forgone cost of a child helping with farming and housework is high – perhaps several times the explicit private cost. These families, with a deficient study environment and fewer job contacts, also feel they receive less benefits from education than rich families (Jimenez, 1986). So while public primary education provides subsidies disproportionately to the poor, it costs the poor to take advantage of them.

African countries provided substantially more subsidies for student living expenses in secondary and higher education than other LDCs. In francophone Africa, these student subsidies represent 23% of total public costs at secondary and 43% at higher education levels; the figures are 14% at both levels in anglophone Africa, and 4% at both levels in Asian LDCs. Student scholarships are 120% of GNP per capita in Côte d'Ivoire, 160% in Senegal, 700% in Mali and the Central African Republic, and 800% in Burkina Faso. In these countries, scholarships and social expenditures exceed even teaching expenses at the higher level.

Improving income distribution calls for abolishing most subsidies. The higher the educational level, the larger the subsidies. Higher education students are privileged in three ways. First, in financing their studies, the state concentrates its resources on a small number of individuals. In francophone Africa (1980), 86% of the population received primary schooling or less, and they obtained 16% of the educational resources; in anglophone Africa, the figures are 83% and 39% respectively. By contrast, the 2% in francophone Africa who attained higher education received 40% of the resources; in anglophone Africa, the figures are 1% and 26%. Second, higher education students tend to come from privileged socio-economic backgrounds; in most African countries they contain a disproportionately high share of children of civil servants, salaried employees, and urban families. Third, these postsecondary students will enjoy higher incomes than average during their active lives and could afford to reimburse the community later for part of the financial aid they received while studying. Even students who have difficulty financing their studies could receive loans rather than scholarships.

The system of allocating school places, based on examination scores, tends to favour the rich. The rich can spend more on books and private tutoring, and are more likely to encourage studying. Rich people are also better able to support repeating a year than poor people (Mingat and Psacharopoulos, 1985; Jimenez, 1986).

The managerial bourgeoisie ensure that their children get the best education, usually university. This is true even in Tanzania, where a university education is available to only 0.02% of the population. In 1968, Nyerere criticised Tanzania's university student attitudes that salary and status are a right conferred by a degree.

Indeed African 'radical' students strike and protest primarily about present living conditions and future job prospects. It would be suicidal for students to attack the privileges of the politico-bureaucratic elites and the benefits of the present economic system they expect to inherit (Markovitz, 1977).

Most African university students see themselves as future members of a technocratic upper-middle class or even the ruling class, not as an alternative one. As long as the governing class guarantees students upper-middle class life styles, they are not likely to challenge it. Thus, before and during the Nigerian civil war, university students strongly supported regional elites they soon expected to join (Barkan, 1975; Sklar, 1963; Nafziger, 1983).

African governments have not reallocated funds away from low-returning university education to high-returning primary education. If higher education subsidies were reallocated to primary schooling, 1985 primary enrolment ratios would increase substantially in most African countries: from 76% to 100% in the Côte d'Ivoire, from 59% to 91% in Malawi, from 68% to 80% in Central African Republic, from 48% to 71% in Senegal, from 27% to 35% in Mali, and (in two countries where spending on higher education is small) from 23% to

26% in Niger, and from 20% to 26% in Burkina Faso (Mingat and Psacharopoulos, 1985; Jimenez, 1986).

KENYA AND TANZANIA

Tanzania, despite its low GNP per capita, has the highest 1980 adult literacy rate (79%) in subsaharan Africa (which has 40%), and a 1982 primary enrolment rate, 98%, compared to subsaharan Africa's 71%. Since 1977, Tanzania has stressed primary educational expansion, hoping to curb the inequality and educated unemployment associated with rapid secondary educational expansion.

Kenya has tried to expand both primary and secondary education rapidly. Yet secondary school leavers are still scarce enough so that returns to secondary education are unusually high. Returns to primary education, on the other hand, are declining because universal primary education's (UPE's) expansion makes primary school leavers relatively abundant (Bigsten, 1984).

Despite the fact that less than one-tenth of Kenya's primary leavers graduate from secondary schools, most primary curricula and examinations ignore the needs of terminating students. Moreover, inter-provincial quality variations (especially teacher credentials) are substantial, depending largely on provincial affluence (ILO, 1972).

The multicorrelation between parental education, income, and ability to provide quality education for one's children reproduces Kenya's class system. Access to secondary and higher education is highly correlated with parental income and education. Those from a higher socio-economic background (especially the urban well-to-do) are more likely to attend high-cost primary schools, with more public subsidy, better teachers, equipment and laboratories, and a higher certificate in primary education (CPE) score, which admits them to the best secondary schools and (eventually) the university. The national secondary schools, which receive more government aid and thus charge lower fees, take only 5% of those with a CPE. Overall, Kenya's 1984 secondary enrolment rate (over ages 12–17) was just over 20%, disproportionately from middle- and upper-class families. Moreover, those with affluent and educated parents can more easily finance education, and are more likely to have the personal qualities, good connections, and better knowledge of opportunities to get higher salaries and non-manual jobs. Investment in education, training, and other forms of human capital explain a sizeable portion of non-property income variance. All in all, income and educational inequalities are likely to be transmitted from one generation to another (Bigsten, 1984).

In 1980, 35.9% of the Kenyan and 20.8% of the Tanzanian manufacturing labour force had some secondary education, while 17.9% of the Kenyan and 30.5% of the Tanzanian force had less than standard 5 primary education. Kuznets (1955) argues that educational expansion, like Kenya's, would reduce equality as increased high incomes are added to a predominantly low-income, traditional agricultural economy. Holding the educational structure of wages constant, Kenya's faster educational expansion's effect on labour's educational composition increased wage inequality more than in Tanzania. However, expansion's effect on compressing wage scales, holding composition constant, outweighed the composition effect. Thus, the overall effect was that Kenya had lower inequality in manufacturing wages than Tanzania (Knight and Sabot, 1983).

Tanzania's policy encouraging primary and limiting secondary educational expansion, though ostensibly to redistribute income to the poor, actually curtailed public secondary opportunities for all income classes, including the poor. With expanding Class 7 primary leavers, the government's restriction of public secondary schools reduced substantially these leavers' opportunity ratio – from 35.8% in 1961 to 10.7% in 1971 to 2.7% in 1981. Some 42.3% of the 1981 primary leavers (compared to 4.6% in 1965 and 24.8% in 1971) enrolled in fee-paying private secondary schools; they were largely the children of affluent parents. Moreover, because the parents could afford the tuition fees to higher-quality primary schools, their children were more likely to be admitted to government secondary schools (Bukuku, 1985). This helps reproduce the class system, enabling privileged parents to convey greater opportunity for wealth and education to their children.

Boissiere's, Knight's, and Sabot's test in Kenya and Tanzania (1985), factoring out returns to education from screening or certification, shows that earning ability increases substantially with greater literacy and numeracy, both in manual and non-manual jobs. These skills enable mechanics, machinists, and fork-lift drivers, as well as accountants, clerks, and secretaries, to do a better job. But cognitive skills, especially literacy and numeracy, that result in wage inequality, are discovered on the job by the employer, who is willing to pay for them. Earnings do not, however, increase much with increased reasoning ability (measured by Raven's Progressive Matrices' pictoral-pattern matching) or increased years of school. While Boissiere *et al.*, think their findings indicate the inefficiency of reducing inequality, they fail to recognise the extent to which acquiring education and experience to increase cognitive ability is correlated with parental class standing.

After 1974, Tanzania limited university entry to high school graduates who had worked in villages, factories, offices, hospitals, or some other job (except for women to compensate for past social disadvantages) (Bukuku, 1985).

NIGERIA

After 1960, Nigeria increased educational enrolments at all levels rapidly, stimulating growth but widening income differences. The greater educational access by children of elites played a major role in transmitting economic status inter-generationally.

A household survey indicated Nigeria's 1967 labour-force educational inequality: 67% were illiterate, 26% had some primary education, 7% some secondary education, and less than 0.5% some university education. Among illiterates, 98% were self-employed and 75% in agriculture. And 92% of the primary educated were self-employed, but only 33% in agriculture. By 1981, 60% were illiterate, 31% primary educated, 8% secondary educated, and 1% university educated.

In 1967, if illiterates' average earnings were the base (100), primary-leavers' earnings were 170, secondary-leavers' 270, and university graduates' 1,220, with discrepancies increasing substantially with age. Government salary structures indicate that as education expanded, the gaps between those no more than primary educated and those at least secondary educated narrowed from 1967 to the late 1970s and early 1980s. While it is unrealistic to reduce university graduates' salaries, the government can hold down their rate of increase relative to that of other groups (Diejomaoh and Anusionwu, 1981a).

Primary-school accessibility in Nigeria was highly unequal depending on location, and highly correlated with income class. In many cities, like Ibadan, schools were located on the peripheries of built-up areas. In 1970, when there were 152 primary schools in Ibadan, there were less than 70 schools in the central city. While the population per school averaged 4,980 in Ibadan, the figure in Central Ibadan (consisting of indigenes usually inhabiting mud houses and slums) was 33,470. Pupils from the centre travelled two to three kilometres to school. In the suburbs, well-to-do families' children were much closer to school. More than one-third of Ibadan's children made trips longer than 1.5 kilometres to primary school. Access was even more unequal for secondary schooling, with no schools in Central Ibadan. Ibadan's unequal access to schooling is typical of Nigerian cities generally (Ayeni, 1981).

During the Third National Plan, 1975–80, in response to an oil boom and growing political demands, the Nigerian government introduced free: UPE, university, teacher-training college, college of education, college of technology, and (in 1979) secondary grammar school. Each September from 1976 through 1981, a new class of primary 1 entered UPE, which encountered shortfalls with the demands for classrooms and teacher training, especially after federal cutbacks in 1977. While UPE redistributes income to the poor, a highly disproportionate share of the fathers of students in secondary school, who received a government subsidy, were highly educated, middle- to upper-income, and professionals, managers, administrators.

This was especially true in federal (first-rate) and highly-reputable private (second-rate) schools, as opposed to third-rate schools (formerly run by private proprietors for profit before state governments took them over). Some 67.2% of the students in the first-rate, 27.5% in the second-rate, and 5.2% in the third-rate secondary schools had gone to private primary schools. Students whose parents could afford private pre-primary and primary schools were more likely to pass the competitive entrance examination for first-rate secondary schools. In 1976–7, the average recurrent annual subsidy per student in first-rate schools was ₦ 1,605, the second-rate ₦ 417, and the third-rate ₦ 220, compared to the annual student fee of ₦ 90. Counting capital subsidies, the rough share of expenditures borne by the student's family was 1% in the first-rate, 18% in the second-rate, and 30% in the third-rate schools. Thus, children of upper-income families were more likely to receive their education virtually free at public expense in the first-rate schools, while middle-income families were shouldering almost a third of their children's expense at much inferior third-rate schools. As annual fees increased after the 1978–9 growth deceleration, the share of school places for low-income children declined. Moreover, the emphasis on students going to school from their home made it more difficult for students located in inaccessible areas. Many poor parents must choose to pay high boarding fees or withdraw their children from secondary school (Diejomaoh and Anusionwu, 1981a).

Subsidies are higher in Nigerian higher education than primary or secondary education. In 1976–7, the average recurrent subsidy per student was ₦ 2,873 in colleges of technology and ₦ 5,130 in universities, each much in excess of first-rate secondary school subsidies. Moreover, the student enjoying the subsidies had been enjoying these for a substantial time. Some 28.2% of the fathers of University of Lagos students had a university degree or equivalent, and 22.0% of fathers of Yaba College of Technology students. Moreover, 28.2% of University of Lagos fathers and 21.8% of Yaba College fathers were professionals, managers, and administrators, a small fraction of the population. While Nigerians' average annual labour-force income was roughly ₦ 1,000, 60.0% of the University of Lagos's students' fathers had incomes above that, and 36.7% above ₦ 3,000 in 1977–8.

In the 1977–8 university academic year, with cutbacks in oil revenues, the federal government dropped a programme of federal loans, bursaries, and scholarships to indigent students. Board and lodging fees of students, subsidised during the 1977–8 academic year, were tripled for the 1978–9 academic year. Low-income students found it even more difficult to attend university. Students protesting these changes clashed with police and soldiers at several universities, resulting in several deaths in 1978.

The colleges of technology, designed to produce middle-level manpower, had been dominated by students from the lower–middle- and middle-income groups. However, after 1978, with a government decree indicating polytechnic graduates as equivalent to university counterparts in initial salaries, technology colleges were increasingly patronised by higher-income groups (*ibid.*; Nafziger, 1983).

Policies to redistribute income would include greater subsidies to primary education, with emphasis on high nation-wide quality, to ensure that public school graduates from low-income backgrounds can compete with those with higher-income backgrounds. Another policy to avoid increased inequality is lower subsidies for secondary and postsecondary education, with scholarships widely available for low-income students.

Medical education in Nigeria in the 1960s and 1970s emphasised expanding high-level professional skills, rather than the wide dispersion of lower-level assistance and information needed to reduce the terrible toll of endemic diseases like gastroenteritis and malaria. In the late 1970s, public health improved dramatically following the introduction of primary care programmes using auxiliary personnel (ILO, 1981).

Field surveys indicate that the non-educated, unskilled, low-income earners have higher fertility rates and dependency burdens than the average, sometimes creating a vicious circle that keeps living standards down. The poor, large family has little capacity to provide resources and incentives to enable its children to escape poverty (Adepoju, 1975). Family planning programmes that are broadly based enough to motivate poor couples to limit family size reduce income inequality.

MALAWI

Until 1976, the Malawian government only accepted responsibility for urban primary schools, leaving rural ones to local initiative (except for teacher salary supplements). Most spending was for the University of Malawi, an expensive institution producing graduates at a recurrent cost per graduate exceeding that of the average US university (Kydd, 1984).

FEMALE EDUCATION

The subsaharan African 1982 primary enrolment rate among males as a percentage of those 6–11 years old was 82% compared to 60% among females. The 1980 secondary rate among males aged 12–17 was 9% compared to 5% among females. Retention rates were also higher among men. Parents may view education for sons as more economically beneficial than for daughters, who either lose marriage chances, or face job discrimination, marry early and stop working, or move to husbands' villages. However, families waste no time in educating girls when cultural change improves their employment opportunities. Moreover, female education substantially improves household nutrition and reduces fertility and child mortality (World Bank, 1986a, 1984a, 1980a).

In Nigeria, the male–female enrolment ratio in primary school in 1973 was 3:2, with 7:3 in North (predominantly Muslim), 10:7 in the East, 3:2 in Lagos state, 4:3 in the West, and 1:1 in the Mid-West. By 1981, UPE had still not yet brought the national ratio to 1:1. The 1973 male–female ratios were higher at the secondary level: 2:1 for Nigeria, 7:2 in the North, 2:1 in the East, Mid-West, and West, and 1:1 in Lagos state. The university male–female ratio was 5:1, with an especially high ratio in the North. Ghana's national ratios are similar to Nigeria's (Diejomaoh and Anusionwu, 1981a; Date-Bah, 1982).

CONCLUSION

Since independence, African elites have used their wealth and access to get superior education for their children, receive disproportionate public educational subsidies, and transmit high class status from one generation to another. Ironically, this class maintenance occurred even in Tanzania, which deliberately restrained secondary education expansion to improve equality of opportunity. Affluent parents could enrol their children in high-tuition primary schools to increase their chances for secondary admission or, if denied admission, send their children to fee-paying private secondary schools. Parents are still more likely to send males than females to school at all levels.

§ 11 §

URBAN BIAS AND RURAL POVERTY

In 1985, Africa's 583 million people included 175 million in urban areas (30%, the world's lowest region, except for South Asia's and Southeast Asia's 24%) compared to a projected 464 million (46.5%) of 997 million in 2008 (Population Reference Bureau, 1986; ECA, 1983b).

Lipton (1977) argues that the most significant class conflicts and income discrepancies are not between labour and capital, as Marx contended, but between rural and urban classes. Despite plans proclaiming agriculture's priority and rhetoric stressing the poor rural masses, government allocates most resources to cities, a policy of urban bias. African politicians respond to the more powerful and articulate urban dwellers. Thus, ruling elites divert farm land from growing millet and beans for hungry villagers to produce meat and milk for urban middle and upper classes, or to grow cocoa, coffee, tea, sugar, cotton, and jute for export. Political leaders spend scarce capital on highways and steel mills, instead of water pumps, tube wells, and other equipment for growing food. Moreover, government uses high-cost administrative talent to design office buildings and sports stadiums rather than village wells and agricultural extension services.

Indeed urban–rural inequalities explain a large proportion of overall inequality in African states. Industry–agriculture productivity differentials are wider in Africa than other world regions. Non-agricultural incomes in Africa are 4–9 times agricultural incomes, compared to 2–2.5 times in other LDCs. The share of the inter-sectoral income disparity in overall income inequality (measured by the Theil index) varies widely: about 10% in Colombia, Mexico, Iran, and Turkey; 20% in Malaysia and in the Philippines; 35% in South Korea; and 40–65% in five African countries – Côte d'Ivoire, Zambia, Madagascar, Senegal, and Swaziland. While agriculture's income share is about the same in Africa and other LDCs, agriculture's employment share in Africa is much more than others. To be sure, these studies may not adjust enough for own consumption in rural areas and urban–rural cost-of-living discrepancies. Yet the share of the population suffering undernourishment (more a function of income than food availability) is higher in Africa's rural areas than in urban areas.[1] Overall, African urban–rural income differentials are not overstated relative to differentials in other LDC regions (Lecaillon *et al.*, 1984; Lee, 1983; FAO, 1977).

In Nigeria, because the rural masses were weak politically, official income redistribution policies focused on inter-urban not urban–rural or intra-urban redistribution. More than 80% of Nigeria's Second Five Year Plan investment (1970–4) was in urban areas. The Third Plan (1975–80) emphasised more even distribution but did not mention rural–urban imbalances (Bienen and Diejomaoh, 1981; Nigeria, 1970; Nigeria, II, 1975).

The ratio of Nigerian industrial to agricultural labour productivity, 2.5:1 in 1966, increased to 2.7:1 in 1970 and 7.2:1 in 1975. (Urban–rural per capita income ratios were greater for all years, largely because incomes from capital, property, and entrepreneurship are far more significant for urban than rural dwellers.) The sharp rise, 1970–5, was due largely to the phenomenal oil output, price, and tax revenue expansion rather than technical change or manpower development. Without oil, 1975's differential would have been 3.0. The terms of trade shifted toward non-agriculture. Moreover, emigration drained the rural areas of the most able-bodied young people, attracted by the oil-fuelled Udoji Commission's doubling of government minimum wages. In fact, emigration selectivity resulted in a decline in inflation-adjusted agricultural productivity, 1970–5. Average rural income was so low that the richest rural fourth were relatively poor by urban standards (Diejomaoh and Anusionwu, 1981b; Matlon, 1981).

Zambian peasant earnings were only a fraction of those by workers (chapter 8). Average annual household income, 1972–3, was ZK 1440 in urban areas, ZK 1188 in semi-urban areas, and ZK 348 in rural areas, with average rural household size (4.2) only slightly smaller than urban (4.9) and semi-urban (5.9) households. Food expenditure constituted 57% of total expenditure in urban areas, 65% in semi-urban areas, and 68% in rural areas (Good, 1986; ILO, 1977b).

Generally, Africa's farmers, especially in the Sahel and central and southern parts, are among the world's poorest people. Isolated farmers work mountainous, desert, and grassland plots, 30 kilometres from a road, and hundreds of kilometres from a seaport. Most barely eke out a living (Markovitz, 1977). While Africa's contemporary agricultural crisis has its roots in colonial policies, the problem has been exacerbated by the continuing inattention to agriculture by independent African governments, whether capitalist, socialist, military, or civilian. Following are the urban policy biases among African governments.

High industrial relative to farm prices

Government may set price ceilings on food, and guarantee minimum prices for industrial goods. High taxes and low prices force agriculture to transfer income and capital to industry and social infrastructure.

The models for transferring farm resources to 'modern' activities have been the past one and one-half century's two most-rapidly industrialising latecomers, Japan and the Soviet Union, which accumulated large sums of industrial capital by squeezing such capital from agriculture (see Nafziger, 1985b; Gregory and Stuart, 1986). In Africa, parastatal corporations and marketing boards draw peasants into the market, capturing the surplus from monopsony farm-good purchases for general government expenditures rather than investing in agriculture or stabilising prices (Bond, 1983). Frequently producers received less than 65% of the income from the sales of the crop.

Studies of African smallholder farmers indicate a substantial positive supply response to price for a wide variety of cash (especially food) crops in all ecological regions of Africa. Farmers respond through labour and land reallocation between farm activities (including subsistence and commercial farming), black market activity, other activities (including urban emigration), and leisure. The cross elasticity of supply for farm goods (e.g., the percentage change in the quantity of coffee supplied divided by the percentage change in the price of wheat) is large, especially in the long run. Moreover, supply response is dependent not only on prices, but also on credit, technologies, inputs, and institutions (Helleiner, 1975; Bond, 1983).

Between the mid 1970s and mid 1980s, even Côte d'Ivoire, which the World Bank's Acharya (1981b) felt provided remunerative price incentives for peasant agriculture, usually paid its coffee producers less than 50% of the world price, and only 18% of the world price in 1976–7. From the early 1960s to the early 1970s, while the terms of trade for export crops deteriorated, marketing boards (Caisses) took an increasingly large share of the world price for its surplus. During the period, the Caisses's surplus was about one-fourth of total government current revenues. By the early 1980s, planters invested in commerce, transport, real estate, and services, but did not replace the existing stock of coffee and cocoa trees.

From 1960 to 1980, Côte d'Ivoire's ruling class used growing agricultural export surplus for expanding employment and credit to develop capital-intensive import-substitution industry and high-cost urban projects to shape alliances and maintain political stability. This surplus, obtained through low prices for the farm exporter, impeded the continuing expansion of agricultural productivity. But by the early 1980s, public revenue stopped growing, creating a crisis of state (Ridler, 1985; Campbell, 1985).

In 1961–2, when the world price of cocoa fell £50 a ton, both Ghana and Nigeria passed the full price reduction to producers, transferring large surpluses accumulated from high prices in prior years to the government. Ghana, whose Cocoa Marketing Board levied heavy taxes on farmers, paid lower producer prices than Côte d'Ivoire and Nigeria, and increased government surpluses as the ratio of producer to export price declined from 49% in 1960 to 39% in 1970 to 22% in 1976. Producer price declines reduced cocoa export volume from an index of 100 in 1965 (the world's leader, one-third of world production) to 44.0 in 1979 (third place in the world, one-sixth of its output), thus reducing foreign exchange earnings and the import of industrial inputs and capital. For Jeffries (1982), Ghana's monopsonistic marketing boards taxed productive peasants heavily to finance highly-paid parasitic bureaucratic, party, and military personnel – a 'kleptocracy' acquiring additional income from corruption and embezzlement. Indeed the net barter terms of trade for Ghana's cocoa farmers declined 90% 1963–80 (ILO, 1982b).

In Nigeria, depressed marketing-board producer prices for cocoa, groundnuts, and palm oil and monopoly returns to intermediate licensed buying agents reduced agricultural growth. Indeed prices for groundnuts, the second leading export in the 1960s, were so unfavourable in the 1970s that their deliveries virtually ceased. Moreover, marketing board surpluses provided capital for subsidised loans to industrial investors, making capital cheap and encouraging capital-intensive technology inappropriate to labour abundance. According to the 1962 Coker Commission of Inquiry into Western Nigerian statutory corporations, many loan beneficiaries were development agencies or politically influential persons. Those in charge of these agencies transferred funds to private banks and corporations in which they held financial interest. Cheap capital led to personal gains and helped build political coalitions (World Bank, 1981a; Eicher and Baker, 1982; ILO, 1981; Bates, 1981; Ghai and Radwan, 1983; Bequele,

1983; Nafziger, 1984). In 1986, however, Nigeria's military government abolished marketing boards, replacing them with a system where farmers directly marketed their own produce.

Kenya's policy after independence required maize sales to the parastatal National Cereals and Produce Board, and forbade sales to private merchants, with imprisonment as the penalty. Since 1978, government has set food prices to avoid urban resistance to large increases in maize and meat prices. But low food prices have caused peasants to switch production to export crops and subsistence output, or sell on the black market (Cowen, 1986).

In 1986, with a bumper maize crop, farmers had to sell at a controlled price, especially low at times of maximum supply for the majority who had little or no storage. Farmers wanted to boycott the board, since payments were delayed, making it difficult to get inputs or pay school fees (*Africa*, Apr. 1986, p. 78).

Kaunda observed in 1983 that Zambia's major problem was being 'born...with a copper spoon in our mouth'. The colonial and postcolonial state's concentration on copper hampered the rest of the economy. The state, by depriving some African peasants of land, paying them low commodity prices, denying them extension services, and levying high tax rates on them, contributed to their underdevelopment, forcing peasants to become a labour reservoir for mines and large-scale commercial farms.

Most of Zambia's commercial farm agricultural goods are marketed domestically. Government set maize prices in the early 1970s at one-half to two-thirds world market prices. In 1980, the farmers gave up three times the agricultural produce for urban necessities that they did in 1965. Moreover, they were unlikely to find basic necessities – cooking oil, salt, matches, soap, and blankets – in the shops, because of serious shortages. Urban pricing bias resulted in a flight from the rural to urban areas (Good, 1986; Ghai and Radwan, 1983; Bates, 1981).

While Tanzania's Ministry of Planning and Economic Affairs (1982) blames unfavourable weather for the threat to economic survival, much of the responsibility rests with large-scale agricultural projects, poor planning, and urban bias. Since 1970, Tanzania's monopsony state crop authorities have levied heavy export taxes on coffee, tea, cotton, sisal, pyrethrum, and tobacco, and imposed large marketing margins (to cover rapidly increasing administrative costs), assuming agriculture would provide a surplus and foreign exchange for the rest of the economy. Subsistence agriculture's share increased from 70.1% in 1972 to 82.8% in 1981 as peasants withdrew from the monetised economy due to the fall in farm producer prices, rampant inflation, and chronic shortages of consumer necessities. Agriculture's commodity terms of trade dropped 15.6% for domestic crops from 1970 to 1980, 42.6% for export crops, and 35.9% overall.

Government tried to keep food prices low, which served as a disincentive to producers, and contributed to a food crisis in 1973, stagnation in average food output (1964–85), and a failure to achieve national self-sufficiency. Yet the urban worker and self-employed did not gain, as after the early 1970s farmers supplied less food or diverted it to black markets, thus driving up food prices. In fact, the bureaucracy and private urban merchants were the major beneficiaries of the surplus appropriated from agriculture (Bukuku, 1985).

Hyden (1980) argues that price incentives are not important in spurring shifts in output mixes. To be sure, the major concern of the peasant is survival, not income maximisation. However, price inducements lure peasants, once they assure subsistence survival, to diversify production into mixed (including commercial) farming (Nafziger, 1984). Tanzania's increase in subsistence food output but decline in marketed food and commercial agricultural outputs since the early 1970s indicates peasants respond to prices. Exports earnings (two-thirds of which were cotton, coffee, cloves, sisal, cashews, tobacco, and tea) were 22% higher in 1966 (25% higher in 1973) than in 1980, and fell from 25% in 1966 to 11% in 1979 as a percentage of GDP. The drop in volume, combined with falling terms of trade, produced a severe balance on current account crisis. Indeed, for subsaharan African generally, discrimination against farm prices and government involvement in providing farm inputs are negatively correlated with agricultural output growth in the 1970s (World Bank, 1981a; Vengroff and Farah, 1985; Cleaver, 1985).

Lemarchand (1979), while travelling in Bandundu province in southwestern Zaïre, observed widespread malnutrition and disease, including the swollen bellies of kwashiokor-ridden infants in villages, the human dregs in rural maternity wards, and the hostile and hungry looks of the unemployed on the Lever plantations. Cash returns on marketable output have not been sufficient to meet the peasants' basic needs, and cultivating cash crops leaves too little time and energy for subsistence farming. The army and political elites appropriate large shares of agricultural production through low prices. But rural people, fearing retribution, do not revolt. Moreover, plantation workers have been marginalised. Consumer prices increased fast, while wages grew slowly. In 1978, real wages for plantation workers were only 15–20% of 1960 real wages.

Urban price bias is only a special case of the ruling class using prices to appropriate resources generated by the working class. The policies of Malawian parastatals and marketing boards using prices to transfer resources from the peasants to the estate sector are analogous to the policies transferring resources from peasants to urban elites discussed in this chapter. Indeed, as chapter 9 indicates, other African countries also use policies to redistribute resources within the farm sector. Urban–rural dichotomies (between peasants and the urban bourgeoisie) are not the most fundamental, as Lipton contends, but merely a part of more general class discrepancies.

Concentration of investment in industry

Although roughly three-fourths of Africa's labour force in the 1960s and 1970s was in agriculture (also including forestry and fishing), less than 10% of public capital investment was in agriculture, a decline from the colonial period. Ghana, during this time, spent 10% of its funds on agriculture, even though 30% of government revenue came from cocoa alone (Bequele, 1983).

During the 1970s' oil boom, Nigerian planners put little priority on agriculture, which stagnated as traditional exports groundnuts and palm oil became net imports. Even though most of the labour force was in agriculture, government devoted only 7.7% of second-plan (1970–4) and 6.5% of third-plan capital outlays to agriculture, primarily for the large commercial farmer. Some 47% of planned agricultural expenditure was on commercial rice and wheat irrigation, which smallholders without funds for expensive complementary inputs of hired labour, high-yielding seeds, tractor use, chemicals and fertiliser could not afford. Moreover, many of the large-scale government farms were costly failures, lacking experienced management and back-up assistance. While the plans indicated goals of more even distribution, policies exacerbated income discrepancies, as planners failed to consider urban–rural or intra-rural redistribution (ILO, 1981; Bienen and Diejomaoh, 1981).

From 1964 to 1977, 75% of Kenya's capital formation (used mostly outside agriculture) was generated from the agricultural surplus. Although the Special Rural Development Programme (SRDP) was launched in 1970 to increase incomes and job opportunities, it was abandoned in 1971 as it ran counter to the Kenyatta government's urban-oriented development strategy. SRDP's orientation toward rural development conflicted with the provincial administration, primarily an agency of political control to support major government clients – large farmers and urban capitalists. Moreover, SRDP implied resource transfer from the affluent to the poor, 'unthinkable' to one person administering the programme (Ghai and Radwan, 1983; Leys, 1974).

Since Malawi spends little on infrastructure investment, research, technology, and extension service for small-farmer foodgrains (maize, cassava, sweet potatoes, rice, and millet), land is the major determinant of rural household survival. With increasing population pressures, the mean household holding declined from 1.54 hectares in the late 1960s to 1.16 hectares in 1980–1, contributing to a decline in food output per capita in the 1970s of 2% annually. Peasants increased off-farm employment to compensate for this decline (Hirschmann, 1987).

In Zaïre, copper production received most government investment, with agriculture's share 2–3% (1970–4) and 5–6% (1975). Mining and processing industries used 70% of electricity in 1973, while less than 2% of Zaïrians had electricity. Most agricultural investments were capital-intensive projects with little relevance for most rural people (Gran, 1979).

Although Mozambique's government after independence in 1975 stressed that agriculture was the base for economic expansion, the 75% of the economically active population in agriculture received only 22% of the 1976–7 capital budget (a proportion that dropped in subsequent years). The government promoted socialisation of agriculture, establishing state farms, communal villages, and cooperatives to replace colonial plantations and large estates, even though the overwhelming majority of agriculturalists were subsistence farmers (Srivastava and Livingstone, 1983).

In the 1970s and early 1980s, the Tanzania government's basic industries strategy, designed to establish engineering, metal-based, chemical, coal, and construction-materials industries, resulted in the neglect of agricultural infrastructure investment and a fall in foodgrain output per capita during the period (Bukuku, 1985).

Tax incentives and subsidies

Most African countries provided government subsidies and concessions, such as tax holidays, accelerated depreciation allowances, price guarantees, import duty relief, equity and loan finance, land acquisition, technical and management assistance, and improved public services to manufacturing, mining, and construction but only rarely to agriculture. Indeed, I have already pointed out above that African state policies transferred large surpluses from agriculture to provide concessions and subsidies for industry, especially parastatals.

Although farmers have a unique need for credit between sowing and harvest, few have the collateral that lending agencies require. Even government loans boards rarely accept land as collateral because of the political difficulty of foreclosing when farmers fail to repay. Moreover, the substantial staff time needed to process and supervise loans and perhaps arrange technical assistance, as well as the risk of bad debts, make it difficult for government farm credit programmes to be self-supporting.

In Nigeria, agriculture contributed almost half the GNP but accounted for only 2.6% of commercial bank loans and advances, and few government and cooperative loans between 1969 and 1975. The banking offices in Nigeria in 1975 were located in less than 120 towns, with 16 towns accounting for more than half the total. Few banks were accessible to rural areas (Teriba, 1981). Furthermore, Nigeria's 1978 land decree edict resting land ownership with government reduced or eliminated land collateral value.

Tariff and quota protection

Free trade improves efficiency of resource use, disperses new ideas, widens markets, improves division of labour, permits more specialised machinery, overcomes technical indivisibilities, utilises surplus productive capacity, and stimulates greater managerial effort because of foreign, competitive pressures. Tariffs and quotas can promote infant industries (by reducing average costs through internal economies of scale), create external economies, facilitate technological borrowing, improve the balance of payments, and increase revenue and employment. Additionally, protection (as well as the above policies of industrial investment concentration and tax inducements) can promote industrialisation and improve the balance of payments by import substitution (replacing imports by domestic industry). However, these arguments for protection are more limited than many African policymakers suppose, as I indicate in detail elsewhere (1984). Moreover, in most African countries, tariff and quota protection against foreign (usually industrial) competition contributes to worsening terms of trade (higher fertiliser, seed, equipment, materials, and consumer-goods prices) and reduced incomes for agriculture.

Ghana and Kenya have written tariff laws to designate protection at the six-digit level of the International Standard Industrial Classification (ISIC) system, in effect extending protection to individual firms.

Firms in Kenya lobby to be listed on a schedule requiring licences to import materials or manufactures, since they can object to these imports by domestic firms, and thus shelter themselves from competition. Moreover, most African governments allocate licences in accordance with historical market shares, thus freezing existing competitive patterns, and preventing the entrance and growth of more efficient firms.

Bureaucratic procedures to protect firms from foreign competition, to allocate imports through licences, and to award tariff rebates for priority-enterprise inputs give an advantage to large firms (often MNCs) with better organisation, information, connections, and more experience in preparing justifications for protection, in devising cost estimates, gathering and analysing supporting data, and handling the volume of paperwork to secure administrative action. While the rationale for protection, licences, and tariff drawbacks was to promote industrialisation, the effect has been to restrict domestic competition and reduce capacity utilisation. Moreover, African governments' lack of explicit criteria for choosing industries to protect and firms to receive licences or rebates gives rise to charges of bribery, influence, and ethnic consideration. Without doubt, these choices increase the power of the political elites and government servants.

These decisions, which frequently carry the power of life or death to the enterprise, are important factors contributing to high industrial concentration. In 1965 in Nigeria, the total value-added of the largest four establishments in the 31 major manufacturing industries as a percentage of total value-added in these industries was 69.0% compared to 3.7% for the same thirty-one industries in the US. This concentration, then associated with foreign dominance of the manufacturing sector, is now, after some indigenisation decrees, associated with parastatal enterprise domination.

In Tanzania, state-associated firms controlled 57% of the manufacturing sector (by value-added) in the late 1960s and early 1970s. Kenya had only 1,972 manufacturing firms in 1972, with only two in textiles, eight in sugar, eight in slaughtering and dressing meat, and ten in ginning cotton. In 1969, Zambia had only 431 manufacturing establishments, with only two leather and footwear units, three spinning establishments, three producing vegetable oils, and three canned goods units. In Ghana in 1969, 83% of the total gross output of state enterprises was produced in industries in which state enterprises contributed 75% or more of the industry's output. African states frequently deny lower-cost firms protection, rebates, or licences needed to survive against inefficient (often politically-favoured) producers, factors which increase the prices farmers pay (Bates, 1981; Nafziger, 1977).

Urban amenities

African governments spend more on education, training, housing, plumbing, sewerage, staple foods, medical care, and transport in urban areas (often with subsidies) than in rural areas. Low agricultural returns, higher industrial wages, and more urban amenities spur rural–urban migration.

Africa, despite its low urbanisation rate, is overurbanised and overconcentrated in one city. The primacy of the capital city has reached extremes in Guinea, where Conakry is almost nine times the population of the next-largest town, and in Senegal, Liberia, and Togo, whose capitals' populations are about seven times those of the next-largest towns.

The concentration of social services in African primate cities has contributed to this overconcentration. With exceptions like Nigeria and Tanzania, a visitor who ventures beyond an African capital city is likely to be shocked by the disparity existing between the city and the hinterlands.

Industrial concentration indicates the primacy of one city. In the early 1970s, 400 of Côte d'Ivoire's 617 industrial enterprises and 60% of modern-sector jobs were located in Abidjan. In Senegal, nearly 80% of industrial enterprises, 66% of all salaried employment, and 50% of civil servants were concentrated in the Dakar area. Nairobi, which increased its dominance of Kenya's modern sector after independence, accounted for two-thirds of the country's wage bill, more than half of the output in manufacturing, electricity, and commerce, two-fifths in transport and services, and two-thirds in construction, while only 5% of the population. Lagos, a federal and state capital with 1.6% of Nigeria's population in 1972, comprised 56% of gross manufacturing output and 53% of manufacturing wages and salaries, both figures increases over 1964.

Governmental health spending in Africa is urban biased. In 1968, Côte d'Ivoire built an 8-storey, 500-bed Centre Hospitalier Universitaire, one of the largest and most modern hospitals in Africa, in the affluent section of Abidjan. But the project's funds, given by the French government, were originally intended for 12 regional hospitals. In 1981–2, the rural population of Senegal, which comprised 81% of the population received only 43% of the government health subsidy (Gugler and Flanagan, 1978; ILO, 1972; Jimenez, 1986).

The lion's share of Kenya's public expenditures goes to urban areas.

In 1977–8, 17.2% of the male urban labour force had no education compared to 42.1% male rural, 34.7% female urban, and 67.4% female rural; 37.2% of the male urban labour force had some secondary education compared to 10.9% male rural, 33.8% female urban, and 2.8% female rural. Returns to secondary and higher education are very high in Kenya's urban areas, but low or negative in rural areas, a reflection of the lack of highly skilled jobs (Bigsten, 1984).

Most of Nigeria's government spending in the 1970s and 1980s was on urban areas, despite a population majority in rural areas. In 1978, 23% of Nigerians (68% urban and 18% rural) had piped water (ILO, 1981). Osuntogun (1975) found poor housing, inadequate or no medical facilities, low educational levels, and poor educational facilities as symptomatic of poverty in five rural villages in Ogbomosho District, Western Nigeria in 1974. Some 76.6% of the houses were mud houses, 6.5% plastered with cement, and the rest partly mud and partly plastered. None of the houses had modern facilities like a decent toilet, kitchen, and bathroom. The five villages averaged twenty kilometres from the nearest hospital, and most had no medical facilities. No village had a primary school, and 69% of the farmers had no formal education.

The emigration decision encompasses such more than the difficulty of keeping youths on the farm once they have seen the 'bright lights' of Lagos. Indeed, it is rare in Nigeria, as well as other African countries, for a rural youth to seek a city job without family or village support. Typically, applicants are sent to the city to diversify family income, often staying with relatives during the job search. The Western stereotype of young, urban immigrants as rebels against the family is not common in Africa, where young people rarely have cars or money essential for independence, and where they depend heavily on the family for employment, a good marriage, and economic security.

Moreover, an urban Nigerian usually retains close connections with his rural roots, often through village and ethnic unions. If he is successful, he proves his success in his rural home by spending lavishly at funerals, weddings, other ceremonies, opening public institutions, or making capital investments in houses and farms. The urban poor return to the village less often from shame, and indeed some continue to receive assistance from rural relatives (Sada, 1981).

Low prices for foreign currency

African states generally set below-market prices for foreign currency, thus reducing domestic currency receipts from agricultural exports.

This policy lowers the price of capital goods and other foreign inputs, benefiting large industrial establishments with privileged access to import licences.

For some in the 1970s and 1980s, the overvalued domestic currency resulted from rapid growth in a booming export sector. This issue is important enough to be discussed separately in chapter 12 on the Nigerian disease, a pathology other African countries have experienced, though frequently in a less virulent form.

Africa's export performance deteriorated from the early 1970s to the late 1970s and early 1980s. Depreciating the domestic currency price of foreign currency to its market rate promotes exports (by making them cheaper to foreigners), as well as rationing imports through the market, encouraging import substitution, increasing labour-intensive production and employment, and improving investment. But Africa experienced overall real domestic currency appreciation (decline in the domestic currency price of foreign currency, adjusted for domestic inflation) from the early 1970s to the 1980s.

Real domestic currency depreciation, 1970–81, was significantly positively related to agricultural growth rates, 1970–81. Chad, Ethiopia, Mali, Malawi, Burkina Faso, Benin, Sierra Leone, Kenya, Senegal, Lesotho, Liberia, and Zambia had real currency depreciation during the period, and a 2.6% average annual agricultural growth, 1970–81. Zaïre, Uganda, Rwanda, Somalia, Tanzania, Guinea, Central African Republic, Madagascar, Niger, Sudan, Ghana, Nigeria, Zimbabwe, Cameroon, Botswana, Congo, and Côte d'Ivoire had real currency appreciation and a 1.5% annual agricultural growth during the same period. Moreover, agricultural growth was highly correlated with economic growth (Cleaver, 1985).

Ghana, during its industrialisation push after 1957, had an overvalued domestic currency, resulting in large deficits on current account. In 1961, in response to this persistent deficit and an international reserve crisis from a decline in cocoa export earnings, Ghana changed to a closed regime with an inconvertible cedi and stringent import licences. The ministers regulating foreign exchange converted privileged access to scarce licences into personal wealth for their private corporations or for political allies or clients.

After 1961, Ghana appreciated the cedi, diminishing the profitability of exports and decreasing effective protection for domestic industry. Even though the real world price of cocoa increased 16-fold from 1960–4 to 1975–9, Ghana's producer prices declined by 70% while Ivorian prices remained constant during the period. Real producer incomes in Ghana fell 75%, but increased 2–3 fold in the

Côte d'Ivoire during the period. The controlled, increasingly overvalued cedi in Ghana reduced real prices and income substantially for the cocoa producers. While Ghana's cocoa output (in tons) dropped 19% from 1960–4 to 1975–9, Ivorian output grew 177%. The fall in Ghana's cocoa export volume played a major role in Ghana's balance of payments problem (Teal, 1986).

Low cocoa prices were related to exchange-rate policy. The real effective exchange rate for cocoa (the number of units of local currency actually received by the producers for a dollar's worth of cocoa exports, adjusted for inflation) declined drastically from 1963 to 1979. Despite Ghana's difficult fiscal situation, adjusting exchange rates would have allowed higher producer prices to be paid without reducing government revenues (World Bank, 1981a).

If Busia government's devaluation in 1971, a decisive break from the Nkrumah years, had been reinforced by civil servant salary and perquisite reductions and increased taxation, as proposed in the 1971 budget, market forces would have improved the balance on current account. But the Acheampong regime (from a 1972 coup to 1979) began a disastrous redirection by revaluing so as to undo two-thirds of the devaluation's effect. Revaluation required comprehensive imports controls, whose maladministration was worse than under Nkrumah. Since Busia's overthrow was justified by the devaluation's unacceptability, the government did not devalue even as the gap between official and black-market exchange rates widened to 1:5 by 1976 (and 1:10 by 1981). Devaluation would have hurt members of government, the rich, and well-connected, who allocate low-priced foreign exchange in return for favours or bribes, but not the majority, who go without foreign inputs or consumer goods (Jeffries, 1982).

In many ways, a price of foreign exchange close to market-clearing appears preferable to compensating duties and surcharges, tax incentives, subsidies, loans, and technical assistance to stimulate import replacements and exports under an overvalued currency regime. But depressing market prices creates opportunities for elites to give privileged access to clients for personal gain or political support. Those who received lower-priced foreign exchange were given special favours, and those who apportioned it amassed political support. Allocating foreign exchange through market prices provides little scope for creating a political clientele. The political attractions help explain why, when given a choice between market and non-market means for achieving the same end, African governments usually choose intervention (Bates, 1981; Nafziger, 1984).

In 1983, in response to an overvalued cedi, Ghana instituted a dual exchange rate (with a surcharge on nonessential imports and a bonus to exporters), increased farm producer prices, removed price distortions on oil and other goods, and reduced deficit financing. By 1984, inflation fell and growth accelerated. Despite protests from the trade unions about its effect on the cost of living, Ghana devalued its cedi 55% in three stages between August 1985 and January 1986 from C40 = $1 to C90 = $1 (ECA, 1985; *African Economic Digest*, 18 January 1986, p. 5). These measures improved the balance of payments in 1986.

POLITICAL FACTORS

Why does government pursue urban-oriented price, investment, spending, tax, subsidy, tariff, and foreign-exchange policies that inhibit agricultural development and increase urban–rural discrepancies? State intervention in the market is an instrument of political control and assistance. Government (attracting foreign investment), parastatals, and business pressure political elites for cheap food policies to keep wages down. Unrest by urban workers over erosion of their purchasing power has threatened numerous African governments. Real wage declines under Nigeria's Balewa government in 1964 and Gowon government, 1974–5, as well as Ghana's Busia government in 1971, contributed to political unrest and violence which precipitated military coups. Politicians may also help emerging industry reduce raw-materials or processing costs. Examples are Ghana's monopsonistic marketing board in the early 1960s to buy copra oils for an oil mill, and Tanzania's low prices of coffee for a local manufacturing firm and cheap sisal for rope and twine manufacturing in the 1970s. Health, educational, and transport programmes, as well as government enterprises in, and business assistance for, industry require substantial public resources – often more than political leaders realise. Awolowo's Western Nigerian AG government, 1954–62, found it administratively convenient to use export marketing board surpluses to fund development programmes and build political support. Market intervention provides political control for elites to use in retaining power, building support, and implementing policies (Bates, 1983; Acharya, 1981a; Nafziger, 1983).

How do we explain the frequent paradox of African governments levying high taxes or setting price ceilings on farm goods while subsidising farm inputs? In 1954 in Ghana, Nkrumah's CPP passed a bill freezing cocoa producer prices for four years, anticipating use of the increased revenues for industry. But the newly-formed opposition party in the cocoa-growing regions was undercut by the allocation of subsidised inputs for support. Additionally, state farm programmes in each political constituency in Ghana and Western Nigeria in the 1960s made available public resources to organise support of the government in power. On the other hand, in Zambia in the 1970s, the cooperative movement, a base for UNIP's political organisation, was the vehicle for small-scale farmers gaining access to loans, seeds, fertilisers, mechanical implements, and other inputs. Rationing access to farm inputs helped the party consolidate political power in the countryside. The state obtained deference to its pricing policy by manipulating subsidy programmes to build political support for the government in power.

Farm market-clearing prices, whose benefits are distributed indiscriminately, erode urban political support and secure little political support from the countryside. In comparison, project-based policies allow benefits to be selectively apportioned for maximum political advantage. Government makes it in the private interest of numerous individuals to cooperate in programmes that are harmful to the interest of producers as a whole (Bates, 1983; Rimmer, 1984).

African governments frequently create industrial monopolies, raising the prices of industry relative to agriculture but creating rents for the political elite and its clients. Thus, in 1969, when Kenya gave Firestone a virtual monopoly of tyre production for a ten-year period, leading ministers were brought into management positions and named distributors to share the monopoly profits. The World Bank (1975) remarked that Kenya's system of protecting a firm from competition was like 'a license to print money'. The profits were shared with the administrators of the public policies that helped create the firm's monopoly. Similarly, Mobutu's power in Zaïre has been based on his capacity to make appointments to state-regulated monopoly enterprises.

Why do not rural dwellers organise themselves to oppose anti-rural government policies? First, they are politically weak and fear government reprisals. While poor peasants have little tactical power, rich ones have too much to lose from protest. Second, they have less costly options like selling in black markets, shifting resources to other commodities, or migrating to urban areas. African relative farm supply response to price is high in the long run. During the early 1970s, when Tanzanian farmers had to abandon established farms and move into villages, government food procurement declined drastically: from 106 thousand tons of maize in 1971–2 to 24 thousand in 1974–5, and from 47 thousand tons each of wheat and rice in 1972–3 to 15 thousand tons each in 1974–5. While the government interpreted this as a production shortfall, the reduction was a result of the massive flight from the government controlled market to private trade channels, as prices offered by government marketing agencies fell as a percent of world market prices (Bates, 1981; Gran, 1979; Markovitz, 1977).

Farmers are less prone to undertake collective action to raise prices. Generally farm producers are numerous and widely scattered, so the costs of organising are high and a single unit gets very little benefit. However, when there are only a few large-scale commercial farmers, the benefits to each from raising prices through lobbying may more than cover the costs. For example, in the 1960s and 1970s, 400–500 Ghanaian commercial rice farmers (with more than 20 hectares average size), accounting for one-third of the total rice acreage, combined in efforts to drive prices up by withholding crops from the market. In response, the government provided subsidies for seeds, fertilisers, credit, and mechanical equipment, as well as ready access to 'unused' land, policies comparing favourably to the assistance given to urban manufacturing (Bates, 1981).

§ 12 §

CATCHING THE NIGERIAN
DISEASE: THE RULING CLASS
AND EXCHANGE RATES

Roemer (1985) analyses 'Dutch disease', named when the booming North Sea gas export revenues in the 1970s appreciated the guilder, exposing Dutch industries to more intense foreign competition and higher unemployment. Analogously, the US suffered from a similar disease, 1980–4, experiencing a farm export crisis, and de-industrialisation from the decline of traditional US export industries (automobiles, capital goods, high technology, railroad and farm equipment, paint, leather products, cotton fabrics, carpeting, electrical equipment and parts, and basic chemicals) during substantial capital inflows strengthening the US dollar.

The pathology might better be called the 'Nigerian disease', a 1970s' economic distortion resulting from dependence on a single booming export commodity, petroleum. In 1974–8, more than 92% of Nigeria's annual export proceeds came from petroleum, in contrast to 1962 and 1966 when 90% and 65% respectively of export value was from non-oil primary products (mainly groundnuts, cocoa, palm products, and rubber). Yet after 1973 these primary products (except cocoa) virtually disappeared from Nigeria's export list.

Like the rest of Africa, Nigeria's 1970s' foreign-exchange rate discouraged agricultural (especially export) growth. But Nigeria's rate was not far from a market rate. Nigeria's petroleum exports rising from ₦ 74 million in 1968 (18% of export value) to ₦ 1,186 million in 1972 (82% of value) to ₦ 9,439 million in 1979 (93% of value) resulted in an enormous influx of foreign exchange, causing the real US dollar price of the naira ($ per ₦) to rise substantially. In 1968 (the base year) $ 1.40 = ₦ 1, while the consumer price indices in both US and Nigeria were 100. By 1979, $ 1.78 = ₦ 1, while the US's consumer price index was 208.5, and Nigeria's was 498.0. The real exchange rate, calculated as

$$\frac{\text{Nigerian consumer price index}}{\text{United States price index}} \times \text{dollar price of naira}$$

was $1.40 = ₦ 1 in 1968, and $4.25 = ₦ 1 in 1979, which was an increase of 3.037, meaning the value of the naira *vis-à-vis* the dollar more than tripled over the eleven-year period. The naira appreciation made imported goods relative to non-tradable goods far cheaper, and naira proceeds of exported agricultural goods (denominated in dollars) much lower in 1979 than in 1968. Appreciation's disincentive slashed the share of traditional agricultural exports – cocoa from 24.5% of total exports in 1968 to 4.1% in 1979, palm kernels from 3.1% to 0.1%, rubber from 3.0% to 0.1%, and groundnuts from 18.0%, groundnut oil and cake from 6.8% and raw cotton from 1.6%, all to 0.0%. All these commodities' export values (in constant naira prices) also fell. In fact, the aggregate index of the volume of output of Nigerian agricultural export commodities declined from 100 in 1968 to 50.1 in 1978 (Nafziger, 1983; Collier, 1983).

The tripling of naira value, 1968–79, greatly reduced the domestic currency price of food and consumer goods purchased from abroad. Thus, food imports increased from ₦ 7.1 million in 1968 to ₦ 126.5 million in 1973 to ₦ 2,115.1 in 1981, and overall consumer goods imports from ₦ 35.6 million to ₦ 417.5 million to ₦ 5,736.3 million, even though the consumer price index during this period only increased 5–6 fold (Central Bank, 1970, 1973, 1983).

The strengthening naira reduced the price of export crops and imported industrial goods relative to that of domestically-produced food, increasing income inequality among food farmers, but diminishing export farm income. And the multiplier and revenue effects of the oil boom had little effect on rural disposable income (Collier, 1983).

Yet the strong naira was optimal for the oil export industry, which has overwhelmed Nigeria's exchange-rate determination. Since oil prices are determined on the world market in dollars, a weaker naira would not increase the dollar value of exports, but would increase essential import costs for the national oil company while reducing the dollar proceeds from selling local inputs to foreign oil companies. One way of retaining the advantages of the strong naira for oil transactions while promoting exports and import substitution with a weak naira would be a dual exchange rate. This achieves greater protection of domestic production without the cost of repressing price signals in a regime of high tariffs and quotas, and eliminates the bias against exports without costly subsidies and tax allowances. While the dual rate could create a black market in foreign exchange, this cost would be less than the benefits of rationalising exports and import substitution.

In Nigeria, as indicated in chapter 11, the sharp increase in labour productivity and per capita differentials between the rural and urban populations during the 1970s' oil boom was the major factor increasing income inequality. Additionally, Nigeria's government spending patterns, fuelled by oil revenue, exacerbated the maldistribution of income. Without oil's impact, Nigeria's income inequality would have been low among LDCs (Bienen and Diejomaoah, 1981).

Other African countries experiencing this disease in the 1970s or 1980s include Zambia, Zaïre (copper), Ghana (cocoa), Côte d'Ivoire (cocoa, coffee), Kenya (coffee, tourism), and Egypt (tourism, remittances, foreign-aid inflows). As in Nigeria, growth in the booming export sector strengthened domestic relative to foreign currency. This reduced incentives to export other goods and substitute imports with domestic production. Moreover, labour moved from the lagging export and import-substitution sectors to the booming and non-tradable sectors. Other ill effects of the export boom have been a neglect of agricultural development (Zaïre and Zambia), relaxed fiscal discipline, increased capital-intensive projects, wage dualism, inability to absorb capital, a crowding out of the private sector's access to scarce managers and technicians, an increased dependence on foreign management of investment projects, instable export earnings and government revenue, and a diversion to quick, high returns from trade and urban real estate.

Cameroon, which began oil production off its west coast in 1978, avoided much of the Nigerian syndrome. While Cameroon's petroleum output was only one-tenth of Nigeria's in the early to mid 1980s, its potential for distortion was as great since its population was about one-tenth of Nigeria's. Indeed by 1984, two-thirds of Cameroon's merchandise exports were crude oil.

Yaounde planned better than the Nigerian government, accumulating substantial foreign-exchange reserves abroad and avoiding some of the painful adjustments of the early 1980s. Moreover, Cameroon used much of its oil revenues for manufacturing and agriculture, including maintaining coffee and cocoa producer prices despite softening world prices (Benjamin and Devarajan, 1986).

Political elites keep the domestic currency overvalued for the non-mineral sector for a number of reasons. In Nigeria, urban middle classes and commercial interests, who had gained from naira appreciation in the 1970s, feared their erosion of purchasing power (for food and other consumer goods), the loss of subsidies, and less profitable commercial opportunities (Forrest, 1986). Moreover, those fortunate enough to get foreign-exchange licences not only get an input in short supply, but also get it at a price below the market rate. But making scarce foreign currency available at a low price, together with poorly stated criteria for awarding it, resulted in charges of bribery, influence peddling, and communal or political prejudice in Nigeria.

The orthodox response to an overvalued domestic currency is to devalue (decrease the price of domestic currency, e.g., from $\$2 = ₦1$ to $\$1 = ₦1$), improving the country's current-account balance, spurring farmers and industrialists to produce more exports and import substitutes, and reducing domestic firms' incentives to import capital goods and inputs. But studies of DCs indicate that the current-account improvement resulting from devaluation usually takes about two years, and that some effects take as long as five years to work out. The lags between changes in relative international prices (from exchange rate changes) and responses in quantities traded include: recognition, decision (time for assessing the change), delivery, replacement (perhaps waiting until inventories are used up and machines wear out), and production (time for increasing output) (Grubel, 1981). The eventual improved current-account balance depends on the price elasticities of demand for exports and imports being sufficiently high. In African countries like Nigeria, import demand elasticities may be low because of trade protection and exchange controls that limit imports primarily to necessities, while export demand elasticities may be low because of licensing restrictions. Thus, export and import elasticities may be too low for devaluation to improve the current-account balance, even in the long run.

It is not difficult to understand the resistance by African countries to devaluation as a tool for improving the international balance of payments. First, the adjustments take so long that domestic discontent with the short-run impact of the devaluation (faster inflation triggered from higher import prices, including imported food) may pressure the government to reverse its policies, or may even topple it. Second, there have been too few studies of African elasticities for us to be confident that elasticities are high enough to improve the balance on current account even after 3–5 years. Third, relying on market-clearing exchange rates reduces government's ability to use subsidies, rebates, and inducements to strengthen alliances and patron–client relationships.

§ 13 §

REGIONAL AND ETHNIC INEQUALITY

Class and ethnic identities cross-pressure African workers and peasants. Indeed elites, especially in Nigeria and Kenya, distribute benefits on an ethnic or regional basis. The communal competition for these benefits transfers potential hostility from class differences to the elites and masses of others. Moreover, when social conflict is organised on ethnic lines, most political and administrative energies focus on competition for resources, rather than innovations essential for economic development (Hyden, 1980).

In Nigeria, the lure of ethnic patrons and parties undercuts labour unity. Although the twelve-day general strike in June 1964 by the Joint Action Committee (JAC) of five superordinate central labour organisations demonstrated the Balewa Government's fragility, labour solidarity soon dissipated. As the pressure of the federal elections of December 1964 neared, the contending political parties and regional governments improved their offers to segments of organised labour, thereby fragmenting it. The Balewa government gave preferential treatment to the moderate United Labour Congress. When the ULC surmised it could not hold its position against the leftists, it lost interest in the JAC. Furthermore, the election alignment between radical labour leaders and the southern-led progressive opposition party coalition miscarried after the latter refused to endorse the candidates of labour parties. Finally, the political strike called by the still-surviving JAC to support the progessive coalition's election boycott largely failed – strengthening the hands of the moderate ULC (Nafziger, 1983). Ethnically-oriented leaders in Nigeria's military governments, 1966–79, 1983–6, used similar tactics of 'divide and rule' to undermine class-based movements.

In Uganda, class and ethnicity coalesced into a ruling coalition at independence (1962). In non-Baganda Uganda, traders, government bureaucrats, and intellectuals dominated colonial politics. But after independence, the expanding bureaucracy obtained direct control of state power in alliance with Bagandan commercial farmers. Non-Baganda traders were blocked by the Indian business class, so the state class began undermining the Indian bourgeoisie in 1966–7 and expelling them in 1972 (Mamdani, 1976).

In Kenya, class and ethnic cross-pressures also resulted in the victory of ethnic politics when in 1969 Bildad Kaggia, leader of the dissident Kenya People's Union, gave in to the ruling party KANU's denying of KPU delegate conferences and public meetings, and joined KANU. The 1969 election, where competition was confined to KANU primaries, was contested mainly on an ethnic basis (Leys, 1974).

NIGERIA

In southern Nigeria, with direct colonial rule the first half of the twentieth century, education was important for producing the clerks and subalterns in the British administrative structure. In Northern Nigeria, where Governor-General Frederick Lugard established a policy of indirect rule in which day-to-day administrative responsibility was delegated to compliant Fulani emirs, education and modernisation were less important to these emirs than maintaining their domestic political hegemony. Thus, as late as 1960s, the male primary enrolment rate (i.e., males enrolled in primary school as a percentage of males aged 6–14), and the corresponding secondary rate (males aged 13–18 as the denominator) were 11% and 1%, respectively in the North, compared with 81% and 11% in the south. Only 84 of the graduates from Nigerian universities in 1966 were from the majority North, compared with 1,249 from the south (Kilby, 1964; Nigeria, Office of Statistics, 1967).

In Nigeria, politics focus on the distribution of public resources among regions and ethnic communities. The Northern government's policy of Northernisation in 1955, which gave priority in many positions to local ethnic communities, was a reaction to the uneven economic and educational development between North and south. As a result of this policy, Northerners in the superscale, administrative, professional, executive, and higher technical classes of the Northern Nigerian civil service increased from virtually none in 1955 to 14% in 1958, surpassing 50% in mid 1961.

Regionalisation was directed more toward southern Nigerians than foreigners because southerners represented a potential long-run rival to Northern political power in the country. From June 1958 to October 1959, southerners in the Northern public sector declined from 294 to 1 (Dudley, 1968).

Regional employment preference helped solidify the bureaucracy as the instrument of the traditional aristocracy and administration, to whom civil servants owed their positions. Northernisation, by expanding the employment of educated Northerners, especially benefited the more advanced Middle Belt (particularly present-day Kwara, Benue, and Plateau states), and expedited an alliance of convenience (at times shaky) between the upper Northern rulers and the educated classes of the Middle Belt.

In the mid 1960s, however, the Northern private modern sector was still dominated by southerners, Lebanese, and Europeans, who were generally sending their earnings out of the North. The alien values, especially of southern Nigerians, threatened the Northern Islamic way of life and social structure. Yet the growing enmity in urban areas was less a conflict of values than competition for the benefits of modernisation, which both groups prized highly, but in which the majority of Northerners were at a disadvantage as a result of arriving late on the scene with less education. In the major Northern centres, there were already the beginnings of a restive group of unemployed, from which political thugs were recruited during the early years of military government, 1966–7.

The resentment against southern migrants peaked after 24 May 1966, when Head of State General J. T. Aguiyi-Ironsi (an Ibo from the East) announced the abolition of regions and the establishment of a unitary administration. The uneasiness concerning the impact of this on economic opportunities for Northerners in their own region helped ignite disorders directed against Easterners that contributed to political disintegration in Nigeria. Elsewhere I have discussed (1983) how ethnic inequalities in representation in the army and the civil service, and regional inequalities in petroleum expansion and inter-regional revenue allocation contributed to the Nigerian civil war, 1967–70.

The 1965 relative regional GDP per capita – £N19 in the North and £N25 in the south (including the East £N20, the West £N25, the Mid-West £N31, and Lagos £N123) – roughly corresponded to 1974 relative wealth holding (Teriba and Philips, 1971; Morrison, 1981). Northern rural farm families had only 58% of energy and protein intake required in 1965, while coastal rural farm families had 83% (ILO, 1981).

Average urban incomes in 1975 were highest in Lagos, East-Central, West, Mid-West, and South-Eastern, southern states with major commercial and industrial centres, or with major resources, like oil. Industrial capacity was also concentrated in Lagos and a few other states.

While revision of the revenue allocation formulas in 1975 reduced the government expenditure per capita (GEPC) ratio of the highest to lowest state from 8:1 in 1969–70 to 6:1 in 1975–6, Rivers, Mid-West (oil-rich coastal states), Lagos, and Kwara states still had a GEPC 4–5 times as high as Kano, North-East, West, and North-West states. Distribution of infrastructure and education by state was unequal. Annual electricity consumption per capita in 1976–7 (43 kwh nationwide) varied widely from 55 kwh in Mid-West, 70 in Rivers, and 728 in Lagos states to 3 in North-East and 6 the North-West (V = 276%). Primary enrolment as a percentage of children aged 6–11 (1976–7, just before UPE) was 61% in the south compared to 20% in the North (V = 58% for 12 states), while secondary enrolment rate as a percentage of children aged 12–17 was 15% in the south compared to 4% in the North (V = 94%). Population per postprimary institutions, 47,119 in the North compared to 25,925 in the south, varied from only 13,752 in Lagos and 17,734 in the Mid-West to 213,889 in Kano (V = 193%). University enrolment rates, highly correlated with primary and secondary rates, were 10 times as high in the highest state (Mid-West or Bendel) than the lowest (North-West) (computed from Diejomaoh and Anusionwu, 1981a; Diejomaoh and Anusionwu, 1981b; Ayeni, 1981).

Nigeria's health indicators varied widely geographically. Hospital beds (1972) ranged from Lagos state's 13 to Kano's, North-Western's, and North-Eastern's 1–2 per 10,000 population. Infant mortality per 1000 in the late 1970s was 79 in Lagos city, 97 in the West, and 170–180 in rural Nigeria. And 41% of the south's population (1978) had piped water compared to 10% of the North's (Diejomaoh, 1975; ILO, 1981).

KENYA

Kenya, with a 1976 GDP per capita of K£90.1, had substantial differences, ranging from K£539.8 in Nairobi and K£123.3 in Coast province to K£17.5 in Northeastern and K£33.1 in Western provinces (V = 116%, more than China's 29%, India's 30%, Nigeria's 76%, and Tanzania's 110% in 1966 and 70% in 1976) (Bigsten, 1977; Datt and Sundharam, 1983; World Bank, 1983, III). Moreover, 45% of Kenya's 1972 modern-sector employment was concentrated in 11 towns with a population exceeding 10,000, yet the share of these towns in the labour force was only 16% (Remple and House, 1978).

Kenya defined poverty among smallholder farm households, 1974–5 as an income falling below the poverty line corresponding to 2,250 calories per day per adult. The Thiel index indicates that only

4% of the variance in smallholder incomes is explained by inter-regional differences. Smallholder poverty rates in four provinces – Nyanza (50.7%), Western (47.7%), Coast (37.7%), and Rift Valley (36.5%) – exceeded the national poverty rate of 35.8%. Yet official data indicate that children in Central and Eastern provinces, with the highest average incomes and lowest poverty rates among smallholders, have the highest incidence of moderate protein energy malnutrition (PEM), while Nyanza, Western, and Coast children suffer the least PEM. Central and Eastern smallholders substituted cash crops for food crops, resulting in high malnutrition in Central and Eastern among children whose parents were farm labourers, village craftsmen, the unemployed, and the poorest smallholders (House and Killick, 1983; Collier and Lal, 1986).

Kenya's postindependence African bourgeoisie has been predominantly Kikuyu, tending to hire fellow Kikuyu for wage employment. By the end of the 1960s, Kikuyu officers with high levels of education and training reached middle ranks in the army and began challenging the previous dominance of Kamba or Kalenjin commanders. Moreover, a new mobile paramilitary force, the General Service unit, created under Kikuyu command, was independent of both the army and police and could be used independently for political control. Kikuyu control over the apparatus of coercion strengthened in June 1971, with the trial of thirteen non-Kikuyu who had plotted a *coup d'etat* (Leys, 1974).

Education, which varies widely among ethnic groups, is a prerequisite for power and economic standing. In 1962, the percentage of children, 5–9 years, with some primary schooling (34.6% nationwide) ranged from 56.0% for the Kikuyu and 50.8% for the Nandi to 14.9% for the Mijikenda and 13.0% for the Masai (V = 40%).

By province, primary school enrolment as a percentage of those aged 5–14, which averaged 40% in 1969 (five years before primary school fees were abolished), varied from 64% in Central and 61% in Nairobi to 4% in Northeastern (V = 34%). Even in 1975, after primary education was free and open to all, enrolment rates for children 6–13 years old (93% for Kenya) ranged from 116% in Central and 113% in Western provinces to 43% in Coast and Rift Valley provinces, and 9% in sparsely populated Northeastern province (V = 22%). (Rates are high not only because of parents mis-stating the age of children during the initial stage of fee abolition, but also because of a population understatement.) The high enrolment rates are in districts with high modern-sector participation and contact with mission schools. While primary schooling opportunities have become more widely available, qualitative differences are substantial, with the best schools in cities and centrally located areas (Court and Kinyanjui, 1980; Bukuku, 1985; Bigsten, 1977).

Secondary education enrolment was even more concentrated in Kenya in 1969, ranging from 46% (of the population, 15–19 years) in Nairobi to 8% in Western, 7% in Eastern and Nyanza, 6% in Rift Valley, and 1% in Northeastern, compared to a national average of 10% (V = 86%). Differences reflect factors discussed above, as well as regional discrepancies in the proportion of students receiving the CPE, which reflects differences in teacher credentials, spending on schools, and so forth.

Kenya has vast differences in access to social services by province. Nairobi, with 4.4% of the population in 1969, had 65.2% of 1970 National Housing Corporation (NHC) housing expenditure, 18.7% of 1970 secondary school enrolment, 152 people per hospital bed compared to 715 nation-wide, and 84 per medical practitioner compared to 871 for the whole country. In contrast, arid and semi-arid Northeastern province, with 2.2% of the population, had no NHC housing spending, 0.2% of secondary enrolment, 1,308 people per hospital bed, and 1,230 people per medical practitioner (ILO, 1972). The inter-provincial distribution of central government recurrent expenditures, 1973–4, was lopsided, ranging from Nairobi's K£70.76 and Coast province's K£13.07 per capita to Western's K£4.09, Northeastern's K£3.54, and Nyanza's K£3.28 (V = 138%) (Bigsten, 1977).

TANZANIA

The Tanganyika colonial government concentrated development efforts in those areas most developed, and neglected those that did not attract colonial interests. Thus in 1966, regional disparities in GDP per capita were wide. The richest region, Dar es Salaam (Tshs. 3,625), had a GDP per capita more than 12 times that of the poorest region, Iringa (Tshs.290) and more than 5 times the mean (Tshs.664). Regions comprising the top third, Dar es Salaam, Arusha, Tanga, Kilimanjaro, Tabora, and Shinyanga, generated 50.2% of GDP, while the poorest third, Mtwara, Ruruma, Singida, Kigoma, Dodoma, and Iringa, accounted for only 18.5%. The five main industrial and agricultural estates regions (Dar es Salaam, Arusha, Tanga, Kilimanjaro, and Morogoro) accounted for 60.4% of total wage employment. Moreover in Tanzania in the 1970s and early 1980s, the location of import-substitution industries with a few highly-skilled jobs in a few cities (mainly in these five regions) increased regional disparities in income and employment opportunities (Ndulu, 1982; Bukuku, 1985).

Since 1973–4, Tanzania promulgated uniform producer prices to equalise income earning opportunities for all farmers, irrespective of location. These policies taxed producers in regions with major local markets or export points, and subsidised producers located in high transport-cost regions, who increased their share of marketed output, especially of high bulk, low value items. Yet overall marketed production declined immediately and grew slowly thereafter, as closer regions reduced production because of lower inducements. Additionally food prices increased. Economies from specialisation due to location were nullified under the policy.

Additionally, Tanzania equalised inter-regional consumer prices on basic necessities like foodgrain, sugar, kerosene, soap, and basic construction materials, creating shortages of the commodities. Private distributors operated close to supply centres, neglecting distant regions. Hawkers bought from public distributors at controlled prices in these regions, selling at higher market prices. Since black market prices dominated, consumers in remote areas paid higher prices than they would have done without the price controls.

The Second Five-year Development Plan (1969–74), just after the Arusha Declaration, committed the government to decentralisation, requiring improved transport, decentralised construction materials, expanded technical training, market development, primary education, hospitals, and other social services in less developed regions, and shifting industrial development away from Dar es Salaam, the capital, major seaport, and largest city. Yet adding ten regional industrial centres to the five already existing had only limited success, as the lack of power, water, transport, markets, and materials resulted in production delays, interruptions, low capacity utilisation, and losses in the new centres.

Before 1972, districts and towns financed health, education, and transport from locally generated taxes, a function of income. This reinforced development polarisation. In 1972, in an attempt to reduce regional inequality, the central government abolished local governments and disbursed expenditures from a national revenue pool based on nationally determined needs. Centralised funding, together with decentralising services narrowed regional differences in income per capita, wage employment opportunities, health services, clean water, and education. Yet this approach proliferated new development projects, mostly externally financed, without corresponding increases in revenues to cover recurrent expenditures.

Population per doctor in Tanzania, a health indicator, ranged from Tanga's 14,725 to Coast region's 111,450, with a mean of 22,985. However, regions with few hospitals and high population–doctor ratios, like Coast, generally provided more dispensaries (Ndulu, 1982).

In Tanzania, wide variations in the regional distribution of education, the basis for modern-sector jobs, resulted from historical differentials in church and government educational activity.

Primary school enrolment in Tanzania (1969) as a proportion of children 15 years and below ranged from 50.7% in Dar es Salaam–Coast regions to 17.7% in Mwanza region, with a mean of 32.6% (V = 28%). Tanzania's 1975 primary rate, 59% (much lower than Kenya's) was an average based on variations from more than 90% for Dar es Salaam, 88% in Ruvuma, and 85% in Kilimanjaro provinces to 39% in Shinyanga and 42% in Mbeya provinces (V = 26%, more than Kenya's 1975 rate).

In 1977, Tanzania enrolled 90% of primary-age children in school and 98% in 1982, not far off the UPE goal. The government concentrated resources on previously neglected areas (especially rural children), pastoralists, and girls. The national school system was more homogeneous in quality than in Kenya, and selected secondary students on a more regional basis, so as to make access easier for underprivileged areas than was the case in Kenya. Yet government and private secondary schools in Tanzania are still concentrated in certain areas: Kilimanjaro and Mbeya regions have far more secondary schools than Lindi, Rukwa, Kigoma, and Singida regions. However, Tanzania's emphasis on mass adult education has brought it closer to the goal of universal literacy than Kenya (*ibid.*; Bukuku, 1985; Court and Kinyanjui, 1980).

CONCLUSION

Communal conflicts and discrepancies originating during colonialism (chapter 5) were often reinforced by postindependent policies that exacerbated regional and ethnic inequalities in income, employment, educational opportunities, and social services. Most elites receive their support from ethnic and regional bases, ally with other communal elites to control the state, and use this power to distribute benefits to their communities. Nigeria's, Kenya's, and Tanzania's ethnic and regional conflicts and inequalities are representative of Africa's generally, which divert attention from class grievances and impede economic development.

INCOME DISTRIBUTION IN THE LATE TWENTIETH CENTURY

POLICIES IN NEWLY INDUSTRIALISING COUNTRIES

Since African countries lack the centralised control and administrative capacity of Maoist China during its rapid growth and declining inequality, I will examine the non-socialist approaches of newly industrialising countries (NICs) Taiwan and South Korea, which improved income distribution and economic growth after World War II by land redistribution and reform, an emphasis on education, family planning programmes, and a focus on labour-intensive expansion in industry, especially in manufactured exports.

ILO research indicates that land redistribution to the poor not only improves distribution but also usually increases agricultural output, at least after a period of adjustment, for two reasons: a farmer who receives security of ownership is more likely to undertake improvements; and small farms often use more labour per hectare – labour that might not otherwise have been utilised. Where small-size farms have a lower productivity per hectare, it is usually because farmers are illiterate and so tend to adopt technological innovations slowly, or because they have virtually no access to credit (Berry and Cline, 1979).

Africa's ratio of higher to primary educational earnings is much higher than any other LDC region. Higher education per student costs more than eight times GNP per capita. Governments could redistribute income by abolishing subsidies (except for the poor) at the secondary and university levels. Moreover, Africa, which has the lowest primary enrolment rate of any world region, could redistribute resources to the poor by diverting spending from low-returning unequal university education to high-returning universal, free, primary education.

In the NICs, population programmes lowering fertility rates increased income equality by decreasing unemployment and increasing per capita expenditures on training and education. Moreover, programmes were sufficiently broadly based to affect the poor, whose living levels were improved by smaller family size since each adult had fewer dependents.

Chapters 9 and 11 indicate substantial scope for Africa to expand industrial employment by using more appropriate technology and promoting exports through market exchange rates. This would improve not only equality among the educated urban classes, but also the incomes of emigrants from rural areas.

The reason for being sceptical about whether the NICs' strategies for land redistribution, education, population programmes, and labour-intensive industry could work in Africa is not so much a technical but a political one. Leaders in African state agencies not only lack the freedom to innovate and design strategy that the NICs' leaders have but also are more likely to use their position to benefit class, regional, and ethnic interests.

We would expect land reform in most African countries, as in India, to fail because of the political opposition of the state bourgeoisie, or because, as in Kenya, it would redistribute not to the poor but to itself, allies, and clients.

Without political pressure from the masses, Africa's managerial bourgeoisie, which uses the advantages of schooling to transmit their high status to their children, is unlikely to spend on education to redistribute income. Even Tanzania's primary educational expansion and secondary educational contraction, while ostensibly to reduce inequality, actually curtailed public secondary opportunities for all income classes, including the poor. But subsidised primary education is not free to the poor student's family, who bears heavy direct and alternative costs. Moreover, Tanzania's use of examination scores to allocate secondary and university places favours the rich, who can spend for private primary education, examination preparation, or even repeating a year. Without wider political participation, we can expect African educational policy to maintain rather than undermine the class system.

Africa's 6.3 total fertility rate (the number of children born to the average women during her reproductive years) is the highest by far of any world region (with all LDCs 4.2). A successful family planning programme requires more than making a supply of contraceptives available; it also requires a demand for birth control, which depends on socio-economic changes like economic modernisation, education and literacy (especially among women), high female wage-force participation, and urbanisation. Africa's large peasant agricultural sector (where children are an economic asset), low literacy, and slow economic improvement for the masses mean that only a tiny (mostly affluent) minority are motivated to use family planning assistance when available. Given Africa's high child mortality rates, workers and peasants are not likely soon to risk insecurity in old age by further reducing family size.

Joint enterprises between foreign capitalists and parastatals in highly-protected import-substitution industry provide mutual benefits, including an expanded patronage base for African elites. Export manufactures, though, must compete on the world market, giving the ruling classes less largess, especially with labour-intensive production, to share with allies and clients. Indeed the export promotional strategy would compel the reduction of parastatal size, waste, and corruption that many African bourgeoisies use to support their rule.

POLICIES TO NARROW URBAN – RURAL DISCREPANCIES

Urban–rural discrepancies explain a large share of African inequality. Feasible techno-economic strategies are numerous. Government must spend more on agricultural investment and amenities. The state can establish separate loans agencies to handle the farmers' unique needs for credit between sowing and harvest. Where farms are too small to afford essential implements, government can rent machinery to several farmers to spread the cost over enough units to be economical. Agricultural research institutions can expand experimentation on ecological zones very different from the West, and reorient toward testing on farms, improving the productivity of crops (especially food) on which low-income farmers depend, and emphasising biochemical technology (fertiliser and new seeds) which, unlike mechanical technology, increases the demand for labour. Governments can improve the wages and career advancement for extension agents (including innovative veteran farmers), provide incentives to work with small farmers and women, and use the farmers' feedback to influence research priorities. Direct social investment in roads, schools, irrigation, drainage, and storage in poor, rural areas can increase income and jobs.

But policies to increase agricultural production, when demand for farm commodities is inelastic, will reduce the agricultural terms of trade and rural real income, and increase urban–rural inequalities in the short run. Thus, to reduce rural poverty, production-oriented programmes must be combined with price and exchange rate policies, improved rural services, land reform, and more rural industry.

Chapter 11 indicates that low-price food and low foreign-exchange price policies discourage domestic production, increase reliance on imports, and widen the urban–rural gap. The managerial bourgeoisie maintains vital urban support (especially among elites) by continuing these anti-agrarian price policies, but provides benefits to selected rural people to maximise the political advantage.

Urban areas have far more schools, medical services, piped water, and other amenities than rural areas. Improving rural services (as well as developing industries and retail enterprises complementary to agriculture) would not only help rural areas, but would also reduce rural–urban migration, thus alleviating urban congestion and blight. But as chapter 11 points out, rural middle and lower classes are rarely united enough to organise collectively to press the (primarily urban) national political leadership to increase their share of social spending.

Thus reducing urban–rural inequalities requires not only recognising techno-economic solutions but also the more difficult problem of finding major political interests who are willing to make changes.

OTHER POLICIES

Other types of programmes to reduce inequality – transfers to the poor, food subsidies or rations, redistribution through the tax system, and emphasis on target groups – face technical, administrative, or political barriers in many African countries.

In DCs (and a few upper-middle income LDCs like Brazil and Turkey), antipoverty programmes include income transfers to the old, the very young, the sick, the handicapped, the unemployed, and those whose earning power is below a living wage. But no black-ruled subsaharan African country can support such programmes. For example, in Uganda, where more than half the population is poor and undernourished (table 3), welfare payments to bring the population above the poverty line would undermine work incentives and be prohibitively expensive.

An alternative approach is to subsidise or ration cheap foodstuffs. Subsidising foods that higher income groups do not eat benefits the poor. For example, sorghum, introduced into ration shops in Bangladesh in 1978, was bought by nearly 70% of low-income households but by only 2% of high-income households (World Bank, 1980a).

Food subsidies or free rations for the poor, as were made available in Sri Lanka in the late 1960s and early to middle 1970s, not only reduce inequality, but lead to better health and nutrition, permit people to work more days in a year, and enhance their effectiveness at work. However, governments often either cannot afford the expense or pay the farmer low prices, creating disincentives that reduce long-run supply.

Africa relies heavily on indirect taxes that are regressive, where the poor pay a higher percentage of income in taxes than the rich. Tanzania is the only African country that has used its tax system to redistribute income to low-income classes. Chapter 8 indicates the trouble that Africa, short on administrative skills, has in enforcing income and other progressive taxes. But more importantly, property owners and upper classes, who comprise the political leadership, resist levying these taxes, introduce tax loopholes beneficial to themselves, or evade tax payments without penalty.

Another strategy is to target certain programmes for the poorest groups. India has schemes to favour the placement of outcastes and other economically 'backward castes' in educational institutions and government positions, industrial incentives and subsidies to help economically backward regions, and institutes to train business people from underprivileged groups. Other programmes aim to improve female literacy and educational rates, and stress health and nutritional programmes for expectant and nursing mothers and their children, provide improvements in social security and pensions for the elderly, and upgrade housing for the poor in urban areas. Of course, targeting the rural areas with programmes would do much to reduce poverty, most of which is concentrated in rural areas.

CONCLUSION

Implementing some of the policies mentioned in this chapter, as well as accelerating economic growth, depends on changing the composition of the state bourgeoisie. African economic stagnation and income inequality are interconnected, linked to a ruling class whose affluence and political survival are threatened by policies promoting decentralised economic decision-making, increased competition, redistribution to the underprivileged, and narrowing urban–rural incomes. The ruling-class use of the state to transfer resources from peasants, small farmers, unskilled workers, and the poor to parastatal managers, civil servants, intermediaries, farm estate owners, large commercial farmers, and other members of the managerial bourgeoisie reduces both growth and equality.

While this poverty and exploitation of the African majority exerts revolutionary pressures, the ruling class can increase repression and foreign support to maintain control. Moreover, the economically disadvantaged are rarely united since their interests vary; and in most instances, the ruling class can usually reward potentially restive groups who cooperate with it and thus remain in control. Even overthrowing this class merely ushers in another privileged elite rather than workers and peasants, who lack the strength and skill to win control of the state.

Africa is not capable of using Soviet-type comprehensive planning to redistribute income and reduce poverty, as it lacks the strong state and skilled administration needed to manage socialist industry. Indeed 'African socialism', initiated by a ruling state bourgeoisie rather than through revolutionary conflict, is really statism. Government enterprises, used to enrich the bourgeoisie and its clients, are plagued by overcapacity, high capital–labour ratios, and inefficiency. A state bureaucracy collectivising an agriculture which barely produces subsistence reduces farm living standards by acquiring resources for its own use, while lowering productivity through severing the link between individual effort and income. Tanzania's state bourgeoisie's authoritarian approach in managing collective and cooperative agriculture in the late 1960s and 1970s resulted in farm output declines. In Africa, the state is the major focus for class struggle by the working class against the bourgeoisie.

The role of the African state ruling class I presented before is not consistent with Huntington's view (1968) of the state as manager of the conflict and above clashes by various special and parochial interests within society. Indeed changing the anti-growth, anti-egalitarian interests of most of Africa's state bourgeoisie requires higher levels of popular mobilisation and mass participation in politics, the opposite of Huntington's prescription.[1]

Chapter 6 indicates that the nationalist movement for independence of African states was class-based, with workers and farmers uniting under bourgeois leadership to struggle against the colonial power for independence. Most African states, who viewed organised social forces outside government control as potential threats, assumed power over the trade unions (chapter 9).[2] Yet sometimes, as in Nigeria in May 1981, labour struck or protested against government control. Doubtless some of the opposition to the ruling bourgeoisie will have to come from the elements which some scholars regard as the 'labour aristrocracy'.

Agrarian leadership will not come from the most downtrodden or the well established, but from small farm holders and middle peasants, who have tactical power, a secure land holding, some education, and some knowledge (perhaps from children living in the city) of what is happening in the larger society (Markovitz, 1977). But rural-based groups are not capable of taking power by themselves, and need to form coalitions with labour leaders as well as elements within the intelligentsia, students, the civil service, politicians, the military, women's groups, religious communities, and aggrieved ethnic groups who stress redistribution and growth. In Africa, reducing poverty and income inequality requires democratising political participation as well as economic control.

NOTES

1 EQUALITY AND GROWTH: TRADEOFF OR INTERLINK?

1 Tariffs have a similar effect to subsidies. Government distorts prices, benefiting special interests, through redistributing income from consumers or merchants to industrialists.
2 In the 1980s, both Korea's and Sri Lanka's income inequalities increased.

4 THE GREAT DESCENT: INEQUALITY AND IMMISERISATION

1 The Middle East, when it includes high-income oil exporters (as in chapter 3's discussion), has greater income inequality than subsaharan Africa. But the Middle East, when it comprises only LDCs (as in table 2), has less inequality than the subsahara.
2 Problems defining a poverty line by the income needed to ensure a given supply of calories include: substantial caloric variation at a given level of expenditure; specifying a single caloric norm; variations in caloric requirements for the same individual; and the lack of consideration of protein, vitamins, minerals, and other nutrients. Furthermore, average caloric intake should vary for populations with different age and sex composition. See Bhanoji Rao, 1981.

Nevertheless, Scrimshaw and Taylor, 1981, indicate that as income rises the consumption of other nutrients rises along with calorie consumption.

5 THE COLONIAL ROOTS

1 Buganda refers to the land and Baganda to the people.

8 THE RULING CLASS AND THE PEOPLE: CONFLICT AND DISCREPANCIES

1 The term 'managerial bourgeoisie' is from Sklar, 1979.

11 URBAN BIAS AND RURAL POVERTY

1 But *severe* malnourishment rates are lower in rural than urban areas in Africa.

14 INCOME DISTRIBUTION IN THE LATE TWENTIETH CENTURY

1 See Nafziger, 1983, for elaboration of this criticism.
2 Leaders of the major South African black trade union organisation (the Congress of South African Trade Unions) indicated to the African National Congress they will not make the same mistake that labour did in other parts of Africa during the struggle for national liberation. They are determined that labour will not lose its independence to the African state bourgeoisie in a free Azania.

BIBLIOGRAPHY

The following abbreviations are used for journals cited frequently:
JMAS   *Journal of Modern African Studies*
ROAPE   *Review of African Political Economy*

BOOKS, MONOGRAPHS, AND ARTICLES

Abelson, P. H., ed. 1975. *Food: Politics, Economics, Nutrition, and Research*. Washington: American Association for the Advancement of Science.

Aboyade, O. 1973. 'Incomes Profile'. Inaugural Lecture delivered at the University of Ibadan. May.

1974. 'Closing Remarks'. In Nigerian Economic Society, *Nigeria's Indigenization Policy: Proceedings of the 1974 Symposium*. Ibadan.

Acharya, S. N. 1981a. 'Perspectives and Problems of Development in sub-Saharan Africa'. *World Development*, 9: 109–47.

1981b. 'Development Perspectives and Problems in sub-Saharan Africa'. *Finance and Development*, 18: 16–19.

Adedeji, A., ed. 1981. *Indigenization of African Economies*. London: Hutchinson.

1985. 'Foreign Debt and Prospects for Growth in Africa during the 1980s'. *JMAS*, 23(1): 53–74.

Adedeji, A., and Shaw, T. M., eds. 1985. *Economic Crisis in Africa: African Perspectives on Development Problems and Potentials*. Boulder, Colo.: Lynne Rienner.

Adelman, I., and Morris, C. T. 1973. *Economic Growth and Social Equity in Developing Countries*. Stanford: Stanford University Press.

Adelman, I., and Robinson, S. 1978. *Income Distribution Policy in Developing Countries: A Case Study of Korea*. Stanford: Stanford University Press.

Adepoju, A. 1975. 'Migration and the Urban Poor in Nigeria's Medium-size Towns'. In Nigerian Economic Society, pp. 125–48.

Ahluwalia, M. S. 1974. 'Income Inequality: Some Dimensions of the Problem'. In Chenery et al., pp. 7–17.

Ahluwalia, M. S., Carter, N. G., and Chenery, H. B. 1979. 'Growth and Poverty in Developing Countries'. *Journal of Development Economics*, 6: 299–341.

Aidoo, T. A. 1983. 'Ghana: Social Class, the December Coup, and the Prospects for Socialism'. *Contemporary Marxism*, no. 6: 142–59.

Ake, C. 1981. 'The Political Context of Indigenization'. In Adedeji, ed., pp. 32–41.

Allen, V. L. 1972. 'The Meaning of the Working Class in Africa'. *JMAS*, 10(2): 169–89.

Aluko, S. A. 1971. 'Prices, Wages and Costs'. In A. A. Ayida and H. M. A. Onitiri, eds., *Reconstruction and Development in Nigeria – Proceedings of a National Conference*. Ibadan: Oxford University Press, pp. 419–41.

Amin, S. 1973. *Neo-colonialism in West Africa*. Trans. F. McDonagh. New York: Monthly Review Press.

Arrighi, G., and Saul, J. 1968. 'Socialism and Economic Development in Tropical Africa'. *JMAS*, 6(2): 141–69.

Ayeni, B. 1981. 'Spatial Aspects of Urbanization and Effects on the Distribution of Income in Nigeria'. In Bienen and Diejomaoh, eds., pp. 237–68.

Bakary, T. 1984. 'Elite Transformation and Political Succession'. In Zartman and Delgado, eds., pp. 21–56.

Barkan, J. D. 1975. *An African Dilemma: University Students, Development and Politics in Ghana, Tanzania and Uganda*. Nairobi: Oxford University Press.

Barongo, Y. R. 1984. 'The De-Embourgeoisement of Ugandan Society: The First State in the Break with International Capitalism'. *JMAS*, 11(3): 100–9.

Bates, R. H. 1981. *Markets and States in Tropical Africa: The Political Basis of Agricultural Policies*. Berkeley and Los Angeles: University of California Press.

Bauer, P. T. 1981. *Equality, the Third World, and Economic Delusion*. London: Weidenfeld and Nicolson.

Benjamin, N. C., and Devarajan, S. 1986. 'Oil Revenues and the Cameroonian Economy'. In Schatzberg and Zartman, eds., pp. 161–88.

Bequele, A., and Van der Hoeven, R. 1980. 'Poverty and Inequality in sub-Saharan Africa'. *International Labour Review*, 119(3): 381–92.

Berg, E. J. 1964. 'Socialism and Economic Development in Tropical Africa'. *Quarterly Journal of Economics*, 78(4): 549–73.

Berry, R. A., and Cline, W. R. 1979. *Agrarian Structure and Productivity in Developing Countries*. Baltimore: Johns Hopkins University Press.

Berry, S. 1984. 'The Food Crisis and Agrarian Change in Africa: A Review Essay'. *African Studies Review*, 27(2): 59–112.

Bettelheim, C. 1976. *Class Struggles in the USSR*, vol. I. New York: Monthly Review Press.

1978. *Class Struggles in the USSR*, vol. II. New York: Monthly Review Press.

Bhanoji Rao, V. V. 1981. 'Measurement of Deprivation and Poverty Based on the Proportion of Food: An Explanatory Exercise'. *World Development*, 9: 337–53.

Bienefeld, M. A. 1975. 'Socialist Development and the Workers in Tanzania'. In Sandbrook and Cohen, eds., pp. 239–60.

1979. 'Trade Unions, the Labour Process, and the Tanzanian State'. *JMAS*, 17(4): 553–93.

Bienen, H. 1981. 'The Politics of Distribution: Institutions, Class, and Ethnicity'. In Bienen and Diejomaoh, eds., pp. 127–71.

Bienen, H., and Diejomaoh, V. P., eds. 1981. *The Political Economy of Income Distribution in Nigeria*. New York: Holmes and Meier.

Bigsten, A. 1977. 'Regional Inequality in Kenya'. Institute for Development Studies Working Paper No. 330, University of Nairobi, Kenya.

1984. *Education and Income Determination in Kenya*. Aldershot, Eng.: Gower.

Birmingham, W., Neustadt, I., and Omaboe, E. N. 1966. *A Study of Contemporary Ghana*, vol. I. [The Economy of Ghana]. Evanston: Northwestern University Press.

Boissiere, M., Knight, J. B., and Sabot, R. H. 1985. 'Earnings, Schooling, Ability, and Cognitive Skills'. *American Economic Review*, 75(5): 1016–30.

Bond, M. E. 1983. 'Agricultural Responses to Prices in Sub-Saharan African Countries'. *IMF Staff Papers*, 30(4): 703–26.

Bowles, S. 1978. 'Capitalist Development and Educational Structure'. *World Development*, 6(6): 783–96.

Bukuku, E. S. 1985. 'Income Distribution in Tanzania'. Paper presented to a UN Conference on Income Distribution. New York.

Callaway, B. 1975. 'The Political Economy of Nigeria'. In R. Harris, *The Political Economy of Africa*. New York: Schenkman, pp. 93–136.

Campbell, B. K. 1985. 'The Fiscal Crisis of the State: The Case of the Ivory Coast'. In H. Bernstein and B. K. Campbell, eds., *Contradictions of Accumulation in Africa*. Beverly Hills, Calif.: Sage Publications, pp. 267–310.

Campbell, J. R. 1984. 'Class and State in the Political Economy of Ghana, 1957–1979'. *Mawazo*, 5(4): 82–97.

Cesaire, A. 1970. 'On the Nature of Colonialism'. In I. L. Markovitz, ed., *African Politics and Society: Basic Issues and Problems of Government and Development*. New York: Free Press.

Chenery, H., Ahluwalia, M. S., Bell, C. L. G., Duloy, J. H., and Jolly, R. 1974. *Redistribution with Growth*. London: Oxford University Press.

Chenery, H., and Syrquin, M. 1975. *Patterns of Development, 1950–1976* London: Oxford University Press.

Cleaver, K. M. 1985. 'The Impact of Price and Exchange Rate Policies on Agriculture in Sub-Saharan Africa'. World bank Staff Working Paper No. 728, Washington.

Clower, R. W., Dalton, G., Harwitz, M., and Walters, A. A. 1966. *Growth without Development: An Economic Survey of Liberia*. Evanston: Northwestern University Press.

Coleman, J. S. 1958. *Nigeria: Background to Nationalism*. Berkeley: University of California Press.

Collier, P. 1983. 'Oil and Inequality in Rural Nigeria'. In Ghai and Radwan, eds., pp. 191–217.

Collier, P., and Lal, D. 1984. 'Why Poor People Get Rich: Kenya, 1960–79'. *World Development*, 12(10): 1007–18.

1986. *Labour and Poverty in Kenya, 1900–1980*. Oxford: Clarendon Press.

Coulson, A. 1982. *Tanzania: A Political Economy*. Oxford: Clarendon Press.

Court, D., and Kinyanjui, K. 1980. 'Development Policy and Educational Opportunity: The Experience of Kenya and Tanzania'. Institute for Development Studies Occasional Paper No. 33, University of Nairobi, Kenya.

Cowen, M. 1986. 'Change in State Power, International Conditions, and Peasant Producers: The Case of Kenya'. *The Journal of Development Studies*, 22(2): 355–84.

Currie, K., and Ray, L. 1984. 'State and Class in Kenya – Notes on the Cohesion of the Ruling Class'. *JMAS*, 22(4): 559–93.

Curtin, P., Feierman, S., Thompson, L., and Vansina, J. 1978. *African History*. Boston: Little, Brown, and Co.

Date-Bah, E. 1982. 'Sex Inequality in an African Urban Labour Market: The Case of Accra-Tema'. Geneva, ILO World Employment Programme 2–21/WP 122.

Datt, R., and Sundharam, K. P. M. 1983. *Indian Economy*. New Delhi: S. Chand.

DeLancey, M. W. 1986. 'Cameroon's Foreign Relations'. In Schatzberg and Zartman, eds., pp. 189–217.

DeLancey, V. 1986. 'Agricultural Productivity in Cameroon'. In Schatzberg and Zartman, eds., pp. 133–60.

Dennis, C. 1983. 'Capitalist Development and Women's Work: A Nigerian Case Study'. *ROAPE*, no. 27/28: 109–19.

Diejomaoh, V. P., and Anusionwu, E. C. 1981a. 'Education and Income Distribution in Nigeria'. In Bienen and Diejomaoh, eds., pp. 373–420.

1981b. 'The Structure of Income Inequality in Nigeria: A Macro Analysis'. In Bienen and Diejomaoh, eds., pp. 89–125.

Dillard, D. 1972. 'Capitalism'. *Encyclopaedia Britannica*, pp. 839–42.

Dobb, M. 1926. *Capitalist Enterprise and Social Progress*. London: George Routledge and Sons.

Dudley, B. J. 1968. *Parties and Politics in Northern Nigeria*. London: Frank Cass.

1972. 'The Politics of Adebo'. *Quarterly Journal of Administration*, 6(3): 131-70.

Eberstadt, N. 1979. 'China: How Much Success?' *New York Review of Books*, (3 May): 38–44.

ECA. 1983a. *Commodity Market Structures, Pricing Policies and Their Impact on African Trade*. E/ECA/TRADE/3, Addis Ababa.

1983b. 'ECA and Africa's Development, 1983–2008: A Preliminary Perspective Study. Addis Ababa.

1983c. *Economic and Survey of Africa, 1958–1983*. E/ECA/CM. 9/20, Addis Ababa.

1985. *Survey of Economic and Social Conditions in Africa, 1983–1984*. E/ECA/CM. 11/16, Addis Ababa.

Eicher, C. K., and Baker, D. C. 1982. *Research on Agricultural Development in Subsaharan Africa: A Critical Survey*. East Lansing, Mich.: Michigan State University International Development Paper No. 1.

Fajana, O. 1981. 'Aspects of Income Distribution in the Nigerian Urban Sector'. In Bienen and Diejomaoh, eds., pp. 193–236.

Falae, S. O. 1971. 'Unemployment in Nigeria'. *Nigerian Journal of Economic and Social Studies*, 13(1): 59–75.

Fanon, F. 1963. *The Wretched of the Earth*. Trans. C. Farrington. New York: Grove Press.

Fieldhouse, D. K. 1986. *Black Africa, 1945–80: Economic Decolonization and Arrested Development.* London: Allen and Unwin.

FAO. 1977. *The Fourth FAO World Food Survey.* Rome.

Forrest, T. 1986. 'The Political Economy of Civil Rule and the Economic Crisis in Nigeria'. *ROAPE*, no. 35: 4–26.

Freund, W. M. 1981. 'Class Conflict, Political Economy and the Struggle for Socialism in Tanzania'. *African Affairs*, 80: 483–500.

Galtung, J. 1971. 'A Structural Theory of Imperialism'. *Journal of Peace Research*, no. 2: 81–118.

Gbetibouo, M., and Delgado, C. L. 1984. 'Lessons and Constraints of Export Crop-led Growth: Cocoa in Ivory Coast'. In Zartman and Delgado, eds., pp. 115–47.

Ghai, D. 1980. 'Basic Needs: From Words to Action – With Illustrations from Kenya'. *International Labour Review*, 119(3): 367–79.

Ghai, D., Godfrey, M., and Lisk, F. 1979. *Planning for Basic Needs in Kenya: Performance, Policies and Prospects.* Geneva: ILO.

Ghai, D., and Radwan, S., eds. 1983. *Agrarian Policies and Rural Poverty in Africa.* Geneva: ILO.

Good, K. 1986. 'The Reproduction of Weakness in the State and Agriculture: The Zambian Experience'. *African Affairs*, 85: 239–65.

Goreux, L. M. 1980. 'Compensatory Financing Facility'. International Monetary Fund Pamphlet Series No. 34, Washington.

Gran, G., ed. 1979. *Zaïre: The Political Economy of Underdevelopment.* New York: Praeger.

Gregory, P. R., and Stuart, R. C. 1986. *Soviet Economic Structure and Performance.* New York: Harper and Row.

Griffin, K. 1978. *International Inequality and National Poverty.* London: Macmillan.

Grosh, M. E., and Nafziger, E. W. 1986. 'The Computation of World Income Distribution'. *Economic Development and Cultural Change*, 34: 347–59.

Grubel, H. G. 1981. *International Economics.* Homewood, Ill.: Irwin.

Gugler, J., and Flanagan, W. G. 1978. *Urbanization and Social Change in West Africa.* Cambridge: Cambridge University Press.

Gutteridge, W. 1985. 'Undoing Military Coups in Africa'. *Third World Quarterly*, 7(1): 78–89.

Hance, W. A. 1967. *African Economic Development.* New York: Praeger.

Harris, J. R., and Todaro, M. P. 1970. 'Migration, Unemployment and Development: A Two-sector Analysis'. *American Economic Review*, 60(1): 126–42.

Hazlewood, A. 1985. 'Kenyan Land-Transfer Programmes and their Relevance for Zimbabwe'. *JMAS*, 23(3): 445–61.

Heilbroner, R. L. 1963. *The Great Ascent: The Struggle for Economic Development in our Time.* New York: Harper and Row.

Helleiner, G. K. 1975. 'Smallholder Decision Making: Tropical African Evidence'. In L. G. Reynolds, ed., *Agriculture in Development Theory.* New Haven: Yale University Press.

Henissart, P. 1973. *Wolves in the City: The Death of French Algeria.* New York: Simon and Schuster.

Higgins, B. 1968. *Economic Development: Problems, Principles, and Policies.* New York: Norton.

Hill, P. 1970. *Studies in Rural Capitalism in West Africa.* Cambridge: Cambridge University Press.

Hinchliffe, K. 1975. 'Education, Individual Earnings and Earnings Distribution'. *Journal of Development Studies,* 11: 149–61.

Hirschmann, D. 1987. 'State, Peasantry and Rural Poverty in Malawi'. To be published in *Policy Studies Journal,* 16(1).

Holtham, G., and Hazlewood, A. 1976. *Aid and Inequality in Kenya: British Development Assistance to Kenya.* London: Croom Helm.

Hopkins, A. G. 1973. *An Economic History of West Africa.* London: Longman.

Hopkins, R. F. 1971. *Political Roles in a New State: Tanzania's First Decade.* New Haven: Yale University Press.

House, W. J., and Killick, T. 1983. 'Social Justice and Development Policy in Kenya's Rural Economy'. In Ghai and Radwan, eds., pp. 31–69.

Hunt, D. 1984. *The Impending Crisis in Kenya: The Case for Land Reform.* Gower: Aldershot.

Huntington, S. P. 1968. *Political Order in Changing Societies.* New Haven: Yale University Press.

Hyden, G. 1980. *Beyond Ujamaa in Tanzania: Underdevelopment and an Uncaptured Peasantry.* London: Heinemann.

IFPRI. 1977. *Food Needs of Developing Countries: Projections of Production and Consumption to 1990.* Research Report 3. Washington.

ILO. 1972. *Employment, Incomes, and Equality: A Strategy for Increasing Productive Employment in Kenya.* Geneva.

Jobs and Skills Programme for Africa. 1977a. *Employment Problems in the Rural and Informal Sectors in Ghana.* Addis Ababa.

Jobs and Skills Programme for Africa. 1977b. *Narrowing the Gaps: Planning for Basic Needs and Productive Employment in Zambia.* Addis Ababa.

1979. *Profiles of Rural Poverty.* Geneva.

Jobs and Skills Programme for Africa. 1981. *First Things First: Meeting the Basic Needs of the People of Nigeria.* Addis Ababa.

Jobs and Skills Programme for Africa. 1982a. *Rural–urban Gap and Income Distribution: Synthesis Report.* Addis Ababa.

Jobs and Skills Programme for Africa. 1982b. *Rural–urban Gap and Income Distribution: The Case of Ghana.* Addis Ababa.

IMF. 1986. *World Economic Outlook.* Washington.

Jackson, H. F. 1982. *From the Congo to Soweto: U. S. Foreign Policy toward Africa since 1960.* New York: William Morrow.

Jackson, R. H., and Rosberg, C. G. 1984. 'Popular Legitimacy in African Multi-Ethnic States'. *JMAS,* 22(2): 177–98.

Jain, S. 1975. *Size Distribution of Income: A Compilation of Data.* Washington: World Bank.

Jeffries, R. 1975a. 'The Labour Aristocracy? Ghana Case Study'. *ROAPE,* no. 3: pp. 59–70.

1975b. 'Populist Tendencies in the Ghanaian Trade Union Movement'. In Sandbrook and Cohen, eds., pp. 261–80.

1982. 'Rawlings and the Political Economy of Underdevelopment in Ghana'. *African Affairs*, 81: 307–17.

Jewsiewicki, B. 1979. 'Zaire Enters the World System: Its Colonial Incorporation as the Belgian Congo, 1885–1960'. In Gran, ed., pp. 29–53.

Jimenez, E. 1986. 'The Public Subsidization of Education and Health in Developing Countries: A Review of Equity and Efficiency'. *World Bank Research Observer*, 1: 111–29.

Kaldor, N. 1975. 'Will Underdeveloped Countries Learn to Tax?' In R. M. Bird and O. Oldman, eds., *Readings on Taxation in Developing Countries*. Baltimore: Johns Hopkins University Press, pp. 29–48.

Kannyo, E. 1979. 'Postcolonial Politics in Zaïre, 1960–79'. In Gran, ed., pp. 54–68.

Kennedy, P. 1977. 'Indigenous Capitalism in Ghana'. *ROAPE*, no. 8: pp. 21–37.

Kenya, Government of. 1978. *Development Plan: 1979–83*, Nairobi.

1983. *Development Plan: For the Period 1984 to 1988*. Nairobi.

Khan, A. U. 1974. 'Appropriate Technologies: Do We Transfer, Adapt, or Develop?' In E. O. Edwards, ed., *Employment in Developing Countries*. New York: Columbia University Press, pp. 223–33.

Kilby, P. 1964. 'Technical Education in Nigeria'. *Bulletin of the Oxford University Institute of Economics and Statistics*, 26(2) (May): 181–9.

1969. *Industrialization in an Open Economy: Nigeria, 1945–1966*. Cambridge: Cambridge University Press.

Killick, T. 1978. *Development Economics in Action: A Study of Economic Policies in Ghana*. London: Heinemann.

Kirkpatrick, C., and Diakosavvas, D. 1985. 'Food Insecurity and Foreign-Exchange Constraints in Sub-Saharan Africa'. *JMAS*, 23(2): 326–42.

Kitching, G. 1980. *Class and Economic Change in Kenya: The Making of an African Petite Bourgeoisie, 1905–1970*. New Haven: Yale University Press.

Knight, J. B., and Sabot, R. H. 1983. 'Educational Expansion and the Kuznets Effect'. *American Economic Review*, 73(5): 1132–6.

Kouadio, Y. 1985. 'Socio-economic Impact of IMF Stabilization Programs: The Case of the Ivory Coast'. Paper presented to a conference on Brazil and the Ivory Coast: the Socioeconomic Impact of International Lending, Investment, and Aid. University of Illinois, Urbana, 15–16 April.

Kravis, I. B. 1986. 'The Three Faces of the International Comparison Project'. *World Bank Research Observer*, 1: 1–26.

Kravis, I. B., Heston, A. W., and Summers, R. 1978. 'Real GDP Per Capita'. *Economic Journal*, 88: 215–42.

Kuznets, Simon. 1955. 'Economic Growth and Income Inequality'. *American Economic Review*, 45(1): 1–28.

Kydd, J. G. 1984. 'Malawi in the 1970s: Development Policies and Economic Change'. Paper presented to a Conference on Malawi: An Alternative Pattern of Development, Edinburgh University, Centre of African Studies.

Kydd, J. G., and Christiansen, R. E. 1982. 'Structural Change in Malawi since

Independence: Consequences of a Development Strategy based on Large-scale Agriculture'. *World Development*, 10(5): 355–74.

Lancaster, C., and Williamson, J., eds. 1986. *African Debt and Financing*. Washington: Institute for International Economics.

Langdon, S., 1980. *Multinational Corporations in the Political Economy of Kenya*. London: Macmillan.

Lardner, G. E.A. 1985. 'Beyond the Neocolonial Nexus: Inheritance, Implementation, and Implications of the *Lagos Plan of Action*'. In Adedeji and Shaw, eds., pp. 35–46.

Lecaillon, J., Paukert, F., Morrisson, C., and Germidis, D. 1984. *Income Distribution and Economic Development*. Geneva: International Labour Office.

Lee, E. 1983. 'Export-led Development: The Ivory Coast'. In Ghai and Radwan, eds., pp. 99–128.

Lemarchand, R. 1972. 'Political Clientalism and Ethnicity in Tropical Africa: Competing Solidarities in Nation-Building'. *American Political Science Review*, 66: 68–90.

1979. 'The Politics of Penury in Rural Zaïre: The View from Bandundu'. In Gran, ed., pp. 237–60.

Leys, C. 1974. *Underdevelopment in Kenya: The Political Economy of Neo-Colonialism*. Berkeley and Los Angeles: University of California Press.

1978, 'Capital Accumulation, Class Formation and Dependency'. *Socialist Register*, 33: 232–47.

Lipton, M. 1977. *Why Poor People Stay Poor: A Study of Urban Bias in World Development*. London: Maurice Temple Smith.

Livingstone, I. 1981. 'The Distribution of Income and Welfare'. In ILO, Jobs and Skills Programme for Africa (JASPA). *Rural Development, Employment, and Incomes in Kenya*. Addis Ababa.

Lofchie, M. F. 1974. 'The Political Origins of the Uganda Coup'. *Journal of Modern African Studies*, 12(4) (Dec.): 489–97.

Loxley, J. 1986. 'The IMF and World Bank Conditionality and sub-Saharan Africa'. In P. Lawrence, ed., *World Recession and the Food Crisis in Africa*. London: James Currey, pp. 96–103.

Luke, D. F., and Shaw, T. M., eds. 1984. *Continental Crisis: The Lagos Plan of Action and Africa's Future*. Lanham, Md.: University Press of America.

McGowan, P., and Johnson, T. H. 1984. 'African Military Coups d'Etat and Underdevelopment: a Quantitative Historical Analysis'. *JMAS*, 22(4): 633–66.

McGrath, M. D. 1977. 'Racial Income Distribution in South Africa'. Black/White Income Gap Research Report No. 2. Department of Economics, University of Natal, Durban.

1984. 'Inequality in the Size Distribution of Incomes in South Africa'. Staff Paper No. 2, Development Studies Unit, University of Natal, Durban.

McLaughlin, M. M. and the Staff of the Overseas Development Council. 1979. *The United States and World Development: Agenda, 1979*. New York: Praeger.

Makala-Lizumu, and Elas, M. 1979. 'Modernization and Urban Poverty: A Case Study of Kinshasa'. In Gran, ed., pp. 108–21.

Mamdani, M. 1976. *Politics and Class Formation in Uganda*. New York. Monthly Review Press.

1983. *Imperialism and Fascism in Uganda*. London: Heinemann.

Manley, J. 1983. 'Neopluralism: a Class Analysis of Pluralism I and Pluralism II'. *American Political Science Review*, 77(2): 368–89.

Mapolu, H. 1984. 'Imperialism, the State, and the Peasantry in Tanzania.' *Mawazo*, 5(3): 3–17.

Marcussen, H., and Torp, J. 1982. *Internationalization of Capital: Prospects for the Third World*. London: Zed Press.

Markovitz, I. L. 1977. *Power and Class in Africa: An Introduction to Change and Conflict in African Politics*. Englewood Cliffs, N. J.: Prentice-Hall.

Martin, C. J. 1984. 'The Agrarian Question and Migrant Labor: The Case of Western Kenya'. *JMAS*, 11(4): 164–74.

Marx, K., and Engels, F. 1953. *On Britain*. Moscow: Foreign Languages House.

Matlon, P. 1981. 'The Structure of Production and Rural Incomes in Northern Nigeria'. In Bienen and Diejomaoh, eds., pp. 323–72.

Mingat, A., and Psacharopoulos, G. 1985. 'Financing Education in sub-Saharan Africa'. *Finance and Development*, 22 (March): 35–8.

Morawetz, D. 1974. 'Employment Implications of Industrialization in Developing Countries'. *Economic Journal*, 84: 491–526.

1977. *Twenty-five Years of Economic Development, 1950 to 1975*. Baltimore: Johns Hopkins University Press for the World Bank.

Morrison, D. G. 1981. 'Inequalities of Social Rewards: Realities and Perceptions in Nigeria'. In Bienen and Diejomaoh, eds., pp. 173–92.

Morss, E. R. 1984. 'Institutional Destruction Resulting from Donor and Project Proliferation in Sub-Saharan African Countries'. *World Development*, 12(4): 465–70.

Mukandala, R. S. 1983. 'Bureaucracy and Socialism in Tanzania: The Case of the Civil Service'. *African Review*, 10(2): 1–21.

Mytelka, L. K. 1984. 'Foreign Business and Economic Development'. In Zartman and Delgado, eds., pp. 149–73.

Nafziger, E. W. 1969. 'The Effect of the Nigerian Extended Family on Entrepreneurial Activity'. *Economic Development and Cultural Change*, 18(1): 25–33.

1976. 'A Critique of Development Economics in the U. S.' *Journal of Development Studies*, 13(1): 18–34.

1977. *African Capitalism: A Case Study in Nigerian Entrepreneurship*. Stanford, Calif.: Hoover Institution Press.

1978. *Class, Caste, and Entrepreneurship*. Honolulu: University Press of Hawaii.

1983. *The Economics of Political Instability: The Nigerian–Biafran War*. Boulder, Colo.: Westview.

1984. *The Economics of Developing Countries*. Belmont, Calif.: Wadsworth.

1985a. 'India vs. China: Economic Development Performance'. *Dalhousie Review*, 65(2): 366–92.

1985b. 'The Japanese Development Model'. In H. F. Didsbury, ed., *The Global Economy: Today, Tomorrow, and the Transition*. Bethesda, Md.: World Future Society, pp. 111–34.

1986. *Entrepreneurship, Equity, and Economic Development,* Greenwich, Conn.: JAI Press.

Nattrass, J. 1979. 'Poverty and Uneven Development in South Africa'. Paper presented to the Conference on Global Poverty in Santa Monica, Calif., 1–2 February.

Ndongko, W. A. 1986. 'The Political Economy of Development in Cameroon: Relations between the State, Indigenous Business, and Foreign Investors'. In Schatzberg and Zartman, eds., pp. 83–110.

Ndulu, B. J. 1982. 'Unequal Regional Distribution of Economic Opportunities in Tanzania and Affirmative Policy Efforts Towards Equalization'. Economic Research Bureau Seminar, University of Dar es Salaam, Dar es Salaam, 20 July.

Newbury, M. C. 1984. 'Dead and Buried or Just Underground? The Privatization of the State in Zaire'. *Canadian Journal of African Studies,* 18(1): 112–14.

Ng'ethe, N. 1980. 'Income Distribution in Kenya: The Politics of Mystification'. In J. F. Rweyemamu, ed., *Industrialization and Income Distribution in Africa.* Dakar, Senegal: Codesria, pp. 191–213.

1984. 'The State and the Evolution of the Peasantry in Kenyan Agriculture: A Summary of Well-known Issues'. *Mawazo,* 5(3): 18–34.

N'Guessan, T. 1985. 'The Socio-economic Impact of the World Bank and the African Development Bank on African Countries: The Case of the Ivory Coast'. Paper presented to a conference on Brazil and the Ivory Coast: the Socioeconomic Impact of International Lending, Investment, and Aid. University of Illinois, Urbana. 15–16 April.

Nicolson, I. F. 1969. *The Administration of Nigeria, 1900–1960: Men, Methods, and Myths.* Oxford: Clarendon Press.

Nigeria, Ministry of Economic Development. 1975. *Third National Development Plan, 1975–80,* 2 vols. Lagos: Central Planning Office.

Nigeria, Ministry of Information. 1970. *Second National Development Plan, 1970–74.* Lagos: Federal Government Printer.

Nigeria, Office of Statistics. 1968. *Population Census of Nigeria, 1963.* 3 vols. Lagos.

Nigerian Economic Society. 1975. *Poverty in Nigeria: Proceedings of the 1975 Annual Conference of the Nigerian Economic Society.* Ibadan University Press.

Nkrumah, K. 1965. *Neo-Colonialism: The Last Stages of Imperialism.* London: Nelson.

1970. *Class Struggles in Africa.* New York: International Publishers.

1973. *Revolutionary Path.* New York: International Publishers.

Nove, A. 1983. *The Economics of Feasible Socialism.* London: George Allen and Unwin.

Nugent, J. B. 1983. 'An Alternative Source of Measurement Error as an Explanation for the Inverted-U Hypothesis'. *Economic Development and Cultural Change,* 31: 385–96.

Nyerere, J. K. 1968. *Ujamaa – Essays on Socialism.* New York: Oxford University Press.

1977. *The Arusha Declaration Ten Years After.* Dar es Salaam: Government Printer.

Nyongo, P. A. 1984. 'Accelerated Development and Industrialization in Africa'. *Mawazo*, 5(4): 3–30.

Odufalu, J. O. 1981. 'The Distributive Impact of Public Expenditures in Nigeria'. In Bienen and Diejomaoh, eds., pp. 455–83.

Ogbuagu, C. S. A. 1983. 'The Nigerian Indigenization Policy: Nationalism or Pragmatism?' *African Affairs*, 82: 241–66.

Ohiorhenuan, J. F. E. 1984. 'The Political Economy of Military Rule in Nigeria'. *ROAPE*, no. 16(2&3): 1–27.

Okigbo, P. N. C. 1975. 'Interpersonal Income Distribution in Nigeria'. In Nigerian Economic Society, pp. 313–29.

Okotie-Eboh, F. S. 1965. *The Redication Budget: Budget Speech, 31st March 1965*. Lagos: Federal Ministry of Information.

Olayide, S. O., and Essang, S. M. 1975. 'Aspects of Rural Poverty in Nigeria: Implications for Policy'. In Nigerian Economic Society, pp. 153–64.

Omorogiuwa, P. A. 1981. 'Personal Income Taxation and Income Distribution in Nigeria'. In Bienen and Diejomaoh, eds., pp. 421–53.

Organisation of African Unity. First Economic Summit of the Assembly of Heads of State and Government. 1980. *Plan of Action for the Implementation of the Monrovia Strategy for the Economic Development of Africa Recommended by the ECA Conference of Ministers Responsible for Economic Development at its Sixth Meeting Held at Addis Ababa, 9–12 April 1980* (called Lagos Plan of Action). Lagos, Nigeria, 28–29 April.

Osuntogun, A. 1975. 'Poverty as an Issue in Rural Development Policy: A Case Study from the Western State of Nigeria'. In Nigerian Economic Society, pp. 191–9.

Papanek, G. F. 1967. *Pakistan's Development: Social Goals and Private Incentives*. Cambridge, Mass.: Harvard University Press.

Parpart, J. L. 1986. 'Women and the State in Africa'. In D. Rothchild and N. Chazan, eds., *The Precarious Balance*. Boulder, Colo.: Westview, pp. 278–92.

Patel, S. J. 1964. 'Economic Transition in Africa'. *JMAS*, 2(1): 329–49.

Peace, A. 1975. 'The Lagos Proletariat: Labour Aristocrats or Populist Militants?' In Sandbrook and Cohen, eds., pp. 281–302.

Pearson, L., *et al.*, 1969. *Partners in Development: Report of the Commission on International Development*. New York: Praeger.

Population Reference Bureau. 1986. *1986 World Population Data Sheet*. Washington.

Price, R. M. 1984. 'Neo-Colonialism and Ghana's Economic Decline: A Critical Assessment'. *Canadian Journal of African Studies*, 18(1): 163–93.

Rajalakshmi, R. 1975. *Pre-school Child Malnutrition*. Baroda, India: University of Baroda Press.

Rawls, J. 1971. *A Theory of Justice*. Cambridge, Mass.: Belknap Press of Harvard University Press.

Remple, H., and House, W. J. 1978. *The Kenya Employment Problem: An Analysis of the Modern Sector Labour Market*. Oxford: Oxford University Press.

Ridler, N. B. 1985. 'Comparative Advantage as a Development Model: the Ivory Coast'. *JMAS*, 23(3): 407–17.

Rimmer, D. 1984. *The Economies of West Africa*. London: Weidenfeld and Nicolson.

Robinson, J. 1949. *An Essay on Marxian Economics*. London: Macmillan.

Rodney, W. 1982. *How Europe Underdeveloped Africa*. Washington: Howard University Press.

Roemer, M. 1985. 'Dutch Disease in Developing Countries: Swallowing Bitter Medicine'. In M. Lundahl, ed. *The Primary Sector in Economic Development*. New York: St. Martin's, pp. 234–52.

Rwegasira, D. G. 1984. 'Exchange Rates and the Management of the External Sector in Sub-Saharan Africa'. *JMAS*, 22(3): 451–67.

Sada, P. O. 1981. 'Urbanization and Income Distribution in Nigeria'. In Bienen and Diejomaoh, eds., pp. 269–98.

Sandbrook, R. 1985. *The Politics of Africa's Economic Stagnation*. Cambridge: Cambridge University Press.

Sandbrook, R., and Cohen, R., eds. 1975. *The Development of an African Working Class: Studies in Class Formation and Action*. London: Longman.

Schatz, S. P. 1978. *Nigerian Capitalism*. Berkeley: University of California Press.

1984. 'Pirate Capitalism and the Inert Economy of Nigeria'. *JMAS*, 22: 45–57.

Schatzberg, M. G., and Zartman, I. W., eds. 1986. *The Political Economy of Cameroon*. New York: Praeger.

Scott, J. C. 1972. *Comparative Political Corruption*. Englewood Cliffs, N. J.: Prentice-Hall.

Scrimshaw, N. S., and Taylor, L. 1980. 'Food'. *Scientific American*, 243 (Sept.): pp. 47–63.

Seers, D. 1974. 'Cuba'. In Chenery *et al.*, pp. 262–8.

Seidman, A., and Makgetla, N. S. 1980. *Outposts of Monopoly Capitalism: Southern Africa in a Changing Global Economy*. Westport, Conn.: Lawrence Hill and Co.

Sewell, J. W., Feinberg, R. E., and Kallab, V., eds. 1985. *U.S. Foreign Policy and the Third World: Agenda, 1985–86*. Overseas Development Council U.S.–Third World Policy Perspectives No. 3. New Brunswick, N. J.: Transaction Books.

Shivji, I. G. 1976. *Class Struggles in Tanzania*. New York: Monthly Review Press.

Silver, M. S. 1985. 'United Republic of Tanzania: Overall Concentration, Regional Concentration, and the Growth of the Parastatal Sector in the Manufacturing Industry'. In UN Industrial Development Organisation. *Industry and Development*, No. 15. New York.

Sklar, R. 1963. *Nigerian Political Parties*. Princeton: Princeton University Press.

1976. 'Postimperialism: A Class Analysis of Multinational Corporate Expansion'. *Comparative Politics*, 9(1): 75–92.

1979. 'The Nature of Class Domination in Africa'. *JMAS*, 17(4): 531–52.

Smith, L. D. 1978. *Low Income Smallholder Marketing and Consumption Patterns: Analysis and Improvement, Policies and Programmes*. Rome: FAO Marketing Development Project.

Spraos, J. 1983. *Inequalising Trade?* Oxford: Clarendon Press.

Squire, L. 1981. *Employment Policy in Developing Countries: A Survey of Issues and Evidence*. New York: Oxford University Press.

Srivastava, R. K., and Livingstone, I. 1983. 'Growth and Distribution: The Case of Mozambique'. In Ghai and Radwan, eds., pp. 249–80.

Stein, H. 1985. 'Theories of the State in Tanzania: A Critical Assessment'. *JMAS*, 23(1): 105–23.

Stewart, F. 1974. 'Technology and Employment in LDCs'. In E. O. Edwards, ed., *Employment in Developing Countries*. New York: Columbia University Press, pp. 80–93.

  1985. *Basic Needs in Developing Countries*. Baltimore: Johns Hopkins University Press.

Streeten, P., Burki, S. J., Ul Haq, M., Hicks, N., and Stewart, F. 1981. *First Things First: Meeting Basic Human Needs in the Developing Countries*. Washington: World Bank.

Stolper, W. F. 1966. *Planning without Facts*. Cambridge: Harvard University Press.

  1970. 'Social Factors in Economic Planning with Special Reference to Nigeria'. In C. K. Eicher and C. Liedholm, eds., *Growth and Development of the Nigerian Economy*. East Lansing: Michigan State University, pp. 221–66.

Swainson, N. 1977. 'The Rise of a National Bourgeoisie in Kenya'. *ROAPE*, no. 8: pp. 39–55.

Sweezy, P. 1976 'More on the Nature of Soviet Society: Replay'. *Monthly Review*, 27(10): 15–24.

Tan, J. 1985. 'Private Enrollments and Expenditures on Education: Some Macro Trends'. *International Review of Education*, 31: 103–17.

Tanzania. Ministry of Finance, Planning and Economic Affairs. 1982. *The National Economic Survival Programme*. Dar es Salaam: Government Printer, January.

Tanzi, V. 1966. 'Personal Income Taxation in Latin America: Obstacles and Possibilities'. *National Tax Journal*, 19: 156–62.

Tawney, R. H. 1938. *Equality*. London: George Allen and Unwin.

Teal, F. 1986. 'The Foreign Exchange Regime and Growth: A Comparison of Ghana and the Ivory Coast'. *African Affairs*, 85: 267–82.

Teriba, O. 1981. 'Financial Institutions, Financial Markets, and Income Distribution'. In Bienen and Diejomaoh, eds., pp. 485–512.

Ul Haq, M. 1966. *The Strategy of Economic Planning: A Case Study of Pakistan*. Karachi: Oxford University Press.

UN. Department of Economic and Social Affairs. 1962 *The United Nations Development Decade: Proposals for Action*. Report of the Secretary-General. New York.

  1977. *Statistical Yearbook, 1976*. New York.

  Family Planning Association. 1979. 'Nigeria: Background Report Needs Assessment for Population Assistance'. Working paper prepared for the Population Council, UNFPA Workshop, New York. October.

  Industrial Development Organisation. 1981. *Appropriate Industrial Technology for Basic Industries*. New York.

  General Assembly. 1986. *Programme of Action for African Economic Recovery and Development, 1986–1990*. New York.

US. Department of Agriculture. Economics, Statistics, and Cooperative Service, International Economics Division. 1980. *Food Problems and Prospects in Sub-Saharan Africa: The Decade of the 1980's*. Washington: US Agency for International Development.

Department of Agriculture, Economic Research Service. 1986. *World Indices of Agricultural and Food Production, 1976–85*. Washington.

Vandemoortele, J. 1982. 'Income Distribution and Poverty in Kenya: A Statistical Analysis'. Institute for Development Studies Discussion Paper No. 275, University of Nairobi.

Vengroff, R, and Farah, A. 1985. 'State Intervention and Agricultural Development in Africa: a Cross-National Study'. *JMAS*, 23(1): 75–85.

Vielrose, E. 1974. 'Distribution of Income in Nigeria'. Nigerian Institute for Social and Economic Research, Ibadan.

Wangwe, S. M. 1984. 'Sub-Saharan Africa: Which Economic Strategy?' *Third World Quarterly*, 6(4): 1033–59.

Waterman, P. 1975. 'The 'Labour Aristocracy' in Africa'. *Development and Change*, 6(3): 57–73.

Wheeler, D. 1984. 'Sources of Stagnation in Sub-Saharan Africa'. *World Development*, 12(1): 1–23.

Willame, J. 1986. 'The Practices of a Liberal Political Economy: Import and Export Substitution in Cameroon (1975–1981)'. In Schatzberg and Zartman, eds., pp. 11–32.

World Bank. 1974. *Senegal: Tradition, Diversification, and Economic Development*. Washington.

1975. *Kenya: Into the Second Decade*. Washington.

1976. *Atlas: Population, Per Capita Product, and Growth Rates*. Washington.

1978a. *Ivory Coast: The Challenge of Success*. Baltimore: Johns Hopkins University Press.

1978b. *World Development Report, 1978*. New York: Oxford University Press.

1980a. *World Development Report, 1980*. Washington.

1980b. *World Tables, 1980*. Baltimore: Johns Hopkins University Press.

1981a. *Accelerated Development in Sub-Saharan Africa: An Agenda for Action*. Washington.

1981b. *World Development Report, 1981*. New York: Oxford University Press.

1983a. *China: Socialist Economic Development*. 3 vols. Washington.

1983b. *World Development Report, 1983*. New York: Oxford University Press.

1984a. *Toward Sustained Development in Sub-Saharan Africa: A Joint Program of Action*. Washington.

1984b. *World Development Report, 1984*. New York: Oxford University Press.

1985. *World Development Report, 1985*. New York: Oxford University Press.

1986a. *Financing Adjustment with Growth in Sub-Saharan Africa, 1986–90*. Washington.

1986b. *World Development Report, 1986*. New York: Oxford University Press.

Young, C. 1982. *Ideology and Development in Africa*. New Haven: Yale University Press.

1984. 'Zaïre: Is There a State?' *Canadian Journal of African Studies*, 18(1): 80–2.

Zartman, I. W., and Delgado, C., eds. 1984. *The Political Economy of Ivory Coast*. New York: Praeger.

PERIODICALS

Africa
Africa Confidential
Africa Insight
African Business
Central Bank of Nigeria. *Annual Reports and Statements of Accounts*, Lagos
Economist Intelligence Unit. *Quarterly Economic Review* for various African countries, London
Nigeria, Office of Statistics. *Digest of Statistics* (Quarterly)
West Africa

INDEX

3 1542 00149 9551

339.2096
N146i   WITHDRAWN

DATE DUE

339.2096
N146i

Nafziger
Inequality in
Africa

Trexler Library
Muhlenberg College
Allentown, PA 18104

DEMCO